# I SPEAK PASCAL TO MY APPLE

# I SPEAK PASCAL TO MY APPLE

AUBREY B. JONES, JR. AND AUBREY B. JONES III

**Hayden Book Company**

A DIVISION OF HAYDEN PUBLISHING COMPANY, INC.
HASBROUCK HEIGHTS, NEW JERSEY / BERKELEY, CALIFORNIA

Acquisitions Editor: KAREN PASTUZYN
Production Editor: ALBERTA BODDY
Design: JIM BERNARD
Compositor: ELIZABETH TYPESETTING
Printer: THE MAPLE-VAIL BOOK MANUFACTURING GROUP

**Library of congress Cataloging in Publication Data**

Jones, Aubrey B.
    I speak Pascal to my Apple.

    Includes index.
    1. Apple II (Computer)–Programming. 2. PASCAL
(Computer program language) I. Jones, Aubrey
II. Title.
QA76.8.A662J68   1985        001.64'24        85-7578
ISBN 0-8104-7590-1

*The Apple Pascal™ system incorporates UCSD Pascal™ and Apple extensions for graphics and other functions. UCSD Pascal is a trademark of The Regents of The University of California.*

*Apple is a registered trademark of Apple Computer, Inc., which is not affiliated with Hayden Book Company,*

*Printed in the United States of America*

| 1 | 2 | 3 | 4 | 5 | 6 | 7 | 8 | 9 | |
|---|---|---|---|---|---|---|---|---|---|
| 85 | 86 | 87 | 88 | 89 | 90 | 91 | 92 | 93 | YEAR |

*To Alyce Carter Jones*

*A beautiful wife*
*A beautiful mother*
*A beautiful person*

# Contents

# *Acknowledgments*

We would like to thank Shawn Parker, a sixteen-year-old student at Bishop McDevitt High School, who did an excellent job of reviewing the material in this book. In fact, Shawn was our first student. He had no prior knowledge of Pascal, so we gave him a draft copy of our manuscript to see if he could understand it. Not only did he understand it well enough to write programs in Pascal by himself, but he made many recommendations for improvements in the course. This book is much improved because of Shawn's assistance.

Our thanks to Ms. Helene Popper, mentor for the Mentally Gifted Program at Central High School in Philadelphia, Pa., for her comments and advice on the manuscript. Also, we thank Ms. Shariah Abduh, who edited the manuscript before it was sent to Hayden Book Company.

Finally, I would like to thank my wife, Alyce, and Denise Durgee for typing the draft of the manuscript. They deserve a lot of credit for being able to translate my sometimes illegible handwriting into a document that can be understood.

*Aubrey B. Jones, Jr.*

# Introduction

## What Is Pascal?

Pascal is a relatively new programming language that combines some of the best features and most useful concepts from other languages. It was developed by Nicklaus Wirth in the early 1970s who named it "Pascal" in honor of the seventeenth-century French mathematician Blaise Pascal.

Pascal is a structured or block-oriented language. That is, any Pascal program, large or small, is comprised of smaller subprograms or blocks, each of which is itself a structured program. Its well-organized structure and its high degree of flexibility in naming variables and subprograms make Pascal programs easy to follow. The Pascal structure offers several advantages over other programs:

- It encourages the programmer to break down a problem into many logical pieces, and thereby encourages good programming habits.

- It makes large programs easy to create, easy to understand, and easy to maintain.

- It is easy enough for beginners to learn.

## What Is UCSD Pascal?

A very popular version of Pascal is the "UCSD," which stands for University of California, San Diego. The UCSD P-System version of Pascal was developed under the direction of Kenneth Bowles for use on mini- and microcomputers in 1978. UCSD incorporates a number of additional features (extensions) to the Pascal language. These extensions allow you to manipulate graphic images and strings of alphabetic information more easily than you can with standard Pascal.

Programs written in UCSD Pascal are readily transferred from one computer system to another—an advantage over other programming languages such as BASIC and FORTRAN.

The UCSD version of Pascal is used with Apple II computers. All references to Pascal in this book refer to UCSD Pascal, unless otherwise stated.

## Why Learn Pascal?

To use a computer, you don't have to know how to program it. But to program a computer, you must learn how to speak its language or a language it can understand. As you will learn later, to program a computer means to write instructions for the computer. These instructions must be written in a language that the computer can understand so that it can perform in the way you wish.

There are many programming languages, and each language has features that make it more appropriate for a particular application. For example, FORTRAN is better suited for scientists and engineers, whereas COBOL is better suited for business applications. Another commonly used language is BASIC, which is used on most microcomputers because of its interactive capability and ease of use. BASIC is probably the easiest language to use and is quite useful for short programs. You might ask, "If BASIC is so easy to learn and so easy to use, why learn Pascal?" The answer is simply this: As you learn to develop more complex programs, BASIC becomes more complex and difficult to follow or debug. The program structure of BASIC is essentially left up to the programmer. If you are a programmer who has good programming habits and good programming techniques, then perhaps you will not have much trouble using BASIC for complex programs. But Pascal is a structured programming language; that is, it has rules that must be followed which encourage you to structure your program logically. Also, it provides you with the flexibility to use a programming style that will enhance the readability and ease of use of your program. In short, Pascal is a programming language that combines structure and style to make programming of large, complex programs easier to write and to read. Anyone who learns to program in Pascal will have no trouble learning any other programming language.

## Equipment Configuration

This book was developed using an Apple II Plus computer with 64K bytes of memory (RAM) and two disk drives. The UCSD Pascal system requires a minimum of 48K RAM with a language card installed and one or more disk drives. Although you can use the UCSD Pascal system with one disk drive, we elected to use a two-drive system because it is much more convenient and practical for Pascal applications.

Apple Pascal can also be used with the Apple IIe. The major differences in using Apple IIe instead of Apple II Plus are:

1. All Pascal commands must be entered with the [CAPS/LOCK] switch in the down position.

2. To cold boot the Apple IIe, press [CONTROL] and [RESET] simultaneously, and then release them. On most Apple II Plus machines, you need only press [RESET].

3. When using Apple IIe with one disk drive, it is tricky to boot the system. See special instructions in Appendix E for booting up Pascal on a one-drive system.

Finally, if your Apple II Plus or IIe has the 80-column text card installed, your screen will display 80 columns instead of 40 columns. This means that you will not have to use [CTRL] [A] to see the right-hand side of the screen. Your text will also appear slightly smaller on the screen.

Here is a checklist for the equipment you will need:

- ☑ 48K Apple computer with a language card installed.
- ☑ A TV set or video monitor connected to your Apple.
- ☑ Two disk drives.
- ☑ APPLE1: system diskette (needed to start the system).
- ☑ APPLE2: system diskette (adds certain extra features to the system).
- ☑ APPLE3: system diskette (contains useful utility programs).
- ☑ Formatted blank diskettes (see Chapter 2).
- ☑ A clear head and an open mind.

*Note:* A diskette marked APPLE0: is also included with the Pascal system diskettes. You will *not* need this diskette since it is normally used with single-disk drive systems.

# I SPEAK
# PASCAL
# TO MY
# APPLE

**2**

# Chapter 1

# A Computer Literacy Mini-Lesson

*Courtesy of Apple Computer Inc.*

**What You Will Learn**

- That the computer is a valuable tool that can solve problems, print words, draw pictures, store information, retrieve information, compare information, play games, and do many other things to help you in everyday life.

- To identify and explain the basic parts of a computer and relate them to a box diagram of a general computer.

- To define and explain the terms: hardware, software, microcomputer, microprocessor, RAM, ROM, EPROM, PROM, object code, source code, IC, input unit, processor unit, storage unit, memory, compiler, and interpreter.

- How IC's are made.

- How data is stored.

- How humans talk to computers via a programming language called Pascal.

## Welcome to the World of Computers

Let's destroy some myths. First of all, despite what you might have heard, people control computers, people design them, people build them, people sell them, and, most of all, people tell the computers what to do (which is another way of saying that people "program" them).

### Terms You Should Know

**Computer program**   A set of instructions that specifies what the computer must do. (Computer programmers write these instructions.)

**Hardware**   The computer and computer-related equipment (the machines).

**Software**   The instructions for the computer (the program).

A computer system consists of three main components: the input, the processor, and the output. Data that is to be processed by a computer is usually stored before it is processed. The main storage unit is part of the processor unit. (See Fig. 1–1.)

**Storage unit (memory)**   Stores both the information and the instructions until needed (requested).

**Central processing unit (CPU)**   interprets (decodes) instructions and regulates (controls) their execution; it also performs all of the calculations.

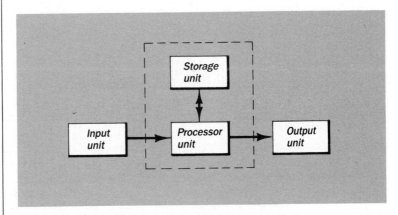

*Fig. 1–1 The basic parts of a computer.*

A computer is capable of basically two types of calculations: arithmetic and logical. *Arithmetic operations* include addition, subtraction, multiplication, and division of data. *Logical operations* include determining whether one number is greater than another number.

## Input Data and Instructions

The most common input device is the keyboard. A keyboard operates much like a typewriter except that the output is a series of electrical pulses which are decoded by the processor instead of a series of characters typed on a sheet of paper.

The number of keys vary from computer to computer, but most have standard typewriter keys plus a few special keys. (See Fig. 1–2.)

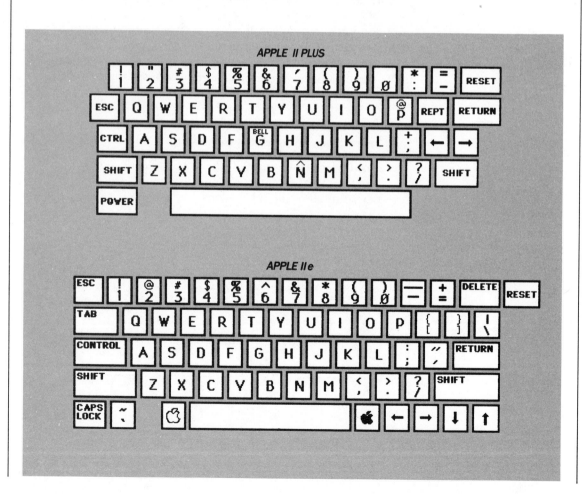

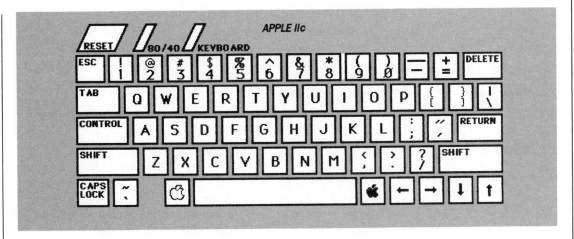

*Fig. 1–2 Three types of keyboards: the Apple II Plus, Apple IIe, and Apple IIc.*

## Output Results and Answers

Two commonly used output units are printers and displays. The display can be a TV screen or a special cathode ray tube (CRT) monitor. A display provides you with an output almost instantaneously, whereas printers are much slower but provide you with a hard copy of the program or its results. (Printers vary in speed, size, and price.)

### More Terms You Should Know

**Microprocessor**   A very small processor.

**Microcomputer**   A very small computer.

**RAM**   Random Access Memory. Information in RAM can be changed by the user. Information stored in RAM will be destroyed if power fails or if the machine is turned off. (It is volatile.)

**ROM**   Read Only Memory. Information in ROM cannot be changed by the user. Information stored in ROM is not destroyed if power fails or if the machine is turned off. (It is nonvolatile.)

**EPROM (Erasable Programmable Read Only Memory)**
Much like ROM, with one added feature. You can erase the information that you have programmed in EPROM by first using ultraviolet light and then reprogramming it with different information.

**PROM (Programmable Read Only Memory)** Like ROM and EPROM, PROM can only be read. But under certain conditions, PROM can be written into through use of a special circuit called a "programmer." Unlike EPROM, once a PROM is programmed, the contents are stored permanently, just as in ROM.

## Historical Notes

The early computer used vacuum tubes for the internal components of its circuits. These machines were known as first-generation computers (1930s to 1950s). The transistor replaced the vacuum tube in the computers of the second generation (1958 to 1964). The third generation of computers was born when several companies managed to combine several transistors on a single silicon chip (1960s to 1970s). Today's technology has already made it possible to contain a computer's CPU on a chip smaller than a fingernail. This chip is called a *microprocessor.*

## How IC's Are Made

Integrated circuits are manufactured in three broad stages: producing a polished blank silicon wafer; creating electrical circuit patterns on the wafer; and selecting, cutting, packaging, and testing the good chips from the wafer.

In stage 1, all semiconductor chips start out as a single crystal ingot of ultrapure material, almost always silicon. An ingot ranges from 3 to 6 inches in diameter with a length of up to 40 inches. Next, the ingot is sliced into wafers of approximately 0.02 inches in thickness.

In stage 2, each of the wafers goes through a series of complex steps which develop the circuit on the wafer. This process is called *photolithography.* (Photolithography is a photomechanical process of printing from a plain surface an impression from a design or picture that is first photographically transferred to a sensitized sheet and then developed for further processing.)

In stage 3, the circuits on the wafer are verified. Each wafer is subjected to a "probe test," which marks or identifies bad chips on the wafer. (Remember, each wafer has several hundred chips on it.) After the "probe test," the wafer is diced into individual chips, keeping the "good chips" and throwing away the bad ones.

Finally, each of the good chips is mounted in a package with fine gold wires connecting the active areas of the chips to the leads of the package. Through these fine gold wires and leads will emit the power and signals that activate the device. After packaging, the chip is tested extensively. *(Note:* The size of the IC and the number of pins or leads on it depend on its complexity and design. An IC may have as few as eight or as many as forty or more metal pins.)

### The Microprocessor

The microprocessor acts as the "heart" of the microcomputer system because all information must flow through or be controlled by it.(See Fig. 1–3.) The microprocessor performs the following functions:

- It gets its instructions from memory.
- It gets the data to process from memory.
- It interprets (decodes) the instructions.
- It regulates (controls) the execution.
- It performs all of the calculations.

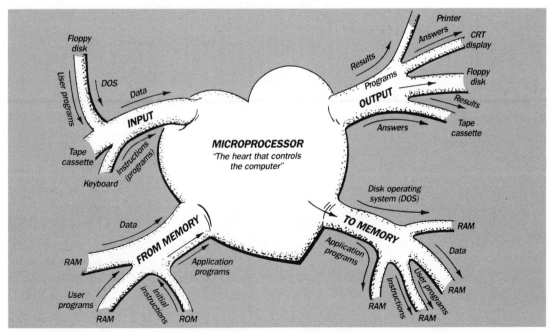

**Fig. 1–3 The microprocessor is the "heart" of the microcomputer system.**

**Data and Memory**

### How Data Are Stored in Memory

Think of *Memory* as a group of mailboxes, each of which has its own address (location). Each location can hold one character (such as a number, letter, space, or punctuation mark).

Think of the services of a mailbox: A person must first go to that specific mailbox (address). Then, he either removes the contents (letters, papers, and so on) or adds (places) something in the box. Essentially, the computer does the same thing. That is, it keeps track of where information is stored in memory, since each location in memory has its own address. When the computer needs to access a memory location, it simply goes to that location and either retrieves the contents or adds new data to the location. Fig. 1–4 shows the concept of memory.

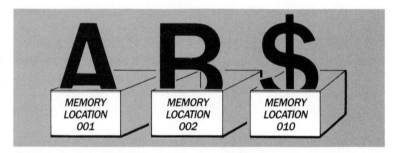

*Fig. 1–4 Storing characters in memory locations.*

### How Data Are Moved to and From Memory

It is important to have enough memory to store the program (instructions) in the computer, and also allow enough space for you to create your own program or to enter new information. Essentially, all information flows through memory under the control of the processor. (See Fig. 1–5.)

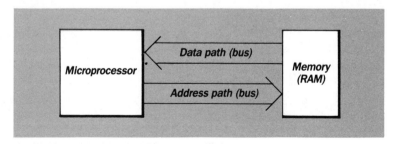

*Fig. 1–5 The movement of data to and from memory.*

**Reading (Retrieving) Data from Memory**   In order for the microprocessor to find information stored in memory, the exact location must be specified. This location, or address, is selected by the program and are sent to the memory via the address "path" or "bus." Once the location is specified and ready to receive data, the microprocessor sends the data to memory via the "data path" or "data bus."

**Writing (Saving) to Memory**   When writing to memory, the microprocessor, under the direction of the computer program, selects an available location for storage and sends this address to memory via the "address bus." Once the location is ready, the contents of its address are sent to the microprocessor via the "data bus."

### Storing Data and Programs Outside of Memory

**Input/Output (I/O) Unit**   Two commonly used I/O units on microcomputers are the cassette tape and the diskette drive. Both devices allow you to store (save) and retrieve information. A cassette tape unit is just like any cassette recorder except that it stores digital data rather than analog (voice) data. A diskette drive is an electromechanical device with motors and moving parts and holds one diskette at a time. Each diskette is small (about 5 inches in diameter) and is coated with plastic so that information may be stored on and erased from its surface. The coating is similar to the magnetic coating on a recording tape. Each diskette is permanently sealed in a square plastic cover that protects it, helps keep it clean, and allows it to spin freely.

The advantage of using diskettes over tapes is that diskettes permit you to store and retrieve information much faster. However, tapes are cheaper to use and usually store more information than diskettes.

### Some Technical Details about Diskettes

The Apple Pascal system stores information on a diskette in thirty-five concentric zones or bands called "tracks." The length of each track on the diskette is divided into sixteen segments, called "sectors." (See Fig. 1–6.)

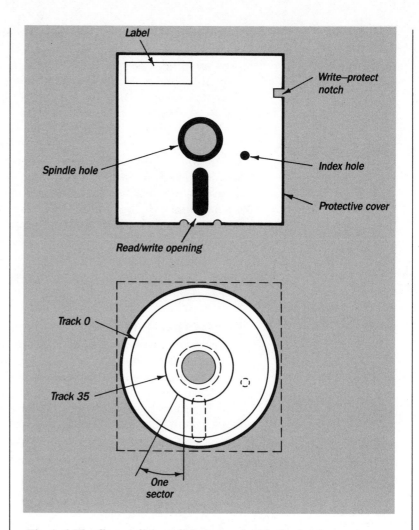

*Fig. 1–6 The floppy disk or diskette used with the Apple.*

Each sector consists of two parts: an "address field" and a "data field." The address field tells the system exactly which sector of which track is about to be read from or written onto the diskette's read/write head. The address fields are written on the diskette just once, when the diskette is formatted for first use. The "data field" is that part of each sector used for storing your data, code, or text information. Up to 256 bytes of information can be stored in each sector's data field.

The protective jacket of the diskette has an opening so that the diskette drive read/write heads can access the diskette. There is a mechanism in the diskette drive that permits the read/write heads to move in and out, and to stop and hover over each of the thirty-five different tracks of the spinning diskette.

Information is stored in two-sector units called "blocks" in the Apple Pascal system. Each block contains 512 bytes and each of the diskette's thirty-five tracks can store eight blocks of information for a total of 280 blocks (that is, 35 tracks × 8 blocks/track = 280 blocks). The total diskette capacity is 140K bytes (that is, 280 blocks × 512 bytes/block = 140K bytes).

Not all of the 280 blocks are available for storing your programs or other files, however. Blocks 0 and 1 are reserved for the bootstrap (start-up) program. In addition, blocks 2 through 5 on the diskette are reserved for the "directory," and may store information for up to 77 different files. Every diskette must contain a directory so that the system can tell what information is stored on that diskette.

A file is stored on the diskette only in contiguous blocks of contiguous tracks. Free blocks that are scattered here and there on the diskette may not be able to store a large file; therefore, you should use the K(RUNCH command from time to time to combine scattered free blocks into one contiguous area that can be used.

## Software (the Programs)

*Software* is the name given to a series of instructions that tells the computer what to do. It is the most important part of a computer system. With the right software, your computer is a valuable tool; without it, it is just a dumb machine.

Software is important because it tells the computer what to do and how to do it and it gives the computer "personality," or a special identity. Without it, the computer is useless: It cannot perform any operation or process any data.

There are basically two kinds of software: systems software and applications software. Systems software manages the resources of your computer and provides a wide variety of services to the user. It manages or controls the peripherals (the disk, printer, and display); it creates and manipulates files on a diskette; it saves and retrieves information; and it does a multitude of "housekeeping" tasks (it initializes, catalogs, and formats diskettes). The system software used with Pascal is called the Apple Pascal operating system.

Applications software causes the computer to do specific jobs or functions such as payroll, mailing lists, word processing, and games. You can write your own application programs, you can purchase them in a store, or you can have a programmer write an application to your specifications.

### Some Terms that Relate to Software

**Compiler**   Translates an entire computer program into machine language before executing the program. Because the compiler translates the entire program into machine language, the output or compiled language program is executed without the need to be translated while running. Thus, a compiled language program runs considerably faster than an interpreted language program, which has to be translated each time before execution. Once a program is compiled, it does not have to be compiled again before execution. The input to the compiler is written in *source code* and the output from the compiler is *object code*.

**Interpreter**   Translates and executes each program statement of a computer program before translating and executing the next statement. Because each line is translated into machine code before it is executed, the interpreted language program executes more slowly than a compiled language program.

**Object code**   A program output from a compiler in executable machine code (machine language).

**Source code**   A program before it has been translated into machine language.

### How Humans Talk to Computers: The UCSD "P-Machine" Approach

The P-Code version of a program can run on virtually any computer for which the P-Machine interpreter has been developed. (See Fig. 1–7.) Use of P-Code has both a major advantage and disadvantage.

The major advantage is that the Pascal programming language is essentially a "portable" language. That is, it can work on virtually any machine because only a short interpreter program (P-Machine) has to be developed for any new machine.

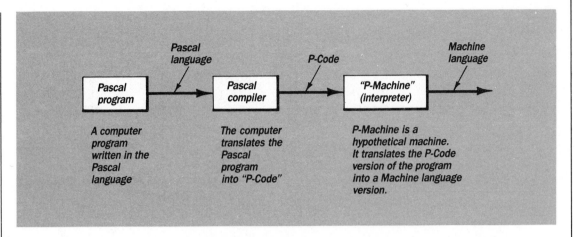

*Fig. 1–7 The translation of the Pascal language into machine language using the P-Code.*

The major disadvantage of the P-Machine approach is that the interpretation step causes programs to run two to three times slower than the same program would run if it were compiled (translated) directly to machine code.

### In Order to Program, You Must First Learn the Language

Learning a computer programming language is similar to learning a foreign language. When you are first introduced to a programming language, it might overwhelm you or appear to be very complicated, but if you relate it to something you know and break it down to small pieces, it might be easier to understand.

As with natural languages, programming languages have a strict set of rules associated with them which describe how a valid program may be constructed in the language. These rules are necessary so that the programmer can be sure of the correctness and effect of the program he writes. Also, rules are necessary so that the program may be understood by both the computer system and anyone who reads the program.

### Learning a New Vocabulary

There are reserved words that have a fixed meaning in Pascal. Here are some of the Pascal reserved words you'll learn.

| | | |
|---|---|---|
| AND | FORWARD | PROCEDURE |
| ARRAY | FUNCTION | PROGRAM |
| BEGIN | GOTO | RECORD |
| CASE | IF | REPEAT |
| CONST | IN | SET |
| DIV | LABEL | THEN |
| DO | MOD | TO |
| DOWNTO | NIL | TYPE |
| ELSE | NOT | UNTIL |
| END | OF | VAR |
| FILE | OR | WHILE |
| FOR | PACKED | WITH |

In this book, the words used to represent reserved words are distinguished by boldface type like **THIS.**

### Summary

Software is the most important part of a computer system because without it, the computer is just a dumb machine.

To use a computer, you do not have to write your own programs; that is, you do not need to become a programmer. Although knowing something about programming computers will help you become computer literate, you do have the option of using application programs written by someone else. These application programs can do specific jobs, such as word processing, mailing lists, and games, and they can be purchased from most computer stores.

If you wish to learn to program a computer, you must learn the language first. The rest of the book will help you learn how to write programs using the Pascal programming language.

*An Apple II system with Apple Pascal diskettes.*

*The Stock Shop/David York*

**Chapter 2**

# Becoming Familiar with the Apple Pascal System

**What You Will Learn**

- To become familiar with components of the Apple Pascal operating system.

- To use the system checklist.

- To boot up Pascal.

- To format new diskettes and to make backup copies of diskettes.

- To become familiar with the keyboard and the video display.

- To become familiar with the Command level and learn how to move around the system from the Command level.

## The Apple Pascal Operating System

In order to write a program, you must first learn the language. But to use the UCSD Pascal system, you must learn more than simply how to write Pascal programs—you must learn how the major pieces of the UCSD Pascal system fit together. You must learn also how to use the FILER, the EDITOR, the COMPILER, and other components of the Apple Pascal operating system.

For those of you who have already programmed computers in other languages, this chapter is a good starting point. For those of you who are learning to program for the first time, it is recommended that you review the material covered up to this point before beginning this chapter.

Fig. 2–1 shows a partial listing of the software components that make up the Apple Pascal operating system. These components are not part of the Pascal programming language itself, but they help to write, store, and execute your programs. We will limit our discussion in this book to the components listed in Fig. 2–1. After you master these components, you will be better prepared to explore other components of the system which are beyond the scope of this book.

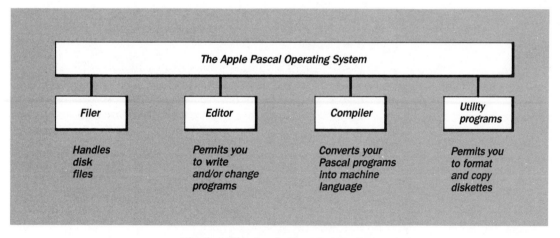

*Fig. 2–1 The Apple Pascal operating system.*

## The Two-Drive System

Check to see that you have the following:

- ☑ A 48K Apple computer with a language card installed.
- ☑ A TV set or video monitor connected to your Apple.
- ☑ Two disk drives. (See note #4 below.)
- ☑ An APPLE1: diskette.
- ☑ An APPLE2: diskette.
- ☑ An APPLE3: diskette.
- ☑ Blank diskettes.
- ☑ One duplicate copy (backup) for each APPLE1:, APPLE2:, and APPLE3: diskette. (See #5 in the list that follows.)

1. The diskette marked APPLE1: contains the EDITOR and other program files needed to start (boot) the system.

2. The diskette marked APPLE2: contains the compiler. You will not need the diskette marked APPLE2: until later.

3. The diskette marked APPLE3: contains a number of utility programs which handle special chores such as formatting, updating software, or reorganizing disk storage to create more space.

4. Pascal assigns a volume number to each of the disk drives. It is a good idea to place tags with these numbers on your disk drives. Volume numbers are assigned to a two-disk drive system (assuming that the two disk drives are attached to a disk controller card in slot #6) in the following manner:

| APPLE DISK DRIVE | PASCAL VOLUME NUMBER |
|---|---|
| Drive 1 | #4 |
| Drive 2 | #5 |

Drive 1 (Pascal volume #4) is the boot or start-up drive.

5. If you are a new owner of the Apple Pascal system, you probably have all of the items on the checklist except the last one: You *must* make backup copies. It would be a big mistake to use your only copy while experimenting with the system, so be sure to follow the backup procedures in the pages that follow.

## Starting Up Pascal

The "boot-up" step is one of the first things you must do to enable your Apple to speak Pascal. The phrase "boot up Pascal" or "booting the system" originates from the expression "pulling oneself up by one's own boot straps." It is simply the procedure used by the Apple computer to get started. Two phrases we will use, which you may have heard programmers use, are *"cold boot"* and *"warm boot."*

### Cold Boot

The system is "cold booted" everytime the Apple's power is turned on, when the RESET key is pressed on,* or when the H(ALT option is selected from the Command prompt line (which you will learn more about later). When the system is cold booted, it loads the program file named SYSTEM.APPLE, which contains the interpreter (or P-Machine). The interpreter is loaded into the language card's memory and is *write-protected* while it is there. Write protection prevents you or someone else from writing over or erasing the information in that part of the memory. SYSTEM.APPLE does not have to be reloaded until the next "cold boot" of the system. This file is normally found on diskette APPLE1: (also APPLE3:), and it must be placed in the boot drive (drive #1 or volume #4) to begin a "cold boot."

* If you are using the Apple IIe, press CONTROL and RESET.

Two additional files needed to complete either a cold boot or a warm boot of the system are SYSTEM.PASCAL and SYSTEM.MISCINFO. These files are also found on APPLE1: diskette.

### Warm Boot

The system is "warm booted" when the I(NITIALIZE option is selected from the Command prompt line or when an error causes the system to be reinitialized (rebooted).

To boot up Pascal on a two-drive system, all you have to do is:

1. Insert APPLE1: diskette into drive 1 (volume #4). Although it is not necessary, it is recommended that you place another Pascal disk in drive 2 (volume #5).

2. Turn on the power. (The programs on APPLE1: will be loaded into memory.)

3. Look for the Command prompt line at the top of the screen. This will tell you that the system was booted up successfully. (The Command prompt line displays the word COMMAND, along with some other information we will discuss later.)

## EXERCISE 2–1

### Booting Up Pascal

| ACTION | DISPLAY |
|---|---|

**ACTION**

Make certain that the system is connected properly.

Place the diskette marked APPLE1: in volume #4 (drive #1), and the diskette marked APPLE2: in volume #5 (drive #2). If you are not familiar with handling diskettes, refer to the material that came with your disk drives. (Make sure you have marked or tagged your disk drives properly.)

Close both doors to the disk drives and turn on the Apple. The message will appear.

(a) The disk drive #1 "IN USE" light comes on. The disk drive makes a clicking sound, which lets you know that everything is working.

(b) The screen lights up for an instant with a display as shown.

**DISPLAY**

```
                APPLE II
```

```
@@@@@@@@@@@@@@@@@@@@@
@@@@@@@@@@@@@@@@@@@@@
@@@@@@@@@@@@@@@@@@@@@
@@@@@@@@@@@@@@@@@@@@@
@@@@@@@@@@@@@@@@@@@@@
@@@@@@@@@@@@@@@@@@@@@
@@@@@@@@@@@@@@@@@@@@@
@@@@@@@@@@@@@@@@@@@@@
@@@@@@@@@@@@@@@@@@@@@
@@@@@@@@@@@@@@@@@@@@@
@@@@@@@@@@@@@@@@@@@@@
@@@@@@@@@@@@@@@@@@@@@
@@@@@@@@@@@@@@@@@@@@@
```

*(c) The other disk drive is turned on as Apple Pascal finds out what is in the drive. A drive with no diskette in it may buzz and clatter a bit.*

*(d) When the disk drive stops, the message shown appears. (The date will be different.)*

```
WELCOME APPLE1, TO APPLE II PASCAL 1.1
BASED ON UCSD PASCAL II.1
CURRENT DATE IS 30-DEC-85




(C) APPLE COMPUTER INC. 1979, 1980
(C) U.C. REGENTS 1979
```

*(e) Finally, in a second or so, the line shown appears at the top of the screen. Note: The line is called the Command prompt line. When you see this prompt line, you know that your Apple computer is running the Apple Pascal system. That is, the system is booted and ready for your use.*

```
COMMAND: E(DIT, R(UN, F(ILE, C(OMP, L(IN
```

The Apple Pascal operating system renames the drives as volume numbers. From now on, drive 1 will be volume #4 and drive 2 will be volume #5. You should label your drives 4 and 5 when using Apple Pascal.

The displays in this book will illustrate 40 characters per line. If you have an 80-column card in your Apple, you will see 80 characters per line.

## Formatting and Copying Diskettes: A Valuable Utility

### Making Backup Copies

If you were to lose or damage one of the system diskettes (APPLE1:, APPLE2:, or APPLE3:), you wouldn't be able to use Apple Pascal on your computer. Therefore, some suggestions follow.

First, make backup copies of your system diskettes. (Two backup copies of each original would be even better.) You should never use the originals; put them in a place where they will not become damaged. If your backups are damaged or erased while in use, find out why they were destroyed before inserting your original copy. (Get help from the dealer if you need it.)

You must format new diskettes before they can be used for backups. The Apple computer system cannot store information on a new diskette in the form that the diskette comes from the computer store. Therefore, the system is supplied with a program that allows you to format a new diskette so that it will work with the Apple Pascal system.

The next exercise will show you the procedure to format new diskettes. After the diskette has been formatted, it will be used to make a backup copy.

## EXERCISE 2–2

### Formatting New Diskettes (Two-Disk System)

| ACTION | DISPLAY |
|---|---|
| 1. Be sure that the Apple is turned off. | |
| 2. Open the disk drive door by gently lifting the door from the bottom. Place diskette APPLE1: in disk drive #1; place diskette APPLE3: in disk drive #2. | |

3. *Turn on the system. The APPLE3: diskette is needed because the FORMATTER program is on APPLE3:. (Note: Check to see that the Command prompt line appears at the top of the screen.)*

```
COMMAND: E(DIT, R(UN, F(ILE, C(OMP, L(IN
```

4. *If you have a 40-character line, hold down the* CTRL *key and then press* A *.*

```
K, X(ECUTE, A(SSEM, D(EBUG,? [1.1]
```

5. *Type* X *. The message shown should appear. This action selects X(ECUTE. Note: If the screen is blank, press* CTRL A *.*

```
EXECUTE WHAT FILE?
```

6. *Type APPLE3:FORMATTER and then press the* RETURN *key. (If you make a mistake before pressing* RETURN *, use* <---- *to erase.)*

```
APPLE DISK FORMATTER PROGRAM
FORMAT WHICH DISK (4,5,9..12) ?
```

7. *Take all of the new blank diskettes that you intend to use with the Pascal system and place them in a pile. (Be sure not to take any diskettes containing precious information.)*

8. *Remove the APPLE3: diskette from volume #5 (drive #2), and put one of the new blank diskettes into that drive.*

9. *Type* 5 *and press*
   RETURN . *If the*
   *diskette in volume #5*
   *has already been*
   *formatted, you will*
   *receive a warning. For*
   *example, if you leave*
   *APPLE3: in that*
   *drive, you will be*
   *warned with the*
   *message shown. If*
   *you do not want to*
   *destroy the directory,*
   *you would type* N
   *(for "no").*

   DESTROY DIRECTORY OF APPLE3:?

10. *Suppose you have a*
    *new unformatted*
    *diskette. In this case,*
    *you will not get any*
    *warning but the*
    *Apple will place this*
    *message on its screen.*
    *(Note: Volume #5 will*
    *make some clicking*
    *and buzzing noise.*
    *The process takes*
    *about 32 seconds.)*

    NOW FORMATTING DISKETTE IN DRIVE 5

11. *When formatting is*
    *complete, the screen*
    *again shows the*
    *message.*

    FORMAT WHICH DISK (4,5,9..12)?

12. *Now you have a*
    *formatted disk. Write*
    *"Pascal" at the top of*
    *the diskette's label,*
    *using a felt-tip pen.*

13. *Repeat the process at*
    *step 9 to format other*
    *new diskettes that you*
    *want to use with the*
    *Apple Pascal system.*

14. When you have
    finished formatting
    all of your new
    diskettes and have
    written the word
    "Pascal" on each of
    them, press RETURN .

THAT'S ALL FOLKS . . .

15. Use CTRL A to
    show the left-most
    part of the screen if it
    is not displayed. The
    Command prompt
    should be at the top
    of the screen.

COMMAND: E(DIT, R(UN, F(ILE, C(OMP, L(IN

16. Remove the newly
    formatted diskettes
    and put them away in
    a safe place until you
    need them. (Note:
    Newly formatted
    diskettes are assigned
    the volume name
    BLANK: by the
    Apple Pascal
    Operating System.)

## EXERCISE 2–3

### Making Backup Copies

**ACTION**

**DISPLAY**

1. If you just finished
   formatting new
   diskettes, the system
   should be at the
   Command level. (That
   is, the Command level
   prompt should be
   displayed.) If it is not,
   make certain that
   APPLE1: is in drive #1
   and then reboot the
   system (that is, just
   press CTRL-RESET).
   Then insert a newly
   formatted blank
   diskette into drive #2.

COMMAND: E(DIT, R(UN, F(ILE, C(OMP, L(IN

2. *Now press* F *for the Filer. (Note: If you forget to put APPLE1: in the diskette drive, you will get the message shown. If this happens, just put APPLE1: in drive #1 and press* F *again.)*

```
FILER: G, S, N, L, R, C, T, D, Q [1.1]
```

```
NO FILE APPLE1:SYSTEM.FILER
```

3. *Now press* T *for T(RANSFER.*

```
TRANSFER ?
```

4. *Suppose you want to make a backup of APPLE1: (to copy APPLE1: onto your newly formatted diskette). Since APPLE1: is already in the volume #4, type APPLE1: and then press* RETURN. *(Note: If APPLE1: is not in the drive when you press* RETURN, *you will see the message shown.)*

```
TRANSFER ? APPLE1:
TO WHERE ?
```

```
NO SUCH VOL ON-LINE <SOURCE>
```

5. *Answer the question "TO WHERE?" by typing in the name of the diskette that is to become an exact copy of APPLE 1:. Type BLANK: and press* RETURN.

```
TO WHERE ?

TO WHERE ? BLANK:
TRANSFER 280 BLOCKS ? (Y/N)
```

   (a) *Remember that BLANK: is the name given to all newly formatted diskettes by the FORMATTER program.*

   (b) *The colon (:) that appears after the diskette name is quite significant: It indicates that the entire diskette is being referred to.*

*(c) The computer checks to see that BLANK: is also in one of the diskette drives. If it is not, you will see the message shown. In this case, put BLANK: into volume #5 and press* SPACEBAR .

```
PUT IN BLANK:
TYPE <SPACE> TO CONTINUE
```

6. *When the computer checks and finds that everything is OK, it displays the message shown. This message gives you a chance to change your mind if you made a typing error in the name of the source (APPLE1:) or the destination (BLANK:) diskettes. The phrase "280 BLOCKS" simply means the "whole diskette." Now type* Y .

```
TRANSFER 280 BLOCKS ? (Y/N)
```

7. *Since you want to turn "BLANK:" into a perfect copy of APPLE1:, the answer to "DESTROY BLANK:?" is "Y." When you type* Y , *the process begins—it takes about 30 seconds.*

```
DESTROY BLANK: ?
```

*When copying is done, this message means the contents of APPLE1:, including the diskette's name, have been copied to the diskette that used to be called BLANK:.*

```
APPLE1:     ---> BLANK:
```

When you have finished copying APPLE1:, be sure to remove the new copy immediately.

Use a felt-tip pen to write "APPLE1:" on the label of the new diskette. It is important to label diskettes immediately so you'll know what information is stored on them.

At this time, make sure that you have at least one backup copy for each of your system diskettes: APPLE1:, APPLE2:, and APPLE3:. Simply repeat steps 3 to 9 for each diskette you want to copy.

## Special Function Keys on the Apple Keyboard

For this section, refer to the Apple keyboards shown in Fig. 1–2 on pages 4 and 5.

**KEY** | **FUNCTION**

CTRL or CONTROL

Several keys have an additional function that is obtained by holding down the CTRL key while the other keys are pressed. Control characters never appear on the display; instead, the computer responds by performing certain actions. (See below.)

ESC

This key represents "Escape." Pressing the ESC key cancels any changes made while in the EDIT mode. You would use the ESC key to escape from accidental key presses. Unlike the CTRL key, ESC does not have to be held down while typing another key.

REPT

This key represents "Repeat." Holding down the REPT key while pressing another key makes the other key's character appear repeatedly on the screen. First, you must hold down the key for the character you wish to be repeated, then hold down the REPT key. The Apple IIe and IIc do not have a REPT key; each key will repeat if held down.

RESET

Press this key if your Apple computer does not respond correctly to your instructions. (If this does not work, try turning your Apple off and on again. Of course, if you do this, you will lose your program.) Pressing the RESET reboots or restarts the system. The Apple IIe and IIc and some Apple Pluses require CTRL and RESET to reboot the system.

SHIFT

Some keys have two characters printed on them. In order to type the upper character shown on such a key, first hold down the SHIFT key and then press the key with the two symbols on it.

| | |
|---|---|
| [ <---- ] | The backspace key moves the cursor back one space at a time. As the cursor moves, one character is erased from the program line that you are currently typing. |
| [ ----> ] | The retype key moves the cursor to the right one space at a time. As it does this, each character it crosses on the screen is entered as if you had typed it—hence its name. |
| [ RETURN ] | This key lets the computer know that you have completed your response. It causes the computer to "look at" the line you just typed in or the response you just made, and to act accordingly. This key must be pressed each time you want to terminate a line you just entered from the keyboard. That is, pressing [ RETURN ] causes the cursor to "return" to the beginning of the next line. (This is very similar to the function of the carriage return on a typewriter.) |
| | The [ RETURN ] key may be pressed to insert a space between program lines typed from the keyboard. If you make a typing mistake before pressing [ RETURN ], you can backspace over the error by pressing the backspace key. |

## Control Key Functions

| **KEY** | **FUNCTION** |
|---|---|
| [ CTRL ] or [ CONTROL ] | Holding down this key while pressing another key causes the computer to perform different actions. The following are some examples of [ CTRL ] key functions that are system commands for the Apple Pascal Operating System. (Note: These commands can be executed at any level of the operating system, unless otherwise noted.) |
| [ CTRL ] [ A ] | On Apple computers that don't have an 80-column card, holding down [ CTRL ] while pressing [ A ] will let you see the right-most 40 characters of the Apple Pascal system's 80-character display. Pressing [ CTRL ] [ A ] again will let you go back to the left-most 40 characters of the display. |
| [ CTRL ] [ F ] | Subsequent program output is not sent to the screen or printer, although the program continues to run. The next [ CTRL ] [ F ] cancels this function. |
| [ CTRL ] [ S ] | This stops any ongoing operating system process or program. When the next [ CTRL ] [ S ] is typed, the process continues. |

| | |
|---|---|
| CTRL Z | This initiates the "Auto Follow" mode; that is, the screen scrolls (moves) right and left to follow the cursor. It is canceled by CTRL A and many other commands. |
| CTRL @ | This causes the current program to be interrupted and issues the message "PROGRAM INTERRUPTED BY USER." To reinitialize the system, you must press the spacebar. |
| CTRL K | This permits you to type the left bracket ([). |
| CTRL M | This permits you to type the right bracket (]). |
| CTRL E | (E stands for "Enable.") This turns the reverse video mode on and changes the case of the keyboard from upper- to lowercase, or vice versa. Thus, it is similar to the "Shift Lock" key on a typewriter. |
| CTRL W | (W stands for "Word.") This turns the reverse video mode on and forces the keyboard into uppercase for the next character typed. After the next character is typed, the keyboard is forced into lowercase. This is useful when you want to capitalize the first letter of a word. |
| CTRL R | (R stands for "Reverse.") This turns the reverse video mode on. *Note that this does not change the keyboard case;* all letters typed on the keyboard are still uppercase unless CTRL E or CTRL W is used to change the case. |
| CTRL T | (T stands for "Turn Off.") This restores normal operation; that is, it turns the reverse video mode off and also forces the keyboard into uppercase. CTRL T can be used from any level of the system *except* the Editor. |

### The 40-Character Display Window*

*\*If your computer has an 80-column card installed, disregard this section.*

Pascal permits up to 80 characters per line to be displayed. But Apple computers without an 80-inch column card permit only up to 40 characters per line to be displayed. Therefore, if the line is greater than 40 characters, only the first 40 characters will be displayed. To see the rest of the line or any information too long to be displayed or seen through the "window" of the display, simply press CTRL A.

Sometimes the display or "window" will be black because there is no text displayed on the right half on the screen. Pressing CTRL A again will shift you back to the left half of the display.

**DISPLAY**                                    **OFF-SCREEN**

COMMAND: E(DIT, R(UN, F(ILE, C(OMP, L(IN          K, X(ECUTE, A(SSEM, D(EBUG, ?

**40 CHARACTERS PER LINE**                     **40 ADDITIONAL CHARACTERS PER LINE**

You can also make the display follow the cursor by pressing CTRL Z. As the cursor moves, the display is automatically adjusted to show the text surrounding the cursor. CTRL Z is canceled by pressing CTRL A, or by using many other commands.

---

## EXERCISE 2–4

### Becoming Familiar With the Apple Pascal Window*

Diskettes needed: APPLE1: in drive #1 (volume #4) and APPLE2: in drive #2 (volume #5).

**ACTION**                                     **DISPLAY**

1. Boot the system. The Command prompt line should be at the top of the screen.

COMMAND: E(DIT, R(UN, F(ILE, C(OMP, L(IN

2. Hold down CTRL and then press A. The other half of the Command prompt line will be shown.

   When you hold down CTRL and press A again, the screen will flip back to the other side. (Try it several times!)

K, X(ECUTE, A(SSEM, D(EBUG, ? [1.1]

*This section applies only to Apples without an 80-column card.

3. *Make sure that you have the left side of the prompt line as shown in step 1 above. Then press* [?] *(don't forget to hold down the shift key).*

```
COMMAND: U(SER RESTART, I(NITIALIZE, H(A
```

4. *Now use* [CTRL] [A] *again. You can now see the right half of these additional command options. Again, use* [CTRL] [A] *to flip back and forth between the left side and the right side.*

```
LT, S(WAP, M(AKE EXEC
```

5. *Press* [RETURN]. *You are now back to the beginning of the Command prompt line.*

```
COMMAND: E(DIT, R(UN, F(ILE, C(OMP, L(IN
```

## Reaching the Command Level

When you see the Command prompt line at the top of the screen, you are at the Command level. This is the most important place in the Pascal system because you enter the system through the Command level.

The Command level is reached whenever one of the following conditions occur:

Whenever you boot or reset the system (by any means).

Whenever the system reinitializes itself after a serious run-time error.

Whenever you quit the Editor or Filer.

Whenever the system finishes C(OMPILING, R(UNNING, or X(ECUTING any other program.

In summary, to go from one part of the Pascal system to another, you will often pass through the Command level. Remember, you can always reach the Command level by rebooting or resetting the computer.

## The Command Level

```
COMMAND: E(DIT, R(UN, F(ILE, C(OMP, L(INK, X(ECUTE, A(SSEM, D(EBUG,? [1.1]
```

### Your Entry Point into Pascal

The following table lists some commands you can access from the command level.*

| COMMAND | PRESS THIS KEY | PURPOSE |
|---------|----------------|---------|
| E(DIT | E | Enter edit mode to write and/or change text. |
| R(UN | R | Execute a program. Will compile a program first, if required. |
| F(ILE | F | Enter Filer, which lets you store, delete, and move diskette files. |
| X(ECUTE | X | Use utility programs such as formatter and calculator. |
| ? | ? | See additional commands. |

*Press CTRL A if you cannot see the right half of the screen.

### Commands Accessible by Pressing ?

```
COMMAND: U(SER RESTART, I(NITIALIZE, H(ALT, S(WAP, M(AKE EXEC
```

The following table lists some commands you can access from the Command level.

| COMMAND | PRESS THIS KEY | PURPOSE |
|---------|----------------|---------|
| U(SER RESTART | U | Reexecutes the last program executed. |
| I(NITIALIZE | I | Performs a "warm boot." |
| H(ALT | H | Performs a "cold boot" (this is similar to turning the power off and then on). |

Pressing ? at the Command level causes new text to be written on the prompt line; it can be used only at the Command and Filer levels only. You must press CTRL A if you can't see the entire Command line.

*The letter in the □ indicates the key you must press to enter or exit the level shown. More details on these commands will be given in subsequent chapters.*

## Moving about the System with Ease

In order to enter the Pascal system, you must start at the Command level. To go from one part of the system to another, you will often pass through the Command level. (See Fig. 2–3.)

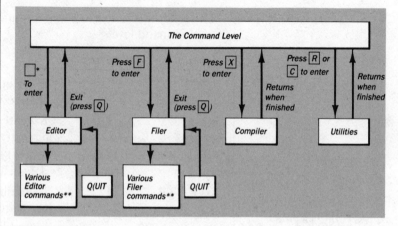

*Fig. 2–2 Using the Command level to move about the system.*

## Summary

The Command level allows you to move in and out of the various levels of the Pascal system. It is the top level of the Pascal system; therefore, you use the various options of the Command level to select any of the main subdivisions or lower levels of the Apple Pascal operating system. Some of the options you can select from the Command level are included in the following list.

| OPTION | FUNCTION |
|---|---|
| **C(OMPILE** | Selects the Pascal compiler, which converts the text of a Pascal program (found in the workfile or other specified textfile) into executable P-code. |
| **E(DIT** | Selects the Editor, which is used to create and modify text. Reads the workfile or other specified textfile into the Apple for editing. |
| **F(ILE** | Selects the Filer, which is used to save, move, and retrieve information stored on diskettes. |
| **H(ALT** | Does a "cold boot" of the system, similar to turning the machine's power off and then on again. |

**I(NITIALIZE**    Does a "warm boot" of the system.

**R(UN**    Executes the current workfile, automatically compiling and linking (from the SYSTEM.LIBRARY) first, if necessary.

**X(ECUTE**    Loads and runs a utility program or other P-code files.

The Command level portion of the operating system is located on diskettes APPLE0: and APPLE1: under the file name SYSTEM.PASCAL. The Command level is reached automatically each time the system is booted, reset, or initialized. It is also reached when any program, including any part of the operating system, is terminated.

## PRACTICE 2–1

### Become Familiar with the Apple Pascal System

1. Boot up (start up) the Apple Pascal system using the start-up procedure (see page 19).

2. What diskette(s) do you need to boot up the system? _____.

3. Which diskette is in drive #1? _____ In drive #2? _____.

4. Drive #1 is also known as volume _____ and drive #2 is also known as volume _____.

5. When you first boot the system, at which level is the Apple Pascal system? _____.

6. Enter the Filer. What level must the system be in to enter the Filer? _____. What key did you press to enter the Filer? _____.

7. Exit the Filer. What key do you press to exit the Filer? _____ When you exit the Filer, to what system level does the Apple Pascal return? _____.

8. Locate the [CTRL] key. Hold down the [CTRL] key and then press [A]. What happened? _____. Now press [CTRL] [A] again. What happened? _____.

9. To see additional commands from the Command level, you must press _____.

10. To exit the Filer or the Editor, press _____ for _____.

*Courtesy of Apple Computer Inc.*

**Chapter 3**

# Under-standing the Filer

**What You Will Learn**

- To understand the concept of a file.

- To understand the difference between program files and data files.

- To become familiar with the Filer and learn how the Filer is used to manipulate diskette files.

- To understand the application and use of the Filer commands used in this book.

- To understand the application and use of the workfile.

- To list the directory.

- To change the date.

- To clear the workfile.

## Files

A file is a collection of information that is stored on a tape cassette or diskette for input to, or output by, a computer. (We will refer only to diskette files in this book.)

Files may be referred to by file names selected by the user or programmer. Information that is used to communicate between the computer and you may also be thought of as an external file. For example, when you type characters at the keyboard, the stream of characters, which are stored in a temporary location called a *buffer*, may be thought of as an input file.

There are two classes of files: program files and data files. *Program files*, as you might expect, contain program statements which must be retained from one program execution to another. *Data files*, on the other hand, contain information that is used by programs; that is, data files are created, written, and read by programs.

Program files are simpler to use than data files because you do not need to know anything about their internal organization— this is a definite advantage. (We will not discuss data files because they are beyond the scope of this book. We will, however, discuss program files briefly so you can better understand how they are used in the Apple Pascal system.)

## The Concept of a Program File

A program file can be any size, limited only by the capacity of the cassette or diskette used as the storage media. A program file should fit on a single tape cassette or diskette. (All files you will use for Apple Pascal in this book will fit on a single diskette.)

To better understand the concept of a file, think of a four-drawer file cabinet typically found in an office. Envision each drawer of the file cabinet with a label on the outside that reads as follows:

| DRAWER NUMBER | LABEL |
|:---:|:---:|
| 0 | APPLE0: |
| 1 | APPLE1: |
| 2 | APPLE2: |
| 3 | APPLE3: |

Now think of each of the diskettes supplied with your Apple Pascal system as one of the drawers in the file cabinet. Just as each file drawer can contain many files (or file folders) with different names, a diskette can contain many program files with different file names. Table 3–1 shows some of the files that are stored on the Apple Pascal diskettes.

**TABLE 3–1. PARTIAL LISTING OF PROGRAM FILES STORED ON APPLE PASCAL DISKETTES**

| FILE NAME | APPLE0: | APPLE1: | APPLE2: | APPLE3: |
|---|---|---|---|---|
| SYSTEM.APPLE | | X | | X |
| SYSTEM.COMPILER | X | | X | |
| SYSTEM.EDITOR | X | X | | |
| SYSTEM.FILER | X | X | | |
| SYSTEM.PASCAL | X | X | | |
| FORMATTER.CODE | | | | X |
| FORMATTER.DATA | | | | X |
| SYSTEM.LIBRARY | X | X | | |

To retrieve a file, you would first select the diskette with the file you want to use and load it into the diskette drive. Next, if you do not know the exact file name of the file you wish to use, get the computer to list the directory of the diskette so that you can see what files are stored on the diskette. After you see the name of the file you want, you merely select the file from the diskette using the designated file names.

Program files are stored on diskettes until you need them, much like files are stored in file cabinets until they are needed. To retrieve a file from a file cabinet or a diskette, you must know which file to use. In the Pascal system, each diskette has a directory which lists its contents. Similarly, some file cabinets have an index in front of each drawer which lists the files stored in the drawer. If, however, you already know the name of the file you are looking for, you can go directly to that file without using the index or a directory.

After you have the desired file, you can either read the information already in the file or you can add new information to it. You can also create new files on the diskette just as you can do with a file cabinet.

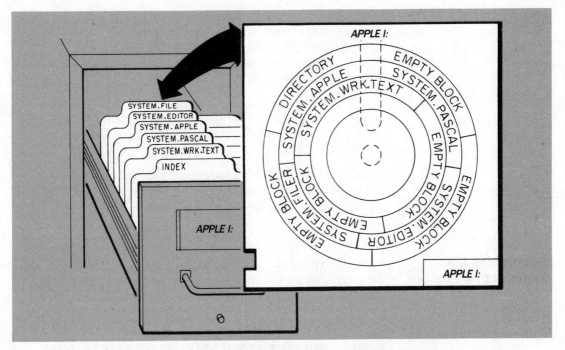

*Fig. 3–1 A cabinet file and a corresponding diskette.*

The difference between diskette and cabinet files is that diskette files are stored and retrieved electronically, and cabinet files are stored and retrieved manually. (See Fig. 3–1.)

Some files are redundant, so you can use the files on either diskette. But as discussed earlier, you will be using APPLE1: and APPLE2: for a two-disk drive configuration. Apple0: is used primarily with single-disk drive systems, and APPLE3: contains files that are used on either single- or dual-disk drive systems.

## Handling the File: The Filer

The Pascal system has a file handler, or Filer, which lets you store, delete, and move diskette files. The Filer handles most of the tasks of transferring information from one place to another, and also keeps track of where files have been placed on the diskettes and what devices and diskettes are available for your system's use.

Each diskette has a "directory," which contains the file names and locations of each file on the diskette. The Filer uses the information contained in the diskette directory to manipulate files.

When you save (write) a program on diskette, it becomes a file that you can subsequently load (read) back into memory. In order to save a file, you must assign a file name to that file. (You would use the same file name to load the program back into memory when needed.)

For Pascal programs, however, one program file is loaded automatically (without your having to specify a file name). This file is called your workfile, and is filed under the name SYSTEM.WRK.TEXT.

SYSTEM.WRK.TEXT is automatically loaded into memory when you select the EDIT mode. We will discuss the Editor and the workfile in more detail later.

**Determining the
Contents of a File**

An Apple Pascal file name normally ends with a suffix that tells the system and you something about the contents of that file. The following list shows the most commonly used suffixes for files.

| SUFFIX | INFORMATION CONTAINED IN FILE IDENTIFIED BY SUFFIX |
| --- | --- |
| **TEXT** | Text or text file read by user: natural language; Pascal program text; 6502 Assembly Language Text; File name example: SYSTEM.WRK.TEXT |
| **CODE** | Code or code file executed by machine: compiled P-code; assembled 6502 machine code; File name example: FORMATTER.CODE |
| **DATA** | Data or data files: information used by programs; File name example: FORMATTER.DATA |

Many Apple Pascal commands deal with various diskette files that you must specify by file name. In those instances where the file being acted on can be only one type (.TEXT, .CODE, and so on), the system allows you to type the file name either with or without the suffix. If you forget to add the suffix, the system will add it for you.

Fig. 3–2 shows a partial listing of the Filer commands. The Filer lets you store, delete, and move diskette files.

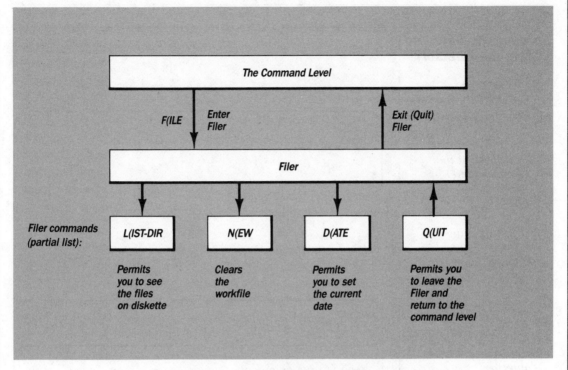

*Fig. 3–2 A partial listing of the Filer commands.*

To enter the Filer, you must first be at the Command level; then press [F] (for Filer). Once you are in the Filer (you should see the Filer prompt at top of screen), you can use any of the Filer commands by simply pressing the first letter of the command. For example, press [D] for D(ATE if you wish to set the date.

In Exercise 3–1, we will enter the Filer, clear the workfile, list the directory, change the date, and then quit the Filer.

## EXERCISE 3–1

### Entering the Filer and Listing the Directory

**ACTION**

1. You must always enter the Filer from the Command level. (If you are not at the Command level, reboot the system or press [ RESET ].*)

   *If you are using the Apple IIe, press [ CONTROL ] and [ RESET ].

2. Press [F] to enter the Filer.

3. Press [L] to list the directory.

4. Type APPLE1: and press [ RETURN ]. Note the following: The bottom line of the display informs you that 13 files out of a total of 13 files on the diskette have been listed, that there are 52 out of a total of 280 diskette blocks left for you to use, and that there are 52 contiguous blocks in the largest unused area on the diskette. (The numbers will vary from machine to machine.)

**DISPLAY**

```
COMMAND: E(DIT, R(UN, F(ILE, C(OMP, L(IN
```

```
FILER: G, S, N, L, R, C, T, D, Q [1.1]
```

```
DIR LISTING OF ?
```

```
FILER: G, S, N, L, R, C, T, D, Q [1.1]
APPLE1:
SYSTEM.APPLE       32      9-NOV-80
SYSTEM.PASCAL      41     22-SEP-80
SYSTEM.MISCINFO     1      4-MAY-79
SYSTEM.EDITOR      47     24-SEP-80
SYSTEM.FILER       28     18-SEP-80
SYSTEM.LIBRARY     34     19-SEP-80
SYSTEM.CHARSET     34     19-SEP-80
SYSTEM.SYNTAX       2     14-JUN-79
13/13 FILES, 52 UNUSED, 52 IN LARGEST
```

The number "32" (just after SYSTEM.APPLE in the listing) tells you that 32 blocks have been used to store that file. (Refer to Appendix A if you want to know more about diskettes.)

The dates shown on your display might be different. Also, there may be other files listed that are stored on your diskette.

5. *Press* RETURN *to erase the directory.*

```
FILER: G, S, N, L, R, C, T, D, Q [1.1]
```

6. *Let's look at the extended directory. Press* ? *to see the rest of the Filer commands first.*

```
FILER: W, B, E, K, M, P, V, X, Z [1.1]
```

7. *Press* E *(for extended directory).*

```
DIR LISTING OF ?
```

8. *Type #4: (or APPLE1:), and then press* RETURN. *Note the following: The SYSTEM.APPLE file starts at block 6 and uses 32 blocks; therefore, the next file (SYSTEM.PASCAL) starts at block 38 (6 + 32 = 38). Three FILE types are shown; DATA, CODE, and TEXT. More files would be shown if they were on the diskette.*

```
FILER: G, S, N, L, R, C, T, D, Q [1.1]
APPLE1:
SYSTEM.APPLE        32      9-NOV-80        6 DATA
SYSTEM.PASCAL       41     22-SEP-80       38 CODE
SYSTEM.MISCINFO      1      4-MAY-79       79 DATA
SYSTEM.EDITOR       47     24-SEP-80       80 CODE
SYSTEM.FILER        28     18-SEP-80      127 CODE
SYSTEM.LIBRARY      34     19-SEP-80      155 DATA
SYSTEM.CHARSET       2     14-JUN-79      189 DATA
SYSTEM.SYNTAX       14      1-AUG-80      191 TEXT
  <UNUSED>          75                    205
```

| # OF BLOCKS USED BY FILE | STARTING BLOCK FOR FILE | FILE TYPES |

9. *Press* RETURN.

```
FILER: G, S, N, L, R, C, T, D, Q [1.1]
```

10. *Press* Q *to QUIT or leave the Filer and return to Command level.*

```
COMMAND: E(DIT, R(UN, F(ILE, C(OMP, L(IN
```

## EXERCISE 3–2

### Entering the Filer and Changing the Date

| ACTION | DISPLAY |
|---|---|

**ACTION**

1. If the Command line is not at the top of your screen with APPLE1: in drive #1, turn your system off and then on again.

2. Press ⬚F⬚ on the keyboard (without pressing the ⬚RETURN⬚ key or any other keys). The screen will go blank, and then the Filer line will appear at the top of the screen.

3. To change the date, press ⬚D⬚. You should see this: What is shown here on the screen doesn't really mean tht today is 5-MAY-83 (or whatever date your screen shows), but it does mean that the Apple thinks that this is today's date. (Note: It is a good habit to reset the date the first time you use the Pascal system on any given day.)

4. Change the date so that it is correct. See the example in the display column.

5. Press ⬚RETURN⬚.

**DISPLAY**

```
COMMAND: E(DIT, R(UN, F(ILE, C(OMP, L(IN
```

```
FILER: G, S, N, L, R, C, T, D, Q [1.1]
```

```
DATE SET: <1:31>-<JAN..DEC>-<00:99>
TODAY IS 5-MAY-83
NEW DATE ? ▮
```
cursor

```
TODAY IS 5-MAY-83
NEW DATE ? 8-MAY-84
```

```
FILER: G, S, N, L, R, C, T, D, Q [1.1]
NEW DATE ?  8-MAY-84
THE DATE IS 8-MAY-84
```

## Clearing the Workfile

One of the first things you will want to do before you start typing a new program is *clear the workfile*. But before you learn how to clear the workfile, let's first discuss some of the unique features of the workfile.

The workfile is just one of many files stored on your APPLE1: (boot) diskette. However, the workfile concept incorporates features that simplify the number of steps it takes to write, edit, compile, and test new programs. The workfile functions as an electronic scratchpad that permits you to save and update the information stored on it. It is a specially reserved file for the program you are currently working on, so you do not have to worry about file-handling procedures and commands.

**NOTE:** *Programs stored in the workfile often consist of both the text version (SYSTEM.WRK.TEXT) and the compiled version (SYSTEM.WRK.CODE).*

The workfile saves you time and trouble when you are working on new programs or changing old ones. That is, the system always stores the workfile on the boot diskette and always uses the same file name SYSTEM.WRK.TEXT. It does all of these things automatically.

When you QUIT (exit) the Editor and ask for an update of the workfile (by pressing [U]), the text you were working on is automatically saved on the diskette under the file name SYSTEM.WRK.TEXT. Any older version of the file is erased from the diskette when you update the workfile.

Whenever you enter the Editor (by pressing [E] from the Command level), the workfile is automatically read (loaded) into the computer memory and displayed on the screen, where it is then ready for editing. The system assumes that there is a workfile on the diskette and that you wish to work with the text stored in the workfile. (If no workfile is present, you will get the message NO WORKFILE IS PRESENT.)

When you press [Q] (for Quit the Editor), [U] (for Update the workfile), and then [R] (for Run), the program in the workfile will compile and run automatically without your having to type file names. If the program is compiled successfully, the compiled version of the workfile (program) is automatically saved under the file name SYSTEM.WRK.CODE.

## EXERCISE 3–3

### Clearing the Workfile

| ACTION | DISPLAY |
|---|---|

1. Boot your system. (If necessary, refer to page 19 and review how to boot up Pascal properly.)

```
COMMAND: E(DIT, R(UN, F(ILE, C(OMP, L(IN
```

2. Enter the Filer by pressing ⬚F.

```
FILER: G, S, N, L, R, C, T, D, Q [1.1]
```

3. Now press ⬚N for NEW, which clears the workfile. One of two things will happen as soon as you press ⬚N:

You will see this message and the Filer prompt line; or you will see this question.

```
FILER: G, S, N, L, R, C, T, D, Q [1.1]
WORKFILE CLEARED
```

This means that the APPLE1: diskette already has some text stored in the workfile. This question is just a precaution to keep you from destroying text you might want to keep.

```
THROW AWAY CURRENT WORKFILE ?
```

If you want to keep the text, press ⬚N for no. Since you are just starting out and you want to enter new text, press ⬚Y for yes.

```
FILER: G, S, N, L, R, C, T, D, Q [1.1]
WORKFILE CLEARED
```

4. When you see the message WORKFILE CLEARED, you can exit the Filer by pressing ⬚Q, which returns you to the Command level.

```
COMMAND: E(DIT, R(UN, F(ILE, C(OMP, L(IN
```

## Summary

### The Filer

The Filer transfers most of the information from one place to another: It saves information on diskette, moves and deletes diskette files, and sends information to either the computer or the printer. The Filer also tells you where files have been placed on the diskettes, and what devices and diskettes are available for your system's use.

Below are some of the Filer commands available for your use.

| COMMAND | FUNCTION |
|---------|----------|
| **C(HANGE** | Renames a file or diskette. |
| **D(ATE** | Sets the current date. |
| **E(XT-DIR** | Shows the directory of a diskette in an extended form. |
| **G(ET** | Designates a file to be used as the next workfile. |
| **K(RUNCH** | Packs all files together on a diskette. |
| **L(IST-DIR** | Shows the directory of a diskette. |
| **M(AKE** | Creates a dummy file on diskette. |
| **N(EW** | Clears the workfile. |
| **Q(UIT** | Leaves the Filer and returns to the Command level. (Be sure your boot diskette is in the boot drive.) |
| **R(EMOVE** | Erases a file from its diskette directory. |
| **T(RANSFER** | Copies a file or an entire diskette to another diskette or device (for example, a printer). Source diskette must be in a drive in order to begin. |
| **S(AVE** | Saves the workfile on diskette. |
| **V(OLUMES** | Shows which devices and diskettes are in the system. |
| **W(HAT** | Tells the original name of the current workfile. |
| **Z(ERO** | Erases a directory and renames the diskette. |

The Filer is found on the diskettes APPLE0: and APPLE1: under the file name SYSTEM.FILER. In order to enter the Filer mode, type [F] while at the Command level. (This assumes that your diskette with SYSTEM.FILER is in the disk drive.) When the Filer prompt line appears, the diskette containing SYSTEM.FILER may be removed from the system to make room for other diskettes.

In order to exit the Filer mode, type [Q] (for Quit). In order to do this, the diskette with the file SYSTEM.PASCAL must be on the boot diskette (that is, APPLE1:) in the boot drive. Therefore, you should place APPLE1: back into drive #1 before you type [Q] to quit the Filer.

## SOME FILES THAT ARE USED WITH THE APPLE PASCAL SYSTEM

| FILE NAME | STORED ON DISKETTE APPLE0: | APPLE1: | APPLE2: | APPLE3: | USE OF FILE |
|---|---|---|---|---|---|
| SYSTEM.APPLE | | X | | X | Executes the P-code (Interpreter). |
| SYSTEM.COMPILER | X | | X | | Converts Pascal program text to P-code. |
| SYSTEM.CHARSET | X | X | | | Lets you put text on the graphics screen. |
| SYSTEM.EDITOR | X | X | | | Lets you create and change text. |
| SYSTEM.FILER | X | X | | | Lets you store, delete, and move disk files. |
| SYSTEM.LIBRARY | X | X | | | Provides standard routines for use by Pascal programs. |
| SYSTEM.PASCAL | X | X | | | Contains the Command level, which lets you pick E(dit, F(ile, or R(un Mode. |
| SYSTEM.SYNTAX | X | X | | | Provides compiler error messages when in E(dit Mode. |
| CALC.CODE | | | | X | A utility program that lets you use the computer as a calculator. |
| FORMATTER.CODE | | | | X | Utility programs that format new diskettes. |
| FORMATTER.DATA | | | | X | |

## PRACTICE 3–1

1. Which system diskettes contain the Filer? _____.

2. The Filer lets you _____, _____, and _____ diskette files.

3. The workfile is loaded automatically when you enter the EDIT mode. The workfile uses the name _____

   _____.

4. When you see the word "TEXT" at the end of the file name (for example, SYSTEM.WRK.TEXT), it means that the contents of the file can be read by the user; and when you see the word "CODE" at the end of a file name (for example, FORMATTER.CODE), it means that the contents are _____ code.

5. a) To enter the Filer, you must first be at the _____ level, and then you must type _____.
   b) To clear the workfile, you must type _____ for

      _____.

   c) To see the contents of a diskette or its directory, you must type _____ for _____.
   d) To set the current date, you must type _____.
   e) To exit the Filer, you must type _____, which returns the system to the _____ level.

6. a) In a two-disk system, what is the volume number of diskette drive #1? _____
   b) of diskette drive #2? _____

# Chapter 4

## Your First Pascal Program

**What You Will Learn**

- To enter and run your first Pascal program.
- To explain the purpose and use of the Editor.
- To explain the purpose and use of WRITE and WRITELN statements.
- To understand how text moves from keyboard to memory to diskette.
- To correct errors in your program.

Here is a checklist for the equipment you will need for this chapter:

☑ 48K Apple computer with Language Card installed.

☑ A TV set or video monitor connected to your Apple.

☑ Two disk drives (with labels).

☑ APPLE1: diskette (backup copy) in drive 1 (volume #4).

☑ APPLE2: diskette (backup copy) in drive 2 (volume #5).

☑ Formatted blank diskettes.

☑ A clear head and an open mind.

## Understanding the Editor Command Structure

To enter text from the keyboard, you must use the Editor; and to use the Editor, you must start at the Command level. Fig. 4–1 shows the levels of commands you can use in the Editor.

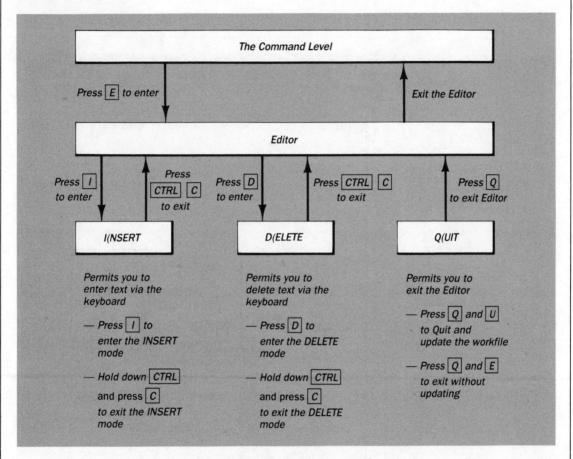

Fig. 4–1 The levels of command in the Editor.

The Editor commands shown in Fig. 4–1 are only some of the commands available when you enter Editor: They are the commands that you will use in this section.

To enter the Editor, you must first be at the Command level; then press [E]. Once you are in the Editor (you should see the EDIT prompt line at the top of the screen), you can use any of the Editor commands by simply pressing the first letter of the command (for example, press [I] for I(NSERT if you wish to enter the INSERT mode).

## How Text Moves from Keyboard to Memory to Diskette and Back

The numbered entries on page 53 refer to the numbers indicated in Fig. 4–2. This diagram will be useful to you in understanding the Apple Pascal system. Study the diagram and refer to it until you thoroughly understand the process.

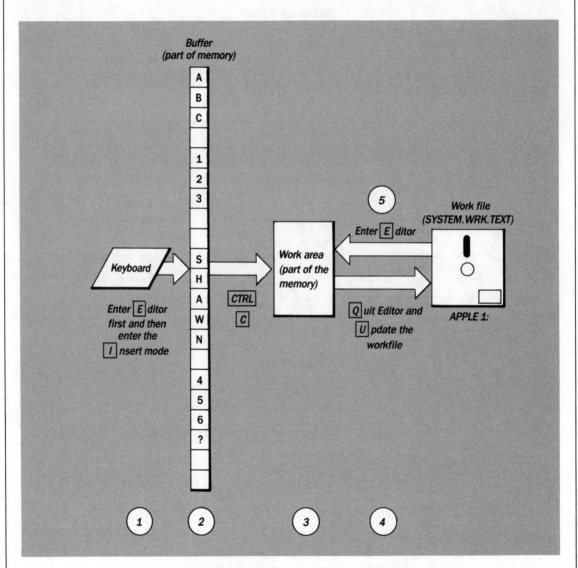

*Fig. 4–2 The movement of text from keyboard to memory to diskette and back.*

1. To enter text, you must first enter the Editor by pressing $\boxed{\text{E}}$ at the Command level, and then enter the I(NSERT mode by pressing $\boxed{\text{I}}$.

2. Each character you type goes into a buffer, which is a temporary storage location in the computer's memory.

3. To exit the INSERT mode, press $\boxed{\text{CTRL}}$ $\boxed{\text{C}}$. A copy of the buffer contents is sent to the work area, which is another part of the computer's memory. But the contents will be lost if either of the following conditions exist: If you press $\boxed{\text{ESC}}$ before pressing $\boxed{\text{CTRL}}$ $\boxed{\text{C}}$, no copy goes to the work area (all text will be lost); if the power is turned off, all information in memory is lost. Therefore, it is important that a copy of the memory content be saved on the diskette from time to time.

4. When you leave the Editor by pressing $\boxed{\text{Q}}$ for Quit, and then press $\boxed{\text{U}}$ for Update, a copy of the contents of the work area is sent to the workfile, where it is written on your APPLE1: diskette and saved there under the file name SYSTEM.WRK.TEXT. (This destroys whatever was there before.)

   If you $\boxed{\text{Q}}$UIT and $\boxed{\text{E}}$XIT without pressing $\boxed{\text{U}}$PDATE (another option), then no copy is sent to the workfile and SYSTEM.WRK.TEXT stays as it was before. The system returns to the Command level whenever you $\boxed{\text{Q}}$UIT the Editor (that is, with or without the Update command). Text on the diskette is least likely to be erased by accident and will not be lost if the power is turned off. However, all text in the computer memory will be lost if the power is turned off.

5. Whenever you are at the Command level and want to enter the Editor, pressing $\boxed{\text{E}}$ causes a copy of the workfile to be sent to the work area. The original copy remains on the diskette. (This is for your convenience, since the material in your workfile is usually the last document you worked on.)

## Entering Your Program Text

**ACTION**

1. *Start at the Command level.*

2. *Enter the EDIT mode by pressing* E. *No workfile is present because you cleared it. (If the workfile is not cleared, then clear it.)*

3. *Press* RETURN.

4. *Enter the INSERT mode by pressing* I. *You are now ready to enter text. (If this prompt line does not appear on the top of the screen, you are* <u>not</u> *in the INSERT mode.)*

5. *Type program text* <u>exactly</u> *as shown, but* <u>do not</u> *press* RETURN *yet!*

   *First examine your program line very carefully. If you made a mistake, use the* <u>&lt;---</u> *to move back to that position, and retype the rest of the line.*

6. *If you typed the first line correctly, press the* RETURN *key twice. (This is done for spacing.)*

**DISPLAY**

```
COMMAND: E(DIT, R(UN, F(ILE, C(OMP, L(IN
```

```
>EDIT: A(DJST C(PY D(LETE F(IND I(NSRT J
NO WORKFILE IS PRESENT. FILE? (<RET> FO
: █
```

```
>EDIT: A(DJST C(PY D(LETE F(IND I(NSRT J
```

```
>INSERT:TEXT [<BS> A CHAR,<DEL> A LINE]
```

```
>INSERT: TEXT [<BS> A CHAR,<DEL> A LINE]
PROGRAM MYFIRST;█
```

```
>INSERT: TEXT [<BS> A CHAR,<DEL> A LINE]
PROGRAM MYFIRST;
█
```

7. *Now type in the rest of the program exactly as shown. (Use the spacebar for indenting.) Note the following:*

   (a) *You indented the keywords **BEGIN** and **END** two spaces from left.*

   (b) *You indented the WRITELN statement four spaces from the left.*

   (c) *A period is required after the keyword **END**.*

   (d) *You inserted your first name. For example, WRITELN ('HELLO AUBREY')*

8. *If you have typed in all lines correctly, hold down* [CTRL] *and press* [C]. *You have left the insert mode and returned to the Editor.*

9. *Exit the EDIT mode (press* [Q]). *Note the options.*

```
PROGRAM MYFIRST;

  BEGIN
    WRITELN ('HELLO NAME')
  END.█
```

```
>EDIT: A(DJST C(PY D(LETE F(IND I(NSRT J

PROGRAM MYFIRST;

  BEGIN
    WRITELN ('HELLO NAME')
  END.
```

```
>QUIT:
  U(PDATE THE WORKFILE AND LEAVE
  E(XIT WITHOUT UPDATING
  R(ETURN TO THE EDITOR WITHOUT UPDATING
  W(RITE TO A FILE NAME AND RETURN
  S(AVE WITH SAME NAME AND RETURN
```

10. *Select the U(PDATE workfile option by pressing* U . *(After the diskette drive whirrs a few seconds and stops, the screen should look like this.)*

```
COMMAND: E(DIT, R(UN, F(ILE, C(OMP, L(IN
```

11. *You have entered the program text. Next, you must see if the program will compile and run.*

## Executing Your Program

### ACTION　　　　　　　　　　　　　　　　DISPLAY

1. *You should now be at the Command level. If you are not, press* CTRL *and* @ *to reinitialize the system.*

```
COMMAND: E(DIT, R(UN, F(ILE, C(OMP, L(IN
```

2. *Be sure APPLE2: is in drive #2.*

3. *Press* R *for R(UN. The screen will clear and then the following will be printed:*

```
COMPILING...

APPLE PASCAL COMPILER 1.1
<   0>
MYFIRST   1923 WORDS
<   3>
4 LINES
SMALLEST AVAILABLE SPACE = 1923 WORDS
```

*The screen will clear again and you will see:*

```
COMMAND: E(DIT, R(UN, F(ILE, C(OMP, L(IN
RUNNING...
HELLO NAME
```

It takes a few seconds for the program to run because it must first be compiled (that is, translated from Pascal to P-code), translated into machine code by the P-machine interpreter, and then executed. Don't worry if you forget the technical aspects of running a Pascal program, because this will not affect the actual running.

## Common Errors

- Forgetting to press `CTRL` `C` after entering your text.

- Forgetting to insert a semicolon at the end of **PROGRAM** statement.

- Forgetting to insert a period after the word **END**.

- Putting a space in the program name.

- Misspelling or using an illegal symbol in the keywords **PROGRAM, BEGIN, END,** and WRITELN.

- Using the letter "O" for the number "zero" (0). (Note: A slash is used to help you recognize a zero. Examine your keyboard closely.)

## Moving the Cursor

In order to edit your programs, it is necessary to move the cursor. You can move the cursor only when one of these prompt lines appears at the top of the screen: EDIT, DELETE, or ADJUST. (The numbers that follow the description of the key in the function column refer to the notes section that follows this list.)

| KEY | FUNCTION |
|---|---|
| `<----` | Moves the cursor one character to the left. (1) |
| `---->` | Moves the cursor one character to the right. (1) |
| `CTRL` `O` | Moves the cursor up one line. (2) |
| `CTRL` `L` | Moves the cursor down one line. (2) |
| `CTRL` `I` | Moves the cursor to the next tab stop in the set direction. (Tab stops are set every eight spaces across the screen.) (3) |
| `P` | Typing `P` while at the EDIT level moves the cursor to the next "page" (that is, a little more than a screenful away from the current cursor position). |

| | |
|---|---|
| <SP> | SP or SPACEBAR moves the cursor in the set direction. (3) |
| RETURN | Moves the cursor in the set direction to the beginning of the next line. (3) |
| = | Moves the cursor to the beginning of the last text inserted, found, or replaced. |
| R-F | The Repeat Factor is a number that is typed immediately before a cursor-move sequence. The cursor move is then repeated the number of times indicated by the Repeat Factor. For example, typing a 2 followed by CTRL L causes the cursor move to be executed twice. (If no RF is typed, RF is assumed to be 1.) |

### Notes

1. Horizontal motion of the cursor is made only within the text of the program.

2. Vertical motion of the cursor is made without regard to the text on the page.

3. The first character (> or <) displayed on most EDITOR prompt lines is a direction indication. A "greater than" character indicates forward direction. A "less than" character indicates backward, or reverse, direction. You can change the set direction when the EDIT or the DELETE prompt line is showing by typing the > or the < key (with or without the shift key).

## Correcting Errors in Your Program

### ACTION

1. *Go to the Command level, if you are not already there.*

2. *Press* E. *(Enter the Editor cursor.) Note that the computer automatically loaded your workfile; it appears on the screen shown.*

### DISPLAY

```
COMMAND: E(DIT, R(UN, F(ILE, C(OMP, L(IN
```

```
>EDIT: A(DJST C(PY D(LETE F(IND I(NSRT J

PROGRAM MYFIRST;

BEGIN
 WRITELN ('HELLO NAME')
END.
```

3. *Move the cursor over the ";" at the end of program's name (MYFIRST).*

**PROGRAM** MYFIRST ⌈;⌉

4. *PRESS* ⌈D⌉ *to select DELETE.*

>DELETE: < > <MOVING COMMANDS> [ <ETX>T
**PROGRAM** MYFIRST ⌈;⌉

5. *Press* ⌈--->⌉ *to delete the ";" and then press* ⌈CTRL⌉ ⌈C⌉ *to exit the DELETE mode. Note: ";" was deleted.*

>EDIT: A(DJST C(PY D(LETE F(IND I(NSRT J
**PROGRAM** MYFIRST

6. *Now exit the Editor and update the workfile by pressing* ⌈Q⌉ ⌈U⌉.

COMMAND: E(DIT, R(UN, F(ILE, C(OMP, L(IN

7. *Run the program by pressing* ⌈R⌉.

COMPILING...

*The program attempted to compile; it reached line 2, where it recognized an ERROR, and then stopped.*

APPLE PASCAL COMPILER [1.1]
<    0>..

  BEGIN<<<<
LINE 2, ERROR 14: <SP> (CONTINUE), <ESC>(

8. *Use* ⌈CTRL⌉ ⌈A⌉ *if you can't see the other half of the screen. You have three options:*

TERMINATE), E(DIT

   (a) *<SP> means press the* ⌈SPACEBAR⌉ *to continue trying to compile the program.*

   (b) *<ESC> means press the* ⌈ESC⌉ *key to quit, and go back to the Command level.*

   (c) *E(DIT means type* ⌈E⌉ *to go to the Editor, and correct the error.*

9. In order to correct the error, press ☐E☐ for Editor. If necessary, press ☐CTRL☐ ☐A☐ again so you can see the left side of the screen.

```
';' EXPECTED (POSSIBLY ON THE LINE ABOVE).
PROGRAM MYFIRST
  BEGIN
    WRITELN ('HELLO NAME')
  END.
```

10. Press the ☐SPACEBAR☐ to enter the Editor.

```
>EDIT: A(DJST C(PY D(LETE F(IND I(NSRT J
PROGRAM MYFIRST

  BEGIN█
    WRITELN ('HELLO NAME')
  END.
```

11. Use ☐CTRL☐ ☐O☐ to move the cursor up, and ☐---->☐ to move the cursor right.

```
PROGRAM MYFIRST█
```

12. Press ☐I☐ (for Insert).

```
>INSERT: TEXT [<BS> A CHAR,<DEL> A LINE]
PROGRAM MYFIRST;█
```

13. Now press ☐;☐ to insert the ";".

14. Press ☐CTRL☐ ☐C☐ to exit the INSERT mode and return to the EDIT prompt line.

```
>EDIT: A(DJST C(PY D(LETE F(IND INSRT J
PROGRAM MYFIRST;█
  BEGIN
    WRITELN ('HELLO NAME')
  END.
```

15. Now exit Editor by pressing ☐Q☐ ☐U☐ (for Quit and Update workfile).

```
COMMAND: E(DIT, R(UN, F(ILE, C(OMP, L(IN
```

16. Let's run the program again. Press ☐R☐.

```
COMMAND: E(DIT, R(UN, F(ILE, C(OMP, L(IN
RUNNING...
HELLO NAME
```

Typing ⬚R⬚ caused the computer to compile the program again before executing it. If other errors existed, the program would stop again and you would repeat the above procedure. This procedure is very important, so make sure you understand it. When an error is encountered in a program compilation, a message usually appears in place of the EDIT prompt line when you return to the Editor.

## Expanding Your Program

### ACTION

### DISPLAY

1. *Enter the Editor. This causes the computer to automatically load the workfile with the program you stored in it.*

```
>EDIT: A(DJST C(PY D(LETE F(IND I(NSRT J
PROGRAM MYFIRST;

  BEGIN
    WRITELN ('HELLO NAME')
  END.
```

2. *Move the cursor to the end of WRITELN line by pressing* ⬚CTRL⬚ ⬚L⬚ *and* ⬚---->⬚, *and press* ⬚I⬚ *(to enter the INSERT mode).*

```
INSERT TEXT [<BS> A CHAR,<DEL> A LINE]
PROGRAM MYFIRST

  BEGIN
    WRITELN ('HELLO NAME')█
```

3. *Now insert a semicolon (press* ⬚;⬚*), and then press* ⬚RETURN⬚.

```
  BEGIN
    WRITELN ('HELLO NAME');
    █
```

4. *Enter another line of text as shown (you can do this since you are still in the INSERT mode). Don't forget the ";" at the end of the line; and be sure to press* ⬚RETURN⬚ *after each line.*

```
  BEGIN
    WRITELN ('HELLO NAME');
    WRITELN ('I SPEAK PASCAL');
    █
```

5. Now type in the last line as shown.

```
>INSERT: TEXT [<BS> A CHAR,<DEL> A LINE]
PROGRAM MYFIRST:

  BEGIN
    WRITELN ('HELLO NAME');
    WRITELN ('I SPEAK PASCAL');
    WRITELN ('DO YOU?')█
```

6. Since this is all the text we wish to insert, let's exit the INSERT mode by pressing [CTRL] [C]. Note that there is no ";" at the end of the third WRITELN statement.

```
PROGRAM MYFIRST;

  BEGIN
    WRITELN ('HELLO NAME');
    WRITELN ('I SPEAK PASCAL');
    WRITELN ('DO YOU?')█
END.
```

7. Let's exit the EDIT mode ( [Q] [U] ).

```
COMMAND: E(DIT, R(UN, F(ILE, C(OMP, L(IN
```

8. Press [R] for Run. If there are no errors, you should see the results as shown.

```
COMMAND: E(DIT, R(UN, F(ILE, C(OMP, L(IN
RUNNING...
HELLO NAME
I SPEAK PASCAL
DO YOU?
```

9. If this worked, let's put spaces between the output lines. Press [E].

```
>EDIT: A(DJST C(PY D(LETE F(IND I(NSRT J
[P]ROGRAM MYFIRST:

  BEGIN
    WRITELN ('HELLO NAME');
    WRITELN ('I SPEAK PASCAL');
    WRITELN ('DO YOU?')
END.
```

10. Move the cursor over the "W" in the second WRITELN statement.

```
  BEGIN
    WRITELN ('HELLO NAME');
    [W]RITELN ('I SPEAK PASCAL');
```

11. Press [I] for Insert.

```
  BEGIN
    WRITELN ('HELLO NAME');
    █
    WRITELN ('DO YOU');
END.
```

*If necessary, press* CTRL A *to see the right side of the screen.*

```
                    WRITELN ('I SPEAK PASCAL');
```

12. *Type in WRITELN, as shown. Press* RETURN *and then press* CTRL C

```
>EDIT: A(DJST C(PY D(LETE F(IND I(NSRT J
PROGRAM MYFIRST;

BEGIN
  WRITELN ('HELLO NAME');
  WRITELN;
  WRITELN ('I SPEAK PASCAL');
  WRITELN ('DO YOU?')
END.
```

13. *Insert another WRITELN. Your screen should look like this.*

```
>EDIT: A(DJST C(PY D(LETE F(IND I(NSRT J
PROGRAM MYFIRST
  BEGIN
    WRITELN ('HELLO NAME');
    WRITELN;
    WRITELN ('I SPEAK PASCAL');
    WRITELN;
    WRITELN ('DO YOU?')
  END.
```

14. *Exit Editor (* Q U *).*

```
COMMAND: E(DIT, R(UN, F(ILE, C(OMP, L(IN
```

15. *Now run the program (press* R *). If the program ran, the message shown here should be on your screen. If it didn't, you probably made an error and will have to enter the Editor to fix it. (Note that there is a space between each of the output lines. The WRITELN; statement caused this to happen.)*

```
COMMAND: E(DIT, R(UN, F(ILE, C(OMP, L(IN
RUNNING...
HELLO NAME

I SPEAK PASCAL

DO YOU?
```

## Understanding the Two Output Statements: WRITE and WRITELN

Pascal features two standard statements—WRITE and WRITELN—to send information to its output devices, such as the display or printer. WRITE simply tells the computer to write out the items specified in the output list and continue to write the output on the same line. (That is, WRITE does not issue a carriage return, so all characters sent to the screen or printer will be on the same line.) WRITELN, which is short for "WRITE A LINE," tells the computer the same thing as WRITE does, except it issues a carriage return so that the next character sent to the screen will start a new line. (Additional differences between WRITE and WRITELN are covered in more detail in subsequent pages of this chapter.)

The format is:

WRITE (output list)

*or*

WRITELN (output list)

The *Output List* is simply a list of things to be written to the display, printer, or other output devices. If the output list is inside apostrophes (single quotes), the computer will print out whatever is within the quotes. For example, in the output statement:

WRITE ('HELLO ADRIENNE')

the computer would display or print HELLO ADRIENNE (without the quotes).

If, however, the output list was *not* inside the quotes, then the computer would consider the output list to include variables that hold some value. Therefore, the computer would print or display the value of the variable. For example, in the output statement

WRITE (LENGTH)

the computer would assume that some value is assigned to the variable length, and would therefore print any value assigned to it. If no value was assigned to the variable, the computer will print out an error message.

*Note: Variables will be discussed in greater detail in Chapter 5.*

If there is more than one variable used in the output list, then commas are used to separate each variable in the list. For example:

WRITE (LENGTH, WIDTH, HEIGHT, AREA)

## EXERCISE 4–1

### *Understanding the Two Write Statements: WRITE and WRITELN*

<table>
<tr><th>ACTION</th><th>DISPLAY</th></tr>
<tr><td>

1. Clear the workfile by entering the Filer from the Command level, and then press [N] [Y]. Exit the Filer by pressing [Q], and then press [E] for EDIT.

</td><td>

```
FILER: G, S, N, L, R, C, T, D, Q [1.1]
WORKFILE CLEARED
```

</td></tr>
<tr><td>

2. Enter the INSERT mode and type in the program shown.

</td><td>

```
>INSERT: TEXT [<BS> A CHAR, <DEL> A LINE
PROGRAM MYSECOND;
```

</td></tr>
<tr><td>

Note that both WRITE and WRITELN statements are used; also, semicolons are used on all WRITE and WRITELN statements except the last one.

</td><td>

```
BEGIN
  WRITE ('I ');
  WRITE ('SPEAK ');
  WRITELN ('PASCAL');
  WRITE ('DO ');
  WRITELN ('YOU?')
END.
```

</td></tr>
<tr><td>

3. EXIT the Editor using [Q] [U] keys, and then press [R] from the Command level to run the program.

</td><td>

```
COMMAND: E(DIT, R(UN, F(ILE, C(OMP, L(IN
RUNNING...
I SPEAK PASCAL
DO YOU?
```

</td></tr>
</table>

WRITE does not issue a RETURN, so it does not start a new line. That is, I SPEAK PASCAL is printed on the same line. WRITELN issues a return; therefore, a new line was started after the first WRITELN (that is, DO YOU? was printed on the second line).

## Summary

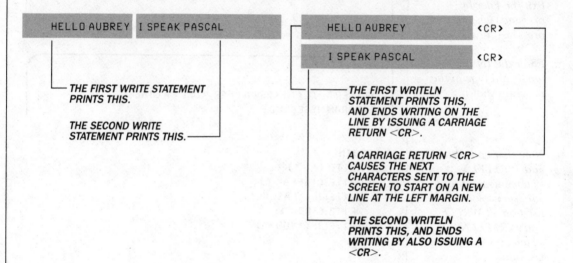

WRITE

```
PROGRAM SAMELINE:
  BEGIN
    WRITE ('HELLO AUBREY');
    WRITE (' I SPEAK PASCAL ')
  END.
```

HELLO AUBREY  I SPEAK PASCAL

*THE FIRST WRITE STATEMENT PRINTS THIS.*

*THE SECOND WRITE STATEMENT PRINTS THIS.*

WRITELN

```
PROGRAM NEWLINE;
  BEGIN
    WRITELN ('HELLO AUBREY ');
    WRITELN (' I SPEAK PASCAL ')
  END.
```

HELLO AUBREY                    <CR>

I SPEAK PASCAL                  <CR>

*THE FIRST WRITELN STATEMENT PRINTS THIS, AND ENDS WRITING ON THE LINE BY ISSUING A CARRIAGE RETURN <CR>.*

*A CARRIAGE RETURN <CR> CAUSES THE NEXT CHARACTERS SENT TO THE SCREEN TO START ON A NEW LINE AT THE LEFT MARGIN.*

*THE SECOND WRITELN PRINTS THIS, AND ENDS WRITING BY ALSO ISSUING A <CR>.*

1. The output is printed on the same line.

2. There is a space between the words "Aubrey" and "I." You must leave a space inside the quote to have proper spacing in your output.

3. Anything you place inside the single quotes will appear on the screen for both WRITE and WRITELN statements.

1. Output printed on different lines.

2. <CR> is not visible on the screen but was placed here to emphasize the difference between WRITE and WRITELN (i.e. WRITE does *not* issue a <CR>).

3. Anything you place inside the single quotes will appear on the screen for both WRITE and WRITELN statements.

**Summary**

### Entering, Editing, and Executing Pascal Programs

Enter the program text (source program) via the keyboard and the text Editor. (See Fig. 4–3.) When you finish entering your program text, Quit (leave) the Editor and save your program on the workfile, which is on a diskette.

After you have Quit ( Q ) and told the computer to Update ( U ) your workfile, your program is automatically saved on the diskette under the file name SYSTEM.WRK.TEXT.

You can also use the Editor if you wish to make changes to your program. When you enter the Editor, the system automatically loads a copy of the workfile from the diskette into memory. If the program you wish to change is not in the workfile but is saved somewhere else (for example, on another diskette or under another file name), you must transfer the program to the workfile first. (This will be demonstrated later.)

When you run your program, the system will attempt to compile it first (if needed). Your program will have to be compiled the first time you try to run it. However, once your program is compiled, it does not have to be recompiled each time you wish to run it; that is, it will be executed without compiling. (Compiling is the process of translating Pascal programming language into machine language so that the computer can execute the program.)

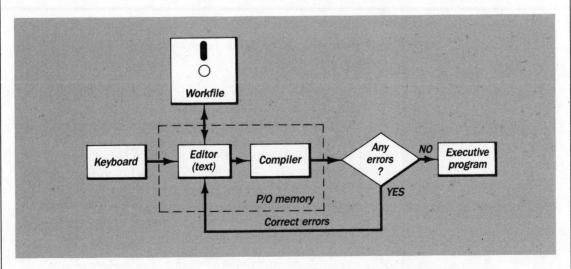

**Fig. 4–3 Entering, editing, and executing Pascal programs.**

Once your program is compiled correctly, the computer will execute the compiled version of the program. Hence, program execution is faster the second time around since the program does not have to be compiled before it is executed.

If errors occur during the compiling process, you must go back to the Editor and correct the errors, and then try to Compile and Run the program again. Repeat this process until the program compiles correctly and executes properly.

### Program Structure

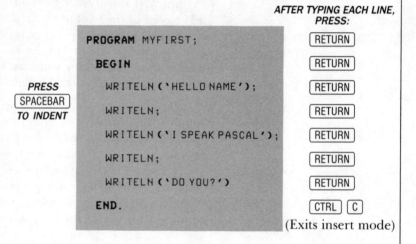

AFTER TYPING EACH LINE, PRESS:

```
PROGRAM MYFIRST;                      RETURN

   BEGIN                              RETURN

      WRITELN ('HELLO NAME');         RETURN

      WRITELN;                        RETURN

      WRITELN ('I SPEAK PASCAL');     RETURN

      WRITELN;                        RETURN

      WRITELN ('DO YOU?')             RETURN

   END.                              CTRL  C
```

PRESS
SPACEBAR
TO INDENT

(Exits insert mode)

Let's summarize some things you have learned about writing Pascal programs:

1. Every Pascal program begins with a program name, which is assigned by the programmer (you). Every name must begin with a letter, and the name must consist of only letters (A to Z) and digits (0 to 9). The letters may be upper- or lowercase. Blank spaces must not be included in names; otherwise, an error will result. (Note: Do not use any of the 42 Pascal reserved words! See page 134 of the Apple Pascal Language Reference Manual for this list.) Only the first eight characters of a name are recognized by the computer, and a semicolon must be inserted after the program name.

2. The reserved words **BEGIN** and **END** serve to bracket program statements. Consecutive Pascal statements between **BEGIN** and **END** must be separated by semicolons. The last program statement does not require a semicolon, but a period is required after the word **END** if it is the last program statement.

3. WRITELN and WRITE statements generate output on your display. The computer will display whatever follows WRITE or WRITELN if it is placed in parentheses and inside single quotes (for example, 'HELLO NAME'). A single WRITELN; statement produces no output but causes the computer to skip a line before displaying the next output line.

4. To significantly enhance your program style and readability, you should use blank spaces and indentation throughout your program.

### Editor Commands

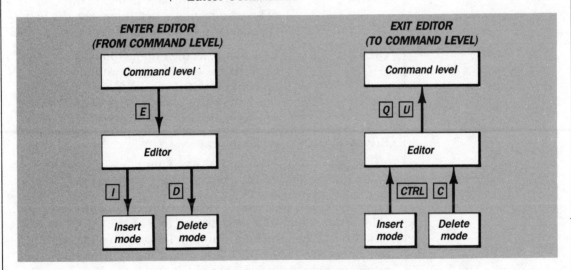

1. To enter the Editor from the Command level, press E .

2. To enter the INSERT mode, press I .

3. To enter the DELETE mode, press D .

1. To exit the Editor and update the workfile, press Q (for Quit) and then U (for Update).

2. To exit the INSERT mode, press CTRL C .

3. To exit the DELETE mode, press CTRL C .

## The Editor

The Editor allows you to create and change text. To enter text from the keyboard, you must use the Editor. Use the Editor commands to I(nsert, D(elete, X(change, and move text. When you are through, Q(uit and U(pdate the workfile. Some Editor commands follow.

| COMMAND | FUNCTION |
|---|---|
| **A(DJST** | Moves the line at the cursor to the right and left. The ADJUST mode makes it easy to adjust the indentation of a line or a whole group of lines. |
| **D(LETE** | Moving the cursor while in this mode erases text. |
| **F(IND /X/** | Moves the cursor to the next "X." |
| **I(NSRT** | Inserts typed text at present cursor position. |
| **P(AGE** | Moves cursor one page in the set direction. (The set direction is determined by the first character displayed on the Editor prompt line.) |
| **Q(UIT** | Leaves or exits the Editor. You may U(pdate the workfile, E(xit without updating, W(rite to any diskette file before returning to the Command level, or S(ave your original file. |
| **R(PLACE /X//Y/** | Replaces next "X" by "Y." |

The Editor is found on the diskettes APPLE0: and APPLE1: under the file name SYSTEM.EDITOR.

Enter the Editor by typing E while at the Command level. (This assumes that your diskette with SYSTEM.EDITOR is in a disk drive.) When the Editor prompt line appears, the diskette containing SYSTEM.EDITOR may be removed from the system to make room for other diskettes.

Exit the Editor by typing Q. This permits you to select one of the following options:

U(PDATE the workfile and leave.
E(XIT without updating.
R(ETURN to the Editor without updating.
W(RITE to a file name and return.
S(AVE with same name and return.

## PRACTICE 4–1

**Writing and Running Your First Program**

1. Write a program to output the following on separate lines:
   a. Your name (first and last)
   b. Your school's name
   c. Your teacher's name

   Hint: If your program does not run, turn to page 58 of this section to review how to correct errors in your program (if needed).

## PRACTICE 4–2

**Editing Your Program**

If you have cleared your workfile, then rewrite the program in Practice 4–1 and do the following (if you still have the program from Practice 4–1, you do not have to rewrite the program):

1. Delete the program lines that output your teacher's name and your school's name.

2. Add (insert) a program line that prints out your home address. (Make sure that each of the following is printed on a separate line).      street name and number
   city and state
   zip code

3. Have the computer insert one space between each of your output lines.

## PRACTICE 4–3

**Understanding WRITE and WRITELN**

1. Trace the program and predict the output. (That is, write the output exactly as the computer would do it.)

```
PROGRAM PRINTOUT;

BEGIN
  WRITE('THIS ');
  WRITE('IS ');
  WRITE('AN ');
  WRITELN('EXAMPLE');
  WRITELN;
  WRITELN('OF');
  WRITELN;
  WRITE('USING WRITE ');
  WRITELN('AND WRITELN')
END. (* PRINTOUT *)
```

2. Enter and run the program. (Did your answer match the computer's answer?)

*Courtesy of Apple Computer Inc.*

## Chapter 5

# Numbers and Data Types Used in Pascal Programs

**What You Will Learn**

- To understand the various number types used in Pascal and to learn how to use them.

- To explain the mathematical operations and order of mathematical operations using the M.D.A.S. rule.

- To understand the structure of Pascal and the Declaration Block, especially the **CONST** and **VAR** parts of the block.

- To enter and run the exercises that help to illustrate the properties of the numbers and data types used in Pascal.

You do not need to be a math major to use or understand computers; one of the major advantages of a computer is that it can perform a lot of calculations very quickly. So far, we have not discussed numbers because some people are intimidated by the thought of having to do mathematics. Nevertheless, we cannot discuss computers without touching on their arithmetic capabilities.

## Types of Numbers in Pascal

Numbers may be represented in either of two forms: integers or real numbers. *Integers* are whole numbers that may be positive, negative, or zero. They may be written as a sequence of digits (ordinary integers range from $-32768$ through $32767$ for Apple Pascal). Integers may or may not be preceded by a sign ($+$ or $-$). Some examples of valid integers are:

| | |
|---|---|
| 2 | $+50000$ |
| 0 | $-600000$ |
| $-2$ | $50000000$ |

Some examples of invalid integers are:

3,256,561    Integers must not contain nondigits (that is, commas).

$-5.0$    Integers must not contain a decimal point.

As a general rule in Pascal, an integer value may be used wherever a real value is expected.

*Real numbers* are numbers with fractional parts. They may be written with a decimal point, and the number may be preceded by a sign. Some examples of valid real numbers are:

$$0.0$$
$$0.774$$
$$-56.8$$
$$13.1376$$

Each of these numbers may be expressed as an integer or a decimal point multiplied by an integral power of 10.

Examples of valid real numbers expressed in scientific notation or exponential forms are:

$$5.73E+02$$
$$0.8567E+2$$
$$25E-5$$

*In Pascal, if an integer value occurs where a real value is required, it is automatically converted to the equivalent real value; however, the converse is not true. That is, if an integer value is required, a real value cannot be used instead. If you are not familiar with scientific notation or exponential form, refer to pages 74 and 75.*

The following are examples of invalid real numbers and why they are not valid:

1.          There is no digit after the decimal point.

.356          There is no digit before the decimal point.

3,476.88     A comma does not appear in a real number.

*Long integers* are made up of a maximum of 36 digits. The long integer is used for business and scientific applications that require extended number lengths with complete accuracy.

If integer and long integer values are mixed in an expression, the integer values are converted to long integer, and the result is a long integer value.

Long integers and real numbers are not compatible; they can never be mixed in an arithmetic expression or assigned to each other.

**NOTE:** *We will not use long integers in the examples in this chapter; however, it is important that you know the difference between ordinary integers, with a range from −32768 to 32767, and long integers, which can extend a range to 36 digits. If you are interested in programs that require long integers, try Extra Practices 5 and 6 at the end of this book.*

## Standard Scientific Notation

Scientists often express large numbers, such as 186,000, and small numbers, such as 0.00015, as the product of two numbers. Some examples follow.

| NUMBER | | EXPRESSED AS PRODUCT OF TWO NUMBERS | MEANING |
|---|---|---|---|
| 186000 | = | $1.86 \times 10^5$ | $10^5$ means move the decimal 5 places to the right. |
| 0.00015 | = | $1.5 \times 10^{-4}$ | $10^{-4}$ means move the decimal 4 places to the left. |
| 764000000 | = | $7.64 \times 10^8$ | $10^8$ means move the decimal 8 places to the right. |
| 0.00347 | = | $3.47 \times 10^{-3}$ | $10^{-3}$ means move the decimal 3 places to the left. |

## Scientific Notation for Pascal

| ORDINARY REAL NUMBER NOTATION | SCIENTIFIC NOTATION | SCIENTIFIC NOTATION FOR PASCAL (REAL NUMBERS ONLY) | MEANING |
|---|---|---|---|
| 5000.00 | $5 \times 10^3$ | 5.000000E3 | Move decimal 3 places to the right. |
| 0.005 | $5 \times 10^{-3}$ | 5.00000E-3 | Move decimal 3 places to the left. |
| 24.375 | $2.4375 \times 10^1$ | 2.43750E1 | Move decimal 1 place to the right. |
| 0.24375 | $2.4375 \times 10^{-1}$ | 2.43750E-1 | Move decimal 1 place to the left. |

Pascal uses scientific notation for real numbers. The table on page 74 compares the regular, or more familiar way, of using scientific notation to the scientific notation used with Apple Pascal.

Review each of the above examples and use other examples, if necessary, until you understand the concept. If you have trouble understanding this, don't worry about it. The most important thing for you to remember is that the E is used for scientific notation when expressing real numbers. More specifically:

En (where n = 1 to 38) means move the decimal n places to the right.

E-n (where n = 1 to 37) means move the decimal n places to the left.

## Math Operators Used with Integers and Real Numbers

| | INTEGER | REAL | LONG INTEGER |
|---|---|---|---|
| Equal | = | = | = |
| Add | + | + | + |
| Subtract | – | – | – |
| Multiply | * | * | * |
| Divide | | / | |
| For whole number part | **DIV** (see note 1) | | **DIV** (see note 2) |
| For remainder part | **MOD** (see note 1) | | (see note 2) |

(1) Since an Integer is a whole number, it cannot have a fractional part. If you divide the integer 7 by the integer 3, the result is 2.33, which is a real number. Therefore, if you are working with integers and want to perform division, you must use the special operators **DIV** and **MOD.** For example, 7 **DIV** 3 is the whole number part of the quotient of 7 divided by 3, which is 2. In contrast, 7 **MOD** 3 is the remainder of 7 divided by 3, which is 1.

(2) Only **DIV** can be used with long integers. **MOD** is not used because overflow (error) occurs if an immediate or final result requires more than 36 decimal digits. That is, long integers do not have a remainder part the way ordinary integers do.

## Order of Mathematical Operation

The order of performing a mathematical operation is to first multiply, then divide, then add, and then subtract. (You can remember this order with the phrase "My Dear Aunt Sally.")

If parentheses are used in the operation, first perform the innermost level operations, and then the next level out. Use the M.D.A.S. order (left to right) inside the parentheses.

If there are no parentheses, the computer performs operations from left to right, first performing multiplication and division. Then, addition and subtraction are done in order from left to right (remember, M.D.A.S.!). For example:

$$4 + 5 * 3 - 4/2 =$$
$$4 + \boxed{15} - 4/2 =$$
$$4 + 15 - \boxed{2} =$$
$$\boxed{19} - 2 = \boxed{17}$$

If there are parentheses, the computer starts at the inner pair of the parentheses and converts everything to a single number. Then, the computer repeats the process with the next pair of parentheses, working inside out, using the M.D.A.S. rule. For example:

$$( (6+4) * 2) / 4 =$$
$$( \boxed{10} * 2) / 4 =$$
$$\boxed{20} / 4 = \boxed{5}$$

## Tips on Using Parentheses

When in doubt, use parentheses. They can't do any harm! Use parentheses around operations you want performed first. Make sure that every left parenthesis has a matching right parenthesis. Count them to be sure.

Work from the innermost pair of parentheses first (the M.D.A.S. rule also applies to operations inside parentheses). Then work form the "inside" out. In the case of a "tie," the computer works from left to right, per the M.D.A.S. rule.

## The Calculator Mode

The calculator mode is a utility program that turns your Apple into a very simple calculator. The file CALC.CODE is normally found on the diskette APPLE3:. It lets you add, subtract, divide, and multiply numbers.

The results are expressed in scientific notation, rounded to six digits followed by a power-of-ten indicator from E37 to E-37. Input numbers must *not* be expressed in scientific notation, however, and should *not* contain more than 36 digits.

When you quit the calculator program, or when an error terminates the program, your boot diskette (APPLE1:) should be in the boot drive. If it is not there, the system may "hang," or you may see the message:

```
PUT IN APPLE1:
```

---

## EXERCISE 5–1

### Using the Calculator Mode

| ACTION | DISPLAY |
| --- | --- |

**ACTION**

1. Put the APPLE1: diskette in your boot drive and the APPLE3: diskette in the other drive, and then boot the system.

**DISPLAY**

```
COMMAND:E(DIT,R(UN,F(ILE,C(OMP,L(IN
```

2. From the Command level, press [X] for Execute. (Note that X(ECUTE command calls the utility program.)

```
EXECUTE WHAT FILE?
```

3. Respond by typing APPLE3:CALC

```
EXECUTE WHAT FILE? APPLE3:CALC
```

4. The system responds by displaying a $\boxed{--\!>}$ . You may now type any simple mathematical expression, using only these operators: add (+), subtract (−), multiply (*), Divide (/).

```
EXECUTE WHAT FILE? APPLE3:CALC
-> ■
```

5. For example, type in the problem shown.

```
-> (4+5)*3/9
```

6. Press $\boxed{\text{RETURN}}$ to get the answer. Note that the cursor drops down to the next line, waiting for you to enter another problem.

```
-> (4+5)*3/9
      3.00000
-> ■
```

7. Make up some problems of your own and try them until you feel comfortable using the CALC mode. (If you can't think of any problems, see Practice 5–3 on page 93.)

8. When you are ready to quit the CALCULATOR mode, respond to the prompt $\boxed{--\!>}$ by pressing the $\boxed{\text{RETURN}}$ key. This returns you to the Command level. Be sure your boot diskette is in the boot drive.

```
COMMAND:E(DIT,R(UN,F(ILE,C(OMP,L(IN
```

## Variables

A variable is simply some location in memory to which you assign a name so that it can hold a value (data) temporarily. Fortunately, you do not have to worry about where the data are stored in the computer because the computer keeps track of it for you. All you have to do is to simply tell the computer the name of each variable you want to use, and then the computer determines the specific location to store the variable.

You *must* remember the names you assign to a variable. Therefore, it is very important to assign a meaningful name or a name that describes the contents of the variable. This will help you to remember the variables used in your program.

A variable has three properties: name, type, and value. You assign the name and the specific data type (for example, INTEGER, REAL, CHAR, and so on). Value is assigned somewhere in the main program either by an assignment statement or via a keyboard input.

To use variables in your program, you *must* declare them in the **VAR** block of your program. You must always declare NAME and TYPE, as you will see in the next few pages.

### Tips on Selecting Names for Variables Used in Pascal

There are thousands of possibilities for names of variables. You are limited only by your imagination for choice of names as long as you comply with the rules. Here are some rules for naming a variable:

- It must begin with a letter (A to Z).

- It must be followed by another letter or a digit (0 to 9).

- Delete spaces and punctuation marks (within names).

- Use meaningful names that relate to your program and the contents of the variable (where possible).

- Do not use any of the 42 Pascal reserve words (if you do not know these words, refer to page 134 in your Apple Pascal Language Reference Manual).

- Only the first eight characters of a variable name are significant, so be careful not to use words that will be treated as equivalent. If you do, an "identifier declared twice" error will result.

Below are some examples of acceptable names for variables:

| | | | |
|---|---|---|---|
| LENGTH | NAME | GROSS | REVENUE |
| WIDTH | ADDRESS | GROSSPAY | SALES |
| HEIGHT | CITY | NET | PROFIT |
| RADIUS | STATE | NETPAY | LOSS |
| AREA | COUNTRY | SALESTAX | EARNINGS |
| PERIMETER | ZIP | FICA | PRICE |
| WEIGHT | STREET | STATETAX | COST |
| MILES | POBOX | RATE | |
| DISTANCE | TELEPHONE | | |

## EXERCISE 5–2

### Using Meaningful Names as Variables

The purpose of this exercise is to help you become familiar with assigning numeric values to variables, and also to understand how a computer stores values.

Variables are like addresses, names, or labels to help you keep track of data location. All variables are declared in the declaration block (**VAR**) as real variables in this program.

The first assignment statement (LENGTH : = 12.5) tells the computer to assign a value of 12.5 to the variable LENGTH. The variable LENGTH is simply some location in memory that the computer keeps track of—so you do not have to worry about where things are stored as long as you remember the variable's name.

You have the freedom of choice to pick the names for your variables (except for reserved words, which cannot be used). But it is a good idea to create meaningful names or names that relate to your program so that you will have an easier time understanding your program.

Fill in the blanks and study the exercise until you understand it. Change the values of LENGTH and WIDTH, and repeat the exercise, if necessary.

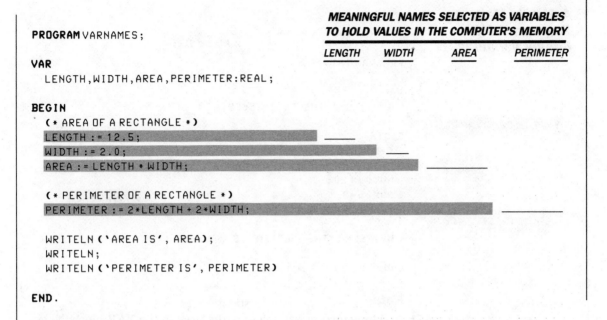

**MEANINGFUL NAMES SELECTED AS VARIABLES TO HOLD VALUES IN THE COMPUTER'S MEMORY**

| LENGTH | WIDTH | AREA | PERIMETER |
|---|---|---|---|

```
PROGRAM VARNAMES;

VAR
  LENGTH,WIDTH,AREA,PERIMETER:REAL;

BEGIN
  (* AREA OF A RECTANGLE *)
  LENGTH := 12.5;
  WIDTH := 2.0;
  AREA := LENGTH * WIDTH;

  (* PERIMETER OF A RECTANGLE *)
  PERIMETER := 2*LENGTH + 2*WIDTH;

  WRITELN ('AREA IS', AREA);
  WRITELN;
  WRITELN ('PERIMETER IS', PERIMETER)

END.
```

## EXERCISE 5–3

### Assigning Numeric Values to Variables

Study the partial Pascal program and then, using the assignment statements, fill in the blanks. Go through the program line by line.

What happens to the data previously stored in location A when the program reaches the assignment statement (A := A*10)?

Go over the exercise until you understand it. Change the value of A and B, and repeat the exercise, if necessary.

**SELECTED VARIABLES USED TO HOLD THE NUMBERS**

| A | B | C | D | E | W |
|---|---|---|---|---|---|

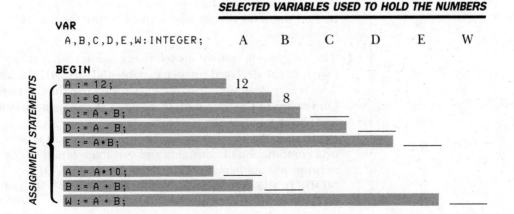

ASSIGNMENT STATEMENTS

```
VAR
  A,B,C,D,E,W:INTEGER;

BEGIN
  A := 12;          12
  B := 8;                8
  C := A + B;
  D := A - B;
  E := A*B;

  A := A*10;
  B := A + B;
  W := A + B;
```

## A Simple Math Program Using Integer Variables

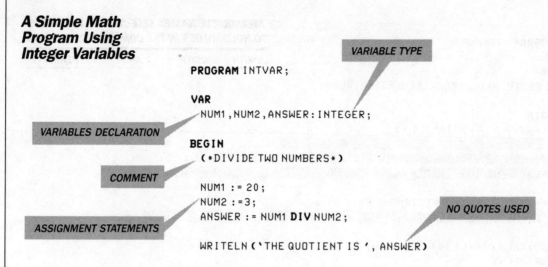

```
PROGRAM INTVAR;

VAR
  NUM1,NUM2,ANSWER:INTEGER;

BEGIN
  (*DIVIDE TWO NUMBERS*)

  NUM1 := 20;
  NUM2 :=3;
  ANSWER := NUM1 DIV NUM2;

  WRITELN('THE QUOTIENT IS ', ANSWER)

END.
```

VARIABLE TYPE

VARIABLES DECLARATION

COMMENT

ASSIGNMENT STATEMENTS

NO QUOTES USED

### Notes

1. Three integer variables are declared in the **VAR** block. Note that a comma separates each variable listed, and a colon (:) separates the variables' names from the data type (integer).

2. Anything between (* and *) is a comment. A comment is not an instruction to the computer; it is simply a remark for you or someone else who may want to inspect the program. Comments may appear anywhere in the program to help you remember or understand what the program is used for and how it is used. For example, the comment here (*DIVIDE TWO NUMBERS*) tells you what this section of the program does.

3. When using integer numbers in a WRITELN statement, leave a space before the final single quote of the label. Integer numbers do not have a space before them as real numbers do.

4. The assignment statements tell the computer what values to assign to the declared integer variable (NUM1, NUM2, and ANSWER). Assignment statements always use the (:=) sign. On the left of the (:=) sign, there must always be a variable; and on the right of the (:=) sign, there must be an expression. An expression can be a constant or a variable, or a combination of constants and variables joined by the appropriate mathematical operation (+, −, *, /, **DIV,** or **MOD**). In the expression NUM1 **DIV** NUM2, NUM1 and NUM2 are joined by the operator **DIV**.

5. The results of this program will show only the whole
number part of NUM1 **DIV** NUM2, which is 6. Of course,
you know that 20/3 is 6.6667 in real numbers, but integer
division does not permit decimals. (To see the remainder,
you would use NUM1 **MOD** NUM2.) The next example will
use real numbers.

```
PROGRAM REALVAR;

VAR
    NUM1,NUM2,ANSWER:REAL;

BEGIN
    (*DIVIDE TWO NUMBERS*)

    NUM1 := 20.0;
    NUM2 := 3.0;
    ANSWER := NUM1 / NUM2;

    WRITELN('THE QUOTIENT IS', ANSWER)

END.
```

VARIABLE DECLARATION

VARIABLE TYPE

COMMENT

ASSIGNMENT STATEMENTS

NO QUOTES USED

### Notes

1. Three real variables are declared in the **VAR** block. Note
that each variable is separated by a comma, and that a colon
(:) is used to separate the variable names and the data type
(REAL).

2. The comments (*DIVIDE TWO NUMBERS*) will be
ignored by the computer, as explained in the previous
example.

3. Assignment statements for real variables in this program are
the same as for the previous program (INTVAR), with the
following exceptions: real numbers must use decimal points
(20.0 and 3.0), whereas integer numbers do not; and the
operator for division is a slash "/" for real numbers, and
either **DIV** or **MOD** for integers.

4. The results of this program (answer) is 6.6667, a real
number. (Compare this result with the previous example
and note the difference.)

5. You do not need to insert a space in the WRITELN
statement before the closing single quote. Positive real
variables automatically have a space in front of them when
they are printed out. You may insert a space before the
closing single quote if the real variable is negative.

## Constants

As with variables, you can also store information in memory by defining constants. Unlike variables, however, the value of constants cannot be changed by the program. If you know the value of the data to be manipulated or processed by your program at the time you are writing the program, you can define these data as constants.

For constants (as with variables), you do not have to worry about where the data is stored in the computer because the computer keeps track of it for you. All you have to do is to simply tell the computer the name and the value assigned to each constant you want to use; then the computer determines the specific location in which to store the constants.

Any name you assign as a constant is known throughout the program, together with its assigned value. As with variables, you do have to remember the names assigned to a constant. Therefore, be sure to use meaningful names when you define your constant.

A constant has two properties: name and value. You assign the name and the value; therefore, a constant allows you to define nonvarying data as part of your program rather than having to ask the user for it or obtaining it from some other source.

You *must* declare or define constants at the top of your program. If you wish to change the value assigned to a constant, you may do so by redefining the constant. Constants are declared in the **CONST** part of the declaration block.

## Tips on Selecting Names for Constants Used in Pascal

As with variables there are thousands of possibilities for names for constants. The same rules for variables apply to constants when you select names for constants. Below are some examples of constants declarations.

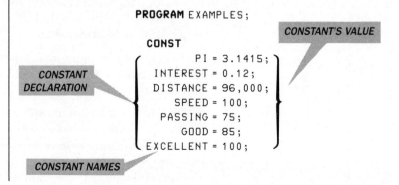

```
PROGRAM EXAMPLES;

CONST
          PI = 3.1415;
    INTEREST = 0.12;
    DISTANCE = 96,000;
       SPEED = 100;
     PASSING = 75;
        GOOD = 85;
   EXCELLENT = 100;
```

CONSTANT'S VALUE

CONSTANT DECLARATION

CONSTANT NAMES

### Notes

1. Constants are declared in the **CONST** part of the declaration block.

2. There must always be a constant name on the left side of the equal sign, and a value on the right.

**A Simple Math Program Using Constants and Variables**

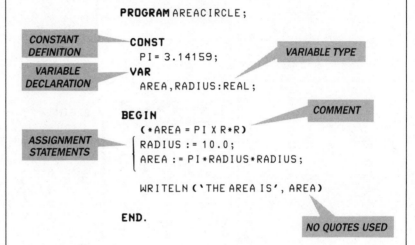

```
PROGRAM AREACIRCLE;

CONST
    PI = 3.14159;
VAR
    AREA,RADIUS:REAL;

BEGIN
    (*AREA = PI X R*R)
    RADIUS := 10.0;
    AREA := PI*RADIUS*RADIUS;

    WRITELN ('THE AREA IS', AREA)

END.
```

CONSTANT DEFINITION

VARIABLE DECLARATION

VARIABLE TYPE

COMMENT

ASSIGNMENT STATEMENTS

NO QUOTES USED

### Notes

1. The constant definition associates the constant, PI, with the value 3.14159.

2. Two real variables are declared in the **VAR** block. The variable declaration tells the computer to allocate memory cells named AREA and RADIUS for storage of real numbers. Note the commas that separate the variables' names, and the colon (:) that separates names from the variable type (REAL).

3. The first assignment statement assigns a value of 10.0 to the variable RADIUS.

4. The second assignment statement assigns the product of PI, RADIUS, and RADIUS to AREA. That is, the result of PI*RADIUS*RADIUS is stored in the memory location named AREA.

Program structure is very important in Pascal. The general form for a Pascal program follows.

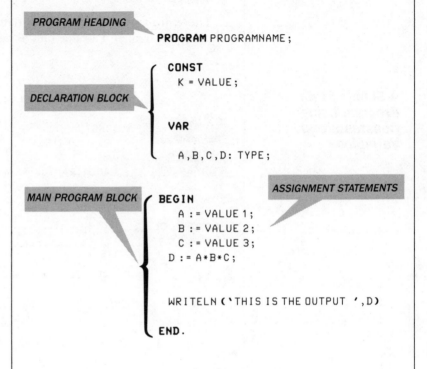

### Notes

1. K is any acceptable name for a constant. A,B,C, and D are any acceptable names for variables used in Pascal.

2. VALUE, VALUE 1, VALUE 2, and VALUE 3 can be any value of the declared type for the variables.

3. A constant has two properties: name and value.

4. All constants are defined at the beginning of the program.

5. An equal sign ( = ) separates the constant's name from the value, and a colon-equal sign ( : = ) separates a variable's name from the value or expression (for example, D : = A*B*C).

6. A variable has three properties: name, type, and value.

## EXERCISE 5–4

### Area of a Circle Program

| ACTION | DISPLAY |
|---|---|

**ACTION**

1. *Boot your system.*

2. *Clear the workfile (that is, press* F N Y Q *from the Command level).*

3. *Enter Editor,* E, *and then the INSERT mode,* I, *and type in the program as shown.*

4. *Quit the Editor and update the workfile (that is, press* Q *and then* U *).*

**DISPLAY**

```
PROGRAM AREACIRCLE;


CONST
  PI = 3.14159;



VAR
  AREA,RADIUS:REAL;



BEGIN
  RADIUS := 15.5;
  AREA := PI*(RADIUS*RADIUS);

  WRITELN ('THE AREA IS', AREA)

END. (*AREA CIRCLE*)
```

5. *Run the program. If your program runs successfully, you will get the results shown. (If you have errors, correct them.)*

```
THE AREA IS 7.54767E2
```

The area was calculated using an assignment statement (Area: = PI*RADIUS*RADIUS), but you could use a WRITELN statement instead. For example:

```
WRITELN ('THE AREA IS',PI*RADIUS*RADIUS)
```

CONSTANTS (**CONST**) are declared before VARIABLES (**VAR**).

Constants use equal signs ( = ) to separate the name from value, but assignment statements use colon-equal sign ( : = ) to separate the variable name from the value.

**Summary**

The general form of the Pascal program follows.

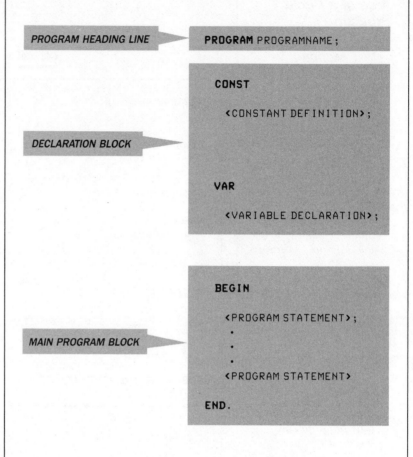

PROGRAM HEADING LINE

    PROGRAM PROGRAMNAME;

DECLARATION BLOCK

    CONST

        <CONSTANT DEFINITION>;

    VAR

        <VARIABLE DECLARATION>;

MAIN PROGRAM BLOCK

    BEGIN

        <PROGRAM STATEMENT>;
        •
        •
        •
        <PROGRAM STATEMENT>

    END.

### Program Name

The name of a Pascal program is always chosen by the programmer. When you program in Pascal, you must assign each program a name. It is best to pick a name that describes what the program does. Here are some examples:

PROGRAM MYFIRST;

PROGRAM SOUND;

PROGRAM MAILING;

PROGRAM PAYROLL;

PROGRAM CLASSAVERAGE;

Every name must begin with a letter, and the name must consist of only letters (A to Z) and digits (0 to 9). The letters may be upper- or lowercase. Blank spaces must *not* be included in names; otherwise, an error will result, thereby preventing the program from being processed by the computer.

Only the first eight characters (that is, letters and digits) of a name are examined by the computer. Therefore, you should restrict your name to eight characters (that is, you should use some shortened form of a name). A program name *cannot* be a reserved word.

### Declaration Block

There are two parts to the declaration block; **CONST** (constants) and **VAR** (variables). Constants are those data items whose values remain fixed during execution of a program. Variables are those data items whose values change during program execution.

Both **CONST** and **VAR** are Pascal reserved words and are set in **bold type.** The declaration block contains the definitions of constants and the declaration of all variables used in your program.

### Constants

A constant is defined by the programmer, and has a name assigned by the programmer. Defining and using a constant in your Pascal programs is a convenient way of replacing long numbers with short names (for example, PI = 3.14159).

Declaring constants at the beginning of your program also makes it easy to change the value of the constants in your program. If the values used as constants were inserted directly into each of the program steps where the value was needed, it would become a very tedious task to replace all of these values—particularly in a large program.

### Variables

A variable is declared by the programmer and is assigned a name by the programmer. A variable declaration creates a variable of a specific type, which holds a value temporarily.

Remember that a variable is a temporary location (in memory) to hold a value at a particular time. Unlike constants, the value of a variable can be changed during program execution.

We will discuss variables in greater detail in Chapter 6.

### Program Block

There may be more than one program block in a Pascal program, but every Pascal program must have only one "main program" block.

A program statement can input data to a program (READ/ READLN statements), output results or answers of a program (WRITE/WRITELN statements), or it can do simple data manipulations (assignment statements). Each of these types of program statements will be discussed in more detail later.

Semicolons must be inserted between any two statements. Semicolons signify the end of one statement and the beginning of another. (Note, however, that the last program statement does not require a semicolon because the reserved word **END** is not a statement.)

### Importance of Program Style

Program style is a very important consideration in Pascal programming because it will make your program look attractive—and a program that looks good is easier to read and understand.

The computer or the compiler does not have specific requirements about how program text is arranged, as long as you follow the rules of Pascal. Pascal allows you to use indentation and blank spaces as needed to make your program neat and clean.

Program *style* should not be confused with program *structure*. You *must* follow the rules for program structure, which involve such things as the use of reserved PROGRAM, BEGIN, and **END;** the placement of semicolons between the Pascal statements; and the placement of a period after the reserved word **END**. On the other hand, program style involves the optional use of indentation and blank spaces to make the program neat and clean. An example of recommended program style is shown in Fig. 5–1.

**NOTE:** *Although use of spacing and indentation is not required in Pascal, we will use it in this book to help you better understand the program.*

Careful and consistent use of spaces can enhance your program significantly. Extra spaces are ignored by your computer; therefore, you can insert spaces as desired to improve the style and appearance of your program. You do not have to follow the program style shown here in Fig. 5–1, but it is the style we like and adopted for this book. Indent lines for clarity; write the reserved words **CONST, VAR, BEGIN,** and **END** on lines by themselves so that they stand out.

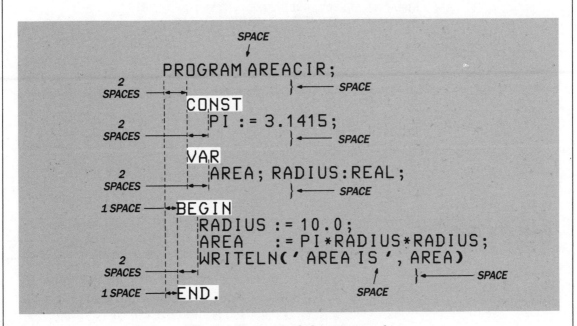

*Fig. 5–1 Recommended program style.*

### Pascal Program Structure

Punctuation marks have special meaning in Pascal programs. A semicolon is required at the end of each line except the last line before the reserved word **END**—a period is required after the reserved word **END**. If you forget to add these punctuation marks, a program error will occur (as you will soon learn).

## PRACTICE 5–1

1. Trace the program below (manually) and predict the output.

2. Enter and run the program. (Did your result match the computers?)

3. Add new program lines to output the following:
   a. The length is 10 inches.
   b. The width is 5 inches.

4. Change the values of L and W in your program, and run the program again.

```
PROGRAM RECTANGLE;

(* AREA OF A RECTANGLE PROBLEM *)
(* AREA(A) = LENGHT(L) X WIDTH(W) *)

  VAR
    L,W,A:INTEGER;

  BEGIN
    L := 10;
    W := 5;
    A := L * W;
    WRITELN('THE AREA OF THE RECTANGLE IS ',A,' SQ.INCHES')
  END. (* RECTANGLE *)
```

## PRACTICE 5–2

1. Using the Pascal programming tools you have learned thus far, write one simple program that will do the following:

   a. Multiply any two integer numbers and label your answer as follows: THE PRODUCT OF (your no.) AND (your no.) IS (your answer).
      Example: THE PRODUCT 5 AND 10 IS 50.

b. Divide any two integer numbers and label your answer as follows: THE QUOTIENT OF (your no.) AND (your no.) IS (your answer).

   Example: THE QUOTIENT OF 12 AND 6 IS 2.

c. Subtract any two integer numbers and label your answer as follows: THE DIFFERENCE BETWEEN (your no.) and (your no.) IS (your answer).

   Example: THE DIFFERENCE BETWEEN 20 AND 15 IS 5.

d. Add any two numbers and label your answer as follows: THE SUM OF (your no.) AND (your no.) IS (your answer).

   Example: THE SUM OF 30 AND 10 IS 40.

**HINTS:** *Declare a separate variable for each number and each result. Use comments such as (\*MULTIPLY TWO NUMBERS\*) to separate each part of the program that does a different operation.*

## PRACTICE 5–3

1. Convert the following to standard scientific notation (example: $5,000,000 = 5 \times 10^6$):

   a. 5,165,123
   b. .000007
   c. .00000008
   d. 6,001,255
   e. 80 000 000 000 000 000 (16 zeros)
   f. 8000 000 000 000 000 (15 zeros)
   g. 9,000,156,000
   h. 7,701,777
   i. 77,701,777,000
   j. 5,612,345,000

2. Use the Apple Pascal calculator mode (a utility program) to solve the problems that follow.

   a. (15.75 \*3)/5
   b. (0.1776\*0.1492)/0.1967
   c. 14 + (27\*3)
   d. 947 \* 914 − 215
   e. (11.37 + 37.11 \* 37.11)/13.71
   f. 0.0001234 \* (−0.5678)
   g. −1555 \* 12/4
   h. 0.456 − 0.89
   i. (−8965 + 137) \* (−17)
   j. 0.6704 \* 0.1378765

# Chapter 6

# *Entering Data Via the Keyboard: READ and READLN Statements*

### *What You Will Learn*

- To explain the purpose and use of the key words READ and READLN.

- To understand how to enter data and use different types of variables such as CHAR, INTEGER, and STRING.

- To write, enter, and run programs using READ and READLN statements with different types of variables.

## Entering Data from the Keyboard

Pascal has two standard input statements: READLN and READ.

The READLN statement format is as follows:

```
READLN (VARIABLE 1)
   or
READLN (VARIABLE 1, VARIABLE 2,---------VARIABLE N)
```

READLN is an abbreviation for "read a line." It is the most commonly used statement for getting input from the keyboard. READLN allows line-oriented reading of characters, strings, and numeric values, and causes a program to stop and wait until you type something (such as a number, integer, or string).

After you type something, the program continues when you press ⎡RETURN⎤, and assigns (or attempts to assign) your input data to the variables specified in the READLN statement. A variable will hold the value entered until a new value is entered or a new value is assigned. If more than one variable is used, commas are used to separate the variables. For example:

```
READLN (LENGTH, WIDTH, HEIGHT)
```

A variable may be one of the following types: CHAR, INTEGER, LONG INTEGER, REAL, or STRING. CHAR is the Pascal abbreviation for character, which means that only the initial character of your typed response to a READLN input request will be assigned to the specified variable. (For example, if a CHAR variable type is used and you typed "YES" as a response, only the "Y" would be assigned to the variable.)

The READ statement format is as follows:

```
READ (VARIABLE 1)
   or
READ (VARIABLE 1, VARIABLE 2,---------VARIABLE N)
```

READ allows characters and numeric values to be read (inputted) from the keyboard in a similar manner to READLN. However only READLN should be used for inputting data. Although either READ or READLN can be used to enter data from the keyboard, we will not use the READ statement in this book except for the CHAR-type data. We found that it is much easier for a beginner to use the READLN statement with Apple Pascal system. There are several reasons for this, but the major reason is as follows.

The READLN statement expects a [RETURN] after the value for the last variable in the list to be read has been entered. The computer will skip over anything else you enter until a [RETURN] is pressed. This means that any other data either entered (read) or printed (WRITE/WRITELN) appears on the next line of the screen. In contrast, READ does not expect a [RETURN]. Reading will automatically proceed to the next line when the values of one line have all been read  unless you remember to press [RETURN] and eliminate the possibility of extra characters on a line when they are not wanted. In short, you will encounter fewer problems when entering data from the keyboard if you use READLN instead of READ.

## Some Things You Should Know about CHAR Variables

CHAR is an abbreviation for character data type. A character is a letter (A to Z), a digit (0 to 9), or a special symbol (for example, !, ?, @).

A character data type can be used to read (input) and store the individual characters that comprise names, addresses, and other information. A character data type is declared by using the word CHAR in the **VAR** declaration block, as you will soon see. (See Fig. 6–1.)

Every computer system communicates with its input and output devices (that is, keyboard, printers, and disks) by means of a set of characters. These character sets are used to transfer readable character information to and from the computer. The number of characters actually read from the keyboard is determined by the type of the variable receiving the data. If the variable is CHAR, then only one character will be read for each READ statement.

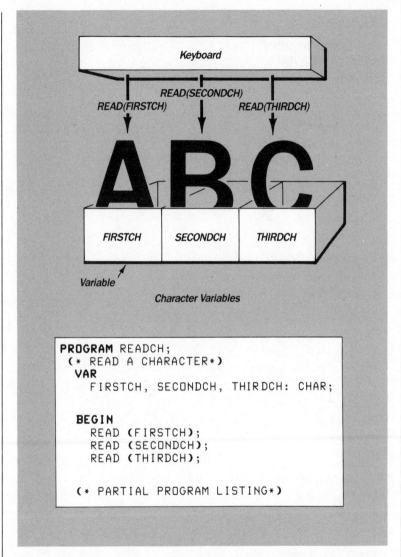

*Fig. 6–1 Reading data from the keyboard (using character variables).*

## EXERCISE 6–1

### A Simple Program Using the CHAR Variable

**ACTION**

1. Clear the workfile and type in this program.

   Note that "RESPONSE" is declared as a CHAR variable.

   "READ (RESPONSE)" is a program statement to input data from the keyboard. (Note: READLN causes the program to wait for the user to press RETURN. When RETURN is pressed, it causes the computer to "look at" the character just entered and to act accordingly.

2. Run the program.
   (a) What happened?
   (b) Try typing in more than one character at a time.

**NOTE:** Character variables store only one character, and any attempt to read more than one character will be ignored by the program.

**DISPLAY**

```
PROGRAM CHARVAR;


VAR
  RESPONSE:CHAR;



BEGIN
  WRITELN ('TYPE IN ANY CHARACTER ');
  READ (RESPONSE);
  READLN;
  WRITELN ('THE CHARACTER IS ', RESPONSE)
END. (*CHARVAR*)
```

## Reading Data from the Keyboard

If the variable receiving data is an integer (or a real number), then the Apple Pascal system must read a numeric variable. To determine if the data read is a numeric value, the Pascal system does the following: It examines all input characters in sequence until the first nonblank character is encountered (any leading blanks and carriage returns are ignored). All characters following the first nonblank character are processed until the computer detects a character that cannot be part of a number (for example, a blank, a letter, a carriage return, and so on). If a nonblank character is detected that is neither a sign nor a digit, an error message is printed. (See Fig. 6–2.)

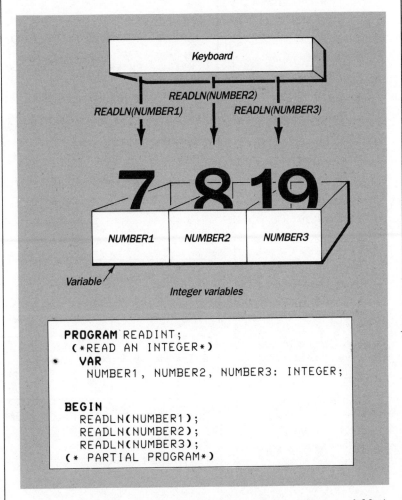

```
PROGRAM READINT;
 (*READ AN INTEGER*)
   VAR
     NUMBER1, NUMBER2, NUMBER3: INTEGER;

BEGIN
   READLN(NUMBER1);
   READLN(NUMBER2);
   READLN(NUMBER3);
(* PARTIAL PROGRAM*)
```

*Fig. 6–2 Reading data from the keyboard (using integer variables).*

## EXERCISE 6–2

### Entering Data Using Integer Variables

**ACTION**

1. Clear the workfile and type in this program.

   Note the following:

   (a) The WRITE statements are included as prompts for the user.
   (b) Only one input value is accepted at a time to minimize input errors (because Pascal is unforgiving if you make an error).
   (c) A space was inserted between the quotes (' ') in the WRITELN statement.

2. Quit the Editor and Update the workfile ( Q  U ). Then run the program.

3. Enter one integer (for example, 1), and press RETURN.

4. Enter two more integers (for example 2 and 3), and press RETURN after each entry.

**DISPLAY**

```
PROGRAM INPUTINT;

  VAR
    A,B,C:INTEGER;

BEGIN
  WRITE ('ENTER 1ST INTEGER: ');
  READLN (A);
  WRITE ('ENTER 2ND INTEGER: ');
  READLN (B);
  WRITE ('ENTER 3RD INTEGER: ');
  READLN (C);

  WRITELN;

  WRITELN (' ',A, ' ',B, ' ',C)
END. (*INPUTINT*)
```

```
RUNNING..
ENTER 1ST INTEGER:
```

```
ENTER 1ST INTEGER:1
ENTER 2ND INTEGER:
```

```
COMMAND:E(DIT,R(UN,F(ILE,C(OMP,L(IN
RUNNING...
ENTER 1ST INTEGER: 1
ENTER 2ND INTEGER: 2
ENTER 3RD INTEGER: 3

1 2 3
```

## EXERCISE 6–3

### Entering Data Using CHAR Variables

| ACTION | DISPLAY |
|---|---|

**ACTION**

1. Clear the workfile and Enter the program as shown.

   Note the following:

   (a) The difference between this program and the program in exercise 6–2 is that you replace the word "INTEGER" with "CHAR" throughout the program.

   (b) This program will accept only one character per input (READLN) statement. You can type in more than one character, but the computer will ignore the extras. (This is because you declared your variable as a CHAR.)

2. Quit and Update the workfile ( Q U ). Then run ( R ) your program.

**DISPLAY**

```
PROGRAM INPUTCHAR;


  VAR
    A,B,C:CHAR;


BEGIN

  WRITE ('ENTER 1ST CHAR: ');
  READLN (A);
  WRITE ('ENTER 2ND CHAR: ');
  READLN (B);
  WRITE ('ENTER 3RD CHAR: ');
  READLN (C);

  WRITELN;

  WRITELN (' ',A,' ',B,' ',C)
END. (* INPUTCHAR *)
```

```
RUNNING...
 ENTER 1ST CHAR:
```

3. *Enter a single character for each input (for example, X, Y, and Z).*

```
COMMAND:E(DIT,R(UN,F(ILE,C(OMP,L(IN
RUNNING...
ENTER 1ST CHAR: X
ENTER 2ND CHAR: Y
ENTER 3RD CHAR: Z


X Y Z
```

4. *Run this program several times until you understand it. Also, try the following and observe what happens.*

   (a) *Enter more than one character per input.*

   (b) *Enter a number for an input.*

   (c) *Enter a symbol such as a !, ?, or @.*

## Strings

A string is a sequence of characters enclosed within single quotes. For example:

```
WRITE('THIS IS AN EXAMPLE ');
WRITELN('OF A STRING');
```

Strings are displayed (printed) exactly as they are typed (with the quotes removed).

Apple Pascal has a new predeclared type called *string*. (Beware! Standard Pascal systems do not use predeclared string variables.)

Declared string variables can be assigned to represent letters, words, numbers, and/or combinations of letters and numbers. The number of characters in a string at any moment is the length of the string itself. Here are some examples of typical string declarations:

**VAR**

A: **STRING;**     (*Defaults to a maximum length of 80 characters*)

B: **STRING 25;**     (*ALLOWS the string to be limited to a maximum of 25 characters*)

C: **STRING 255;**     (*Maximum limit of a string*)

A string variable may be compared to any other string variable or to a string constant, regardless of its current dynamic length.

Strings can be declared as type CONSTANT:

```
PROGRAM HELLO;
  CONST
    GREETINGS = 'HI THERE, I SPEAK PASCAL!';
  BEGIN
    WRITELN (GREETINGS)
  END.
```

If the data to be received is a STRING, then the Apple Pascal system must read a string variable. All input characters are examined in sequence until a carriage return is encountered. This lets the computer know that all characters in the string have been entered. (See Fig. 6–3.)

**Built-in String Functions and Procedures**

Strings can be manipulated using Apple Pascal built-in functions and procedures. Here are some things you can do with strings. You can

• Determine the length of strings using the LENGTH function.

• Send strings for a pattern (substring) using the POS function.

• Join strings together (concatenate) using the CONCAT function.

• Select only part of a string using the COPY function.

• Insert strings in the middle of other strings using the INSERT procedure.

• Delete characters from strings using the DELETE procedure.

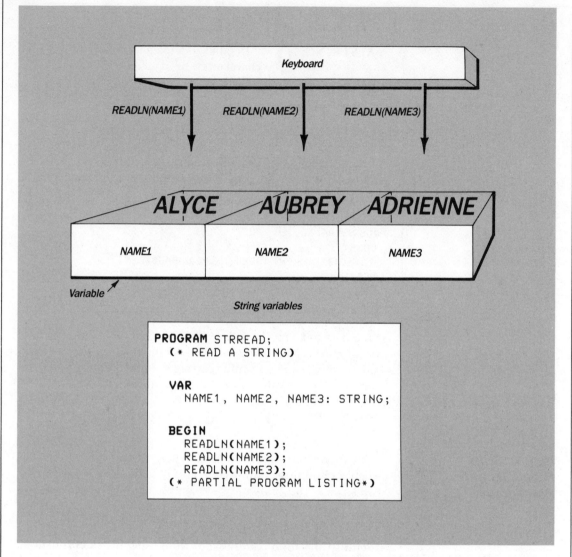

**Fig. 6–3 Reading (entering) data from the keyboard (using string variables).**

The following pages provide more details on the built-in string functions and procedures. Programs using the built-in functions and procedures are included in the Extra Practices at the end of the book.

### The LENGTH Function

The LENGTH function determines the current length of a string. The working length of a string variable is determined by the data stored in it. This function returns the integer value of the length of a string. The format is

```
LENGTH (STRG)
```

where STRG is a string value. A string with zero characters is called a null string. For example:

```
NUMSTRING := '1234567';
WRITELN (LENGTH (NUMSTRING));
```

This will print 7.

### The POS Function

The POS function searches a string from left to right for a substring (pattern). That is, it determines the location of the first occurrence of the string pattern. If the pattern (substring) is found, the integer value returned is the position in the string of the first character of the pattern. If the pattern is not found, POS returns zero. The format is

```
POS (PATTERN STRING, SOURCE STRING)
```

where both the pattern string and the source string are string values. Some examples are:

```
SOURCE := 'NOW IS THE TIME TO TRY IT';
PATTERN : 'IME';
WRITELN (POS (PATTERN, SOURCE));
```

This will print 13.

```
POS ('STEP', 'SIDESTEPPED')
```

results in 5.

### The CONCAT Function

The CONCAT function concatenates or joins together two or more short strings to form a longer string. The format is

```
CONCAT (STRING 1, STRING 2, STRING 3 . . . STRINGN)
```

There can be any number of string values separated by commas. For example:

```
WORD1 := 'UP';
WORD2 := 'TIME';
WORD3 := 'DOWN';

WRITELN (CONCAT (WORD1, WORD2));
WRITELN (CONCAT (WORD3, WORD2));
```

The display reads:

```
UPTIME
DOWNTIME
```

### The COPY Function

The COPY function permits you to select parts of strings. That is, you can break a part of a string into sections or substrings. This function returns a string value. The format is:

```
COPY (STRG, START POSITION, LENGTH OF SUBSTRING)
```

where STRG is a string value, and START POSITION and LENGTH OF SUBSTRING are integer values. For example:

```
WORD := 'BILLION';
SENTENCE := 'BUILT-IN STRING FUNCTIONS ARE USEFUL';

WRITELN (COPY (WORD, 2, 3));
WRITELN (COPY (SENTENCE, 31, 6));
```

This will display

```
ILL
USEFUL
```

### The INSERT Procedure

The INSERT procedure permits you to insert strings in the middle of other strings. The format is:

`INSERT (STRING TO BE INSERTED, DESTINATION STRING VARIABLE, POSITION WHERE INSERTION IS TO START)`

The position where insertion is to start may be any expression that has an integer value. For example:

```
SENTENCE := 'HAVE A GOOD DAY';
INSERT (' VERY', SENTENCE, 7);
WRITELN (SENTENCE);
```

This will print

`HAVE A VERY GOOD DAY`

### The DELETE Procedure

The DELETE procedure permits you to delete characters from strings. The format is:

`DELETE (DESTINATION STRING VARIABLE, WHERE TO START DELETION, NUMBER OF CHARACTERS TO BE DELETED)`

For example:

```
WORDS := 'I DO SPEAK PASCAL!';
DELETE (WORDS, 2, 3);
WRITELN (WORDS);
```

This will print

`I SPEAK PASCAL!`

## EXERCISE 6—4

### Entering Data Using String Variables

| ACTION | DISPLAY |
|---|---|

*1. Clear the workfile.*

```
PROGRAM INPUTSTRING;


VAR
  A,B,C:STRING;
BEGIN
  WRITE('ENTER 1ST STRING: ');
  READLN(A);
  WRITE('ENTER 2ND STRING: ');
  READLN(B);
  WRITE('ENTER 3RD STRING: ');
  READLN(C);
  WRITELN;
  WRITELN(' ',A,' ',B,' ',C)
END. (*INPUTSTRING*)
```

*2. Enter the program as shown (you might want to modify the existing programs, if you know how!).*

*Note that you used basically the same program for all three of the data entry programs. You merely changed the type of variable used from INTEGER to CHAR to STRING.*

*3. Quit the Editor and update the workfile ( [Q] [U] ). Then Run ( [R] ) your program.*

```
RUNNING...
```

*4. Enter a string for each input. For example, enter your first, middle, and last names on each line. Don't forget to press [RETURN] after each entry.*

```
COMMAND:E(DIT,R(UN,F(ILE,C(OMP,L(IN
RUNNING...
ENTER 1ST STRING: AUBREY
ENTER 2ND STRING: BRIGHT
ENTER 3RD STRING: JONES

AUBREY BRIGHT JONES
```

## EXERCISE 6–5

### Area of Rectangle Problem

**ACTION**

**DISPLAY**

1. Clear the workfile.

2. Type in the program as shown. You may omit comment lines, which are the lines containing the (*). These lines are to aid you in understanding what the program is doing.

3. Quit the Editor and Update the workfile ( ⎡Q⎤ ⎡U⎤ ).

   (a) Each input prompts the user.

   (b) The area was calculated using an assignment statement, but we could have used the WRITELN statement. For example,

WRITELN ('THE AREA IS', LENGTH*WIDTH).

4. Run the program.

```
PROGRAM AREARECT;


VAR
  LENGTH,WIDTH,AREA:INTEGER;


BEGIN
  (*INPUT YOUR DATA*)
  WRITE ('THE LENGTH IS: ');
  READLN (LENGTH);
  WRITE ('THE WIDTH IS: ');
  READLN (WIDTH);

  (*CALCULATE AREA*)


  AREA : = LENGTH*WIDTH;


  (*PRINT YOUR ANSWER*)
  WRITELN;
  WRITELN ('THE AREA IS ',AREA)


END. (*AREARECT*)
```

## EXERCISE 6–6

1. Modify Exercise 6–5 to calculate the area using the statement WRITELN instead of using the assignment statement (AREA := LENGTH*WIDTH). Run the program.

2. Modify the program to input the dimensions to be used (that is, ft., in., or yds.) and print the answer with its dimension (that is, sq.ft., sq.in., or sq.yds.). Run the program.

**Summary of READ and READLN**

Pascal is unforgiving and can cause disastrous errors when using READ and READLN to enter data. For example, when entering numbers from the keyboard, Pascal does not allow you to enter commas to separate them. If you forget and enter a comma, an error will result, which will cause you to reinitialize your system, and consequently you will lose any data already entered. (See Fig. 6–4.)

Be careful if you use READ and READLN with numeric variables in any program intended for use by other people. If someone other than you will use your program, make sure you do the following: Always prompt the user for each number separately and only accept one value at a time. For example,

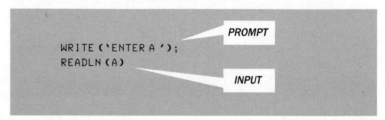

```
WRITE ('ENTER A ');          PROMPT
READLN (A)                   INPUT
```

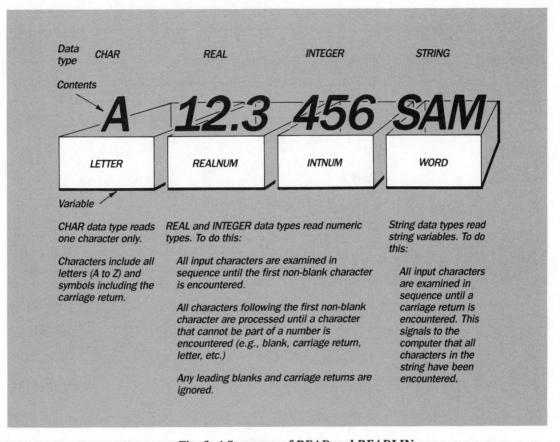

*Fig. 6–4 Summary of READ and READLN.*

CHAR data type reads one character only.

Characters include all letters (A to Z) and symbols including the carriage return.

REAL and INTEGER data types read numeric types. To do this:

All input characters are examined in sequence until the first non-blank character is encountered.

All characters following the first non-blank character are processed until a character that cannot be part of a number is encountered (e.g., blank, carriage return, letter, etc.)

Any leading blanks and carriage returns are ignored.

String data types read string variables. To do this:

All input characters are examined in sequence until a carriage return is encountered. This signals to the computer that all characters in the string have been encountered.

## PRACTICE 6–1

**Volume of a Rectangle Problem (Using the READLN Statement)**

1. Write a new program using the READLN statements to find volume (volume = length × width × height).

2. Include a statement: THE VOLUME IS *your answer.*

## PRACTICE 6–2

### More READLN Statement Programs

### Part I

1. Using READLN statements, write a program to change meters to centimeters (centimeters = 100 × meters).

2. Include a statement: _____ METERS EQUALS _____ CENTIMETERS.

### Part II

1. Using READLN statements, write a new program to do the following:

   a. Input the number of members of your family.
   b. Input the age of the oldest member of your family.
   c. Input the age of the youngest member of your family.
   d. Input the average age of your family.

2. Print each with the proper labels. For example, THE YOUNGEST MEMBER OF MY FAMILY IS…

## PRACTICE 6–3

### String Variables

#### Part I

1. Write a program using READLN statements, string
   variables, and a space between each output line to do the
   following:

   a. Input and print your first name.
   b. Input and print your middle name.
   c. Input and print your last name.
   d. Print your first, middle, and last name on one line.
   e. Input and print your full name.

#### Part II

1. Write a new program using READLN statements and string
   variables to print the following information (Example: MY
   BEST FRIEND IS _____):

   a. Your best friend.
   b. Your favorite subject.
   c. Your favorite food.
   d. Your favorite movie star.
   e. Your favorite color.
   f. Your zodiac sign.

*Freelance Photographers Guild/Jeffery Sylvester*

**Chapter 7**

# IF–THEN– ELSE *and* CASE Statements

**What You Will Learn**

- To understand how computers make decisions based on logical and relational operations, which return the value TRUE or FALSE. You will learn how to compare one value with another using the logical operators (**AND, OR, NOT**) and relational operators ( $=$ , $<$ , $>$ , $<>$ , $<=$ , $>=$ ).

- To explain the purpose and use of the key words **IF–THEN, IF–THEN–ELSE,** and **CASE**.

- To understand how the **IF–THEN–ELSE** and **CASE** statements work.

- To compare the decision-making statements and explain how they relate to one another; specifically:

Single-option decision     $<$**IF–THEN**$>$

Double-option decision     $<$**IF–THEN–ELSE**$>$

Multiple-option decision   $<$**CASE**$>$

So far, all of the programs that have been considered have been executed sequentially. That is, each program statement has been executed in turn, starting with the statement immediately following the reserved work **BEGIN** and continuing until the end of the program is reached. Although you can still write some useful and worthwhile programs this way, you will learn that many more problems can be solved if the computer can be programmed to make decisions when certain specified conditions are met.

## Relational Operators

Relational operators allow the computer to compare one value to another. The three relational operators include:

| SYMBOL | MEANING | EXAMPLES |
|--------|---------|----------|
| = | Equal | A = B |
| > | Greater than | A > B |
| < | Less than | A < B |

*To distinguish between < and >, just remember that the symbol points to the smaller of the two quantities being compared.*

Combining the three operators above, we have:

| | | |
|--------|---------|----------|
| <> | Not equal to | A <> B |
| <= | Less than or equal to | A <= B |
| >= | Greater than or equal to | A >= B |

The computer makes decisions by comparing values held in variables, and then takes the desired action based on the results of the comparison. To compare the value held in a variable, it is necessary to use the relational operators. These operators allow the computer to compare the value of two arithmetic expressions and return the following values:

If the conditions are met, a value of TRUE is returned.

If the conditions are *not* met, a value of FALSE is returned.

## Boolean Data Type

Boolean values are binary; Boolean data uses two values, TRUE and FALSE, which define a value as being either true or false.

Boolean values may be compared with one another using the logical operators **AND, OR,** and **NOT.** This produces a Boolean result. Boolean values can also be compared with one another using the relational operators $=$, $<$, $>$, $<>$, $<=$, and $>=$.

### Logical Operators

Pascal provides the standard logical operators shown in the following table.

| OPERATOR | EXAMPLE | MEANING |
|---|---|---|
| **AND** <br> (logical AND) | A **AND** B | If the values of both A and B are TRUE, then the result is TRUE. Conversely, if the value of either A or B is FALSE the result of A **AND** B is FALSE. |
| **OR** <br> (logical inclusive OR) | A **OR** B | If the value of either A or B is TRUE the result of A **OR** B is TRUE. The value of both A and B must be FALSE for A **OR** B to be FALSE. |
| **NOT** <br> (logical negation) | **NOT** A | If the value of A is FALSE, then **NOT** A is TRUE. If the value of A is TRUE, then **NOT** A is FALSE. Therefore, **NOT** A gives the negative (opposite) value as the result. |

## Truth Table

The best way to examine what will happen when Boolean values are compared logically is to use a truth table. Below is a truth table, which shows the results of applying these operators to the Boolean argument A and B.

| IF VALUES OF | | THEN RESULTS OF | | |
|---|---|---|---|---|
| *A* | *B* | *A AND B*[a] | *A OR B*[b] | *NOT A*[c] |
| False | False | False | False | True |
| False | True | False | True | True |
| True | False | False | True | False |
| True | True | True | True | False |

[a]Both values (A and B) must be True for the results to be True.
[b]Either value (A or B) must be True for the results to be True.
[c]If value A is False, the result is True. Also, if value A is True, the result is False. (That is, **Not** A gives the negative or opposite logical truth value as a result.)

## IF–THEN (Single-Option Decision)

**IF–THEN** is used to tell the computer to take some action only if certain conditions are met; that is, the program will evaluate the specified condition first. If the condition is evaluated to be true, then the designated program statement is executed. If the condition is evaluated to be false, the rest of the program statement is skipped. The format is as follows:

```
IF <CONDITION> THEN
        <STATEMENT>
```

This means that if the <conditon> is true, then execute the program <statement>; otherwise, skip the <statement>. (See Fig. 7–1.)

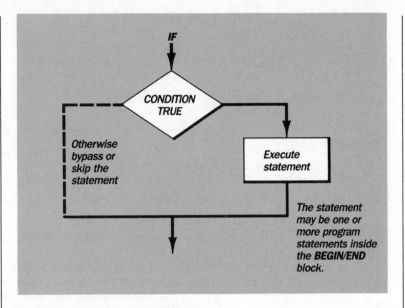

**Fig. 7–1 A simple IF-THEN statement.**

## EXERCISE 7–1

### IF–THEN

Given:

```
CONST
  A = 10;
  B =  5;
  C = 30;
```

Use the **IF–THEN** statement below to complete Exercises 1 through 10.

```
BEGIN
  IF <CONDITION> THEN
  WRITELN('TRUE')
END.
```

| EXERCISE NUMBER | IF <CONDITION> | THEN WRITELN ('TRUE')* | OTHERWISE* SKIP |
|---|---|---|---|
| 1 | A > B | TRUE | |
| 2 | A > C | | SKIP |
| 3 | A <> B | | |
| 4 | A = B | | |
| 5 | C <= A+B | | |
| 6 | C >= A+B | | |
| 7 | B DIV A > C DIV A | | |
| 8 | A*B <= A*C | | |
| 9 | C DIV A <= A*B | | |
| 10 | A > C − B | | |

*If the <condition> is true, then execute the program statement—that is, <WRITELN('TRUE')>; otherwise, skip the statement.

## EXERCISE 7–2

### IF–THEN *Program*

1. Boot the system.

2. Clear the workfile.

3. Type in this program:

```
PROGRAM IFGPA;
  VAR
    AVERAGE:INTEGER;
  BEGIN
    WRITE('INPUT YOUR AVERAGE 0-4 ');
    READLN(AVERAGE);
    WRITELN;
    WRITE('YOUR LETTER GRADE IS ');
    IF AVERAGE = 4 THEN
       WRITELN('A');
    IF AVERAGE = 3 THEN
       WRITELN('B');
    IF AVERAGE = 2 THEN
       WRITELN('C');
    IF AVERAGE = 1 THEN
       WRITELN('D');
    IF AVERAGE = 0 THEN
       WRITELN('F')
  END. (* IFGPA *)
```

*A semicolon is used after each WRITELN statement except the last one. No semicolon is needed immediately before the reserved word* **END**. *However, if you add a semicolon, it will have no effect on the program. There are five conditions to be tested and there are five simple IF statements. (See Fig. 7–2.)*

4. Press Q, U, and R (Quit, Update, and Run).

5. Did your program run successfully? If not, correct your errors and then run it again.

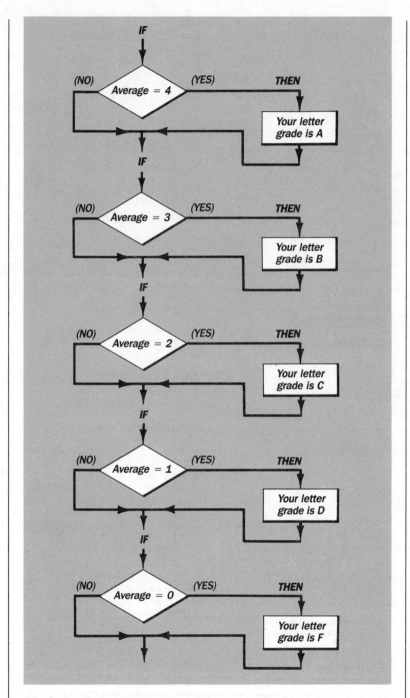

*Fig. 7–2 A series of IF-THEN statements.*

## IF–THEN–ELSE

The **IF–THEN–ELSE** statement is used to tell the computer to take one action if a specified condition is met, and take another action if the condition is *not* met. (That is, the computer has two options or choices.) **IF–THEN–ELSE** allows the computer to select one of two different options. That is, the program will evaluate the specified condition first. If the condition is evaluated to be true, then the first option or designated program statement is executed. If the condition is evaluated to be false, the second option or alternative program statement is executed.

The format is as follows:

```
IF <CONDITION> THEN
      <OPTION 1>
ELSE
      <OPTION> 2
```

This means that if the <condition> is true, then execute <OPTION 1 >; if the <condition> is false, execute <OPTION 2> (where <OPTION 1> and <OPTION 2> are designated program statements). (See Fig. 7–3.)

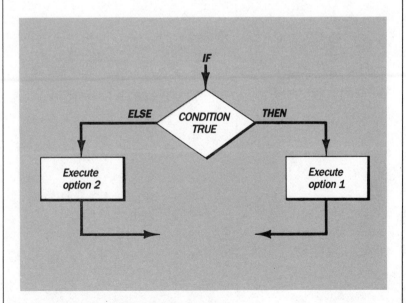

*Fig. 7–3 The IF-THEN-ELSE statement.*

## EXERCISE 7–3

### IF–THEN–ELSE

Given:

```
CONST
  A = 20;
  B = 10;
  C = 60;
```

Use the **IF–THEN–ELSE** statement below to complete Exercises 1 through 10.

```
BEGIN
  IF <CONDITION> THEN
      WRITELN ('TRUE')
  ELSE
      WRITELN ('FALSE')
END.
```

**NOTE:** *No semicolons are required here because* **IF–THEN–ELSE** *is considered to be one program statement. Semicolons are required only between consecutive statements.*

| EXERCISE NUMBER | IF <CONDITION> | THEN WRITELN ('TRUE') | ELSE WRITELN ('FALSE') |
|---|---|---|---|
| 1 | A > B | TRUE | _____ |
| 2 | A < B | _____ | _____ |
| 3 | A <> B | _____ | _____ |
| 4 | A = B | _____ | _____ |
| 5 | C <= A+B | _____ | _____ |
| 6 | C >= A+B | _____ | _____ |
| 7 | B DIV A > C DIV A | _____ | _____ |
| 8 | A*B <= A*C | _____ | _____ |
| 9 | C DIV A <= A*B | _____ | _____ |
| 10 | A > C – B | _____ | _____ |

The following is an example of an **IF–THEN–ELSE** statement:

*REFERENCE*

```
1  PROGRAM STATUS;

2    VAR
3      ANSWER:CHAR;

4    BEGIN

5      WRITE('DO YOU SPEAK PASCAL? ');
6      READLN(ANSWER);

7      IF ANSWER = 'Y' THEN
8        WRITE('GOOD, SO DO I!')
9      ELSE
10       WRITE('HANG IN THERE.')

11   END.
```

## Explanation

Based on the response to the question (line 6), the computer will take some action. If the response is "Y" (for yes), then the computer will execute Option 1 (line 8); otherwise, it will execute line 10.

Note that the declared variable type in line 3 is a CHAR, which means the program will evaluate the first character only, even if you type in "YES."

## EXERCISE 7–4

1. Enter the above program and run it several times until you understand it.

## EXERCISE 7-5

**IF–THEN–ELSE**
*Program*

1. Boot your system.

2. Clear the workfile.

3. Type in this program:

```
PROGRAM ELSEGPA;

  VAR
    AVERAGE:INTEGER;

  BEGIN
    WRITE('INPUT YOUR AVERAGE 0-4 ');
    READLN(AVERAGE);
    WRITELN;
    WRITE('YOUR LETTER GRADE IS ');
    IF AVERAGE = 4 THEN
        WRITELN('A')
    ELSE
        IF AVERAGE = 3 THEN
            WRITELN('B')
        ELSE
            IF AVERAGE = 2 THEN
                WRITELN('C')
            ELSE
                IF AVERAGE = 1 THEN
                    WRITELN('D')
                ELSE
                    IF AVERAGE = 0 THEN
                        WRITELN('F')
  END. (* ELSEGPA *)
```

4. Press ⎡Q⎤, ⎡U⎤, and ⎡R⎤ (Quit, Update, and Run).

5. Did your program run successfully? If not, correct your errors and then run the program again.

No semicolons were needed in the fourteen lines containing the **IF–THEN–ELSE** statements. None is needed or permitted because each **THEN** branch is followed by a simple WRITELN statement, and each **ELSE** branch is followed by a simple **IF** statement. Since the WRITELN and **IF** statements are simple statements, no semicolon separators are needed.

These **IF–THEN–ELSE** statements look complicated, but they are not. Since there are five conditions to be tested, there are actually five **IF** statements. However, these five **IF** statements are combined into one long statement. Such long, conditional statements are called "cascaded" **IF** statements. (See Fig. 7–4.)

If you can view the **IF** statements as one long simple statement, it might be easier to understand why no semicolons are needed, since semicolons are not needed for simple statements.

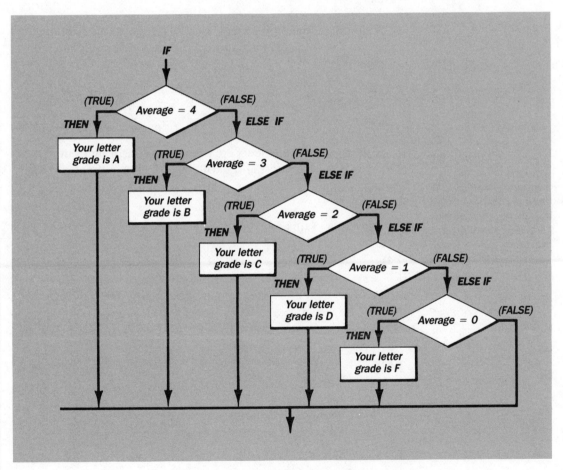

*Fig. 7–4 A Cascaded IF-THEN-ELSE statement.*

## Some Terms You Should Know

A compound statement is a sequence of one or more statements bracketed by the reserved words **BEGIN** and **END**. A semicolon is used to separate statements in a sequence. No semicolons are required after **BEGIN** or before **END**. For example:

```
BEGIN
  WRITE('ENTER YOUR NAME ');
  READLN(NAME);
  WRITELN('HELLO, 'NAME);
  WRITELN('I SPEAK PASCAL, DO YOU? ')
END.
```

A simple statement is a single statement that specifies one action. No semicolon is required after a simple statement. For example:

```
BEGIN
  WRITELN('AUBREY ')
END.
```

Null or empty statements are statements consisting of no symbols or characters and having no effect on a program. For example:

```
BEGIN
  WRITELN ('AUBREY');
END.
```

*Since a semicolon is not required here, the computer assumes that there is an empty or null statement preceding the end. Therefore, program execution is not affected.*

Nested **IF** statements consist of one **IF** statement contained or nested within another. The format for a nested **IF** statement is as follows:

```
BEGIN
    <OTHER PROGRAM STATEMENTS>
  IF <CONDITION 1> THEN
```

> **OUTER BRANCHES**

```
    IF <CONDITION 2> THEN

        <EXECUTE OPTION 1>

    ELSE
        <EXECUTE OPTION 2>
```

```
  ELSE
```

```
    IF <CONDITION 3> THEN

        <EXECUTE OPTION 3>

    ELSE

        <EXECUTE OPTION 4>
```

> **NESTED IF STATEMENT**

```
END.
```

## Notes

1. Note that there is one outer **IF** statement and two inner (nested) **IF** statements. The outer **IF** statement contains a **THEN** branch and an **ELSE** branch.

2. The outer **IF–THEN** branch is a simple **IF** statement, also containing **THEN** and **ELSE** branches; similarly, the outer **ELSE** branch is another simple **IF** statement with **THEN** and **ELSE** branches.

3. It is important that you use indention and spacing to clarify the nesting of **IF** statements. Each **ELSE** statement is indented the same amount as its corresponding **IF–THEN** statement. To determine which **ELSE** goes with a particular **IF–THEN,** all you have to do is look directly above it to locate the **IF** that has the same indention.

4. Options 1, 2, 3, and 4 can be simple or compound statements. If each of the options is a simple statement, however, no semicolons are needed or permitted.

5. Conditions 1, 2, and 3 are Boolean conditions (that is, TRUE and FALSE).

### Punctuation for IF—THEN—ELSE Statements

```
IF <CONDITION> THEN
    WRITELN('THIS IS A SIMPLE STATEMENT')


ELSE
    WRITELN('NOTE THAT ELSE LINES UP WITH IF')
```

No semicolons are required or permitted in the example because the **THEN** branch and the **ELSE** branch consist of simple statements.

```
IF <CONDITION> THEN
  BEGIN
    WRITELN('THIS IS A COMPOUND STATEMENT');
    WRITELN('BECAUSE IT CONSISTS OF');
    WRITELN('MORE THAN ONE STATEMENT');
    WRITELN('SEPARATED BY SEMICOLONS');
    WRITELN('AND BRACKETED BY BEGIN AND END')
  END
ELSE
    WRITE('THIS IS A SIMPLE STATEMENT')
```

*NO SEMICOLON NEEDED*

A semicolon is not permitted after the reserved words **THEN, BEGIN,** or **ELSE**. A semicolon is not required after the reserved word **END** or after the last WRITELN statement before **END.**

If a semicolon was added to the WRITELN statement before the reserved word **END,** a null or "empty" statement is assumed to follow. An empty statement is a statement consisting of no symbol and having no effect on the program execution.

The following is a program example of a nested **IF** statement:

```
PROGRAM NESTEDIF;

  VAR
    A,B,C:INTEGER;

  BEGIN
    WRITE('ENTER 1ST NUMBER: ');
    READLN(A);
    WRITE('ENTER 2ND NUMBER: ');
    READLN(B);
    WRITE('ENTER 3RD NUMBER: ');
    READLN(C);
    IF A<B THEN
        IF A<C THEN
            WRITELN(A,' IS THE SMALLEST')
        ELSE
            WRITELN(C,' IS THE SMALLEST')
    ELSE
        IF A>B THEN
            IF B<C THEN
                WRITELN(B,' IS THE SMALLEST')
            ELSE
                WRITELN(C,' IS THE SMALLEST')
    ELSE
        IF A=B THEN
            IF A=C THEN
                WRITELN('ALL NUMBERS ARE EQUAL')
            ELSE
                WRITELN('FIRST TWO NUMBERS ARE EQUAL')
  END. (* NESTEDIF *)
```

This example clearly illustrates how a nested **IF** statement would appear in a program. Note that after the first **IF—THEN** statement, the program branches into another **IF** statement. That is, the second **IF—THEN** statement is nested within the first.

---

## EXERCISE 7–6

1. Enter and run the above program.

### The CASE *Statement*

The **CASE** statement is used when there are more than two options or actions to be considered if certain specified conditions are met. That is, while most problems can be broken down into a series of single- or double-option **IF** statements, it is sometimes necessary to select one of a whole series of possible actions dependent upon the value of some expression.

The format for a **CASE** statement is as follows:

```
CASE <EXPRESSION> OF
  <VALUE 1>:<OPTION 1>;
  <VALUE 2>:<OPTION 2>;
  <VALUE 3>;<OPTION 3>;
  <VALUE 4>:<OPTION 4>
END;(*CASE*)
```

where <EXPRESSION> following the reserved word **CASE** is known as the *selector:* It represents anything that has an INTEGER, CHAR, or BOOLEAN value. <EXPRESSION> can be the name of a variable, a function, a constant, or an arithmetic function.

<VALUE 1>, <VALUE 2>, <VALUE 3>, and <VALUE 4> are allowed values of <EXPRESSION>. These values represent one or more constants, which must be the same type as the <EXPRESSION>. If there are several values for the same option, they must be separated by commas.

<OPTION 1> through <OPTION 4> represents any Pascal statement.

Note the ";" after the reserved word **END** and the optional comment (*CASE*), which tells you it is the end of the **CASE** statement.

In standard Pascal, if there is no **CASE** <VALUE> equal to the <EXPRESSION>, the result of the **CASE** statement is undefined. In Apple Pascal, however, if there is not a **CASE** matching the value of the <EXPRESSION>, then the next statement following the **CASE** statement is executed. (See Fig. 7–5.)

The first thing that happens when a **CASE** statement is executed is that the <EXPRESSION> or selector is evaluated. Next, a match is looked for between the values and the <EXPRESSION>.

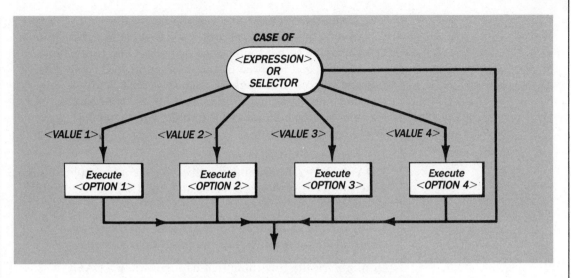

*Fig. 7–5 Execution of the CASE statement.*

If a match is found (for example, <EXPRESSION> = <VALUE 1> or <VALUE 2>), the corresponding option is executed. Then the next statement following the case statement is executed. If no match is found, the next statement following the **CASE** statement is executed without executing any of the options.

The following is an example of a **CASE** statement:

```
PROGRAM WEEK;

  VAR
    DAYNUM:INTEGER;

  BEGIN
    WRITE('INPUT A NUMBER 1-7 ');
    READLN(DAYNUM);
    WRITELN;
    WRITE('THE DAY IS ');
    CASE DAYNUM OF
        1:WRITELN('SUNDAY');
        2:WRITELN('MONDAY');
        3:WRITELN('TUESDAY');
        4:WRITELN('WEDNESDAY');
        5:WRITELN('THURSDAY');
        6:WRITELN('FRIDAY');
        7:WRITELN('SATURDAY')
        END; (* CASE *)
  END.
```

The **CASE** statement begins with the reserved word **CASE** followed by the selection expression <DAYNUM>, which must be a data type with a finite range of values. The expression <DAYNUM> is followed by the reserved word **OF** and a list of possible choices (1 through 7). Each choice starts wtih a constant value to be matched followed by a colon. The executable statement follows the colon. For example: WRITELN('MONDAY').

If the constant (or value) matches the expression <DAYNUM>, the statement is executed. (For example, if 2 is a match with expression <DAYNUM>, then TUESDAY would be displayed on the screen.)

If none of the values matches the option, then the Pascal program continues with the next program statement.

In summary, the first thing that happens when a **CASE** statement is executed is that the <EXPRESSION> is evaluated. Next, a match between the resultant value <DAYNUM> and one of the constants is sought. If no match is found, the Pascal program continues to the next statement. If a match is found, the corresponding option is executed.

## EXERCISE 7–7

1. Enter and run the above program (**PROGRAM** WEEK).

## Summary    The **IF–THEN** and **IF–THEN–ELSE** Statement

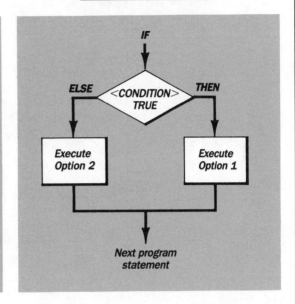

1. If <CONDITION> is true, execute the program statement; otherwise skip to the next program statement.

2. Any statement, including another **IF** statement, can be a program statement.

3. If more than one program statement is required (that is, a compound statement), it must be bracketed by **BEGIN–END.**

**4. The format is:**

```
IF <CONDITION> THEN

    <STATEMENT>
```

1. If <CONDITION> is true, the first option is executed. If the <CONDITION> is false, the second option is executed.

2. Any statement, including another **IF** statement, can be executed as Option 1 and/or Option 2.

3. If a compound statement is used in Option 1 or Option 2, it must be bracketed by **BEGIN–END.**

4. The format is:

```
IF <CONDITION> THEN
    <EXECUTE OPTION 1>

ELSE
    <EXECUTE OPTION 2>
```

### The Nested IF Statement

If you have a nested **IF–THEN** statement of the form:

```
IF <CONDITION 1> THEN
   IF <CONDITION 2> THEN
      <EXECUTE OPTION 1>

   ELSE
      <EXECUTE OPTION 2>
```

it might appear ambiguous whether execution of <OPTION 2> is controlled by the value of <CONDITION 1> or by the value of <CONDITION 2>. To resolve this ambiguity, you should bracket the entire inner **IF** statement between **BEGIN** and **END**. For example:

```
IF <CONDITION 1> THEN
   BEGIN
      IF <CONDITION 2> THEN
         <EXECUTE OPTION 1>

   END
ELSE
         <EXECUTE OPTION 2>
```

No semicolons are needed before or after the reserved word **END**. You need semicolons only if a compound statement is present in the **IF** statement. Any other semicolon will erroneously signal the end of the **IF** statement; and as a result, the computer will try to interpret the word following the semicolon as the start of a new statement outside the **IF** statement. Also, don't forget to align the **ELSE** statement with its corresponding **IF** statement for clarity.

### The CASE *Statement*

The format for a **CASE** statement is:

```
CASE <EXPRESSION> OF

    <VALUE 1> : <OPTION 1>;
    <VALUE 2> : <OPTION 2>;
    <VALUE 3> : <OPTION 3>;
        .
        .
        .
    <VALUE N> : <OPTION N>;

END; (*CASE*)
```

When there are more than two options in a selection statement, a **CASE** statement can be more direct than a set of nested **IF–THEN–ELSE** statements.

When a **CASE** statement is encountered in a program, the <EXPRESSION> is evaluated and a match between the <VALUE> and the <EXPRESSION> is sought. If a match is found, the corresponding option is executed. If no match is found, the next statement following the **CASE** statement is executed (Apple Pascal only).

### Punctuation and Programming Style

Watch out for extra semicolons within your **IF** statements. Do not use semicolons immediately before or after the reserved words **THEN** or **ELSE**.

The one exception where a semicolon may be required within an **IF** statement is inside a compound statement. An extra semicolon will indicate the end of an **IF** statement, and the computer will try to interpret the word following the semicolon as the start of a new statement outside of the **IF** statement, which is an undetected program error.

It is important that you make your program as clear and easy to read as possible. Use indentation and spacing wherever possible. For example, the statements inside **IF** statements should be indented to make the overall program organization apparent to anyone reading the program.

## PRACTICE 7–1

1.  Trace the program below manually and predict the output.

```
PROGRAM TRACE;

  VAR
    A,B,C:INTEGER;

  BEGIN
    A:=1;
    B:=2;
    C:=5;
    IF A<B THEN
        BEGIN
          WRITELN(A);
          A:=A+C
        END (* IF *)
    ELSE
        WRITELN(A);
    B:=B-A;
    IF A<B THEN
        WRITELN(B)
    ELSE
        BEGIN
          WRITELN(A);
          WRITELN(B);
          C:=C+B;
          IF (A+B) = (C+1) THEN
              WRITELN(A+B+C);
          WRITELN(C)
        END (* ELSE *)
  END. (* TRACE *)
```

2.  Enter and run the program. (Did your answer match the computer's answer?)

## PRACTICE 7–2

Using the **IF–THEN–ELSE** statement, write a program to input two integers. If the first number is less than the second number entered from the keyboard, then add the two numbers. If the two numbers are equal, then multiply them. If the first number is greater than the second number, then subtract the second number from the first. Print the answer.

## PRACTICE 7–3

Using the **CASE** statement, write a program to input a number (1 to 12), and print out the corresponding month for each input number. Include an error message to be printed out if the number inputted is not between 1 and 12. Also, include a statement to prompt the user for the input.

**Chapter 8**

# Loop Statements

**What You Will Learn**

- To explain the purpose and use of the key words **WHILE-DO, REPEAT-UNTIL,** and **FOR-DO.**

- To compare the **WHILE-DO, REPEAT-UNTIL,** and **FOR-DO** loops, and explain how they relate to one another.

- To develop, enter, and run programs using each of the loop statements.

**The Loop
Statements While-
Do/Repeat-Until/
For-Do**

The computer is most useful when a particular calculation is repeated many times. To do this, it is necessary to use loop statements in which certain sequences of operations are performed many times. That is, loops or repetitive statements allow the computer to do the same thing over and over any number of times (and to do it quickly).

In Pascal, there are several loop statements, each of which operates in a slightly different way. This allows you to choose the most appropriate statement for your intended application. Your choice will depend on a number of different factors, but will typically be made on the basis of precise conditions that must be met before the execution of the loop can be terminated. The three loops or repetitive-type statements we will discuss are:

**WHILE-DO**

**REPEAT-UNTIL**

**FOR-DO**

It is important that the conditions to be met are determined very carefully, since the computer will continue to perform the operations programmed within the loop until it is told to stop. (Since the computer can't think, you must tell it where and when to stop, or the loop will continue forever, or at least until the power fails or is turned off.)

### The While-Do Loop Statement

Use the **WHILE-DO** statement if you want the loop to be executed as long as the condition to be met exists or remains true. The format for the **WHILE-DO** statement is:

```
WHILE <CONDITION> DO
     <STATEMENT>
```

If the **WHILE** <CONDITION> is true, continue to execute the<STATEMENT>. Terminate the loop as soon as the value of the expression becomes false. The <STATEMENT> can be any Pascal statement. (See Fig. 8–1.)

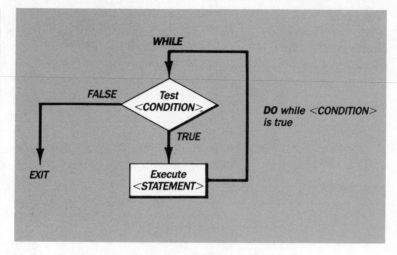

*Fig. 8–1 Execution of the WHILE–DO loop statement.*

An example of a **WHILE-DO** statement follows:

REFERENCE

```
1     PROGRAM WHILECOUNT;

2       VAR
3         COUNT:INTEGER;

4     BEGIN
5       COUNT:=0;
6       WHILE COUNT <> 10 DO
7         BEGIN
8           COUNT:=COUNT+1;
9           WRITELN(COUNT)
10        END; (* WHILE *)
11    END.
```

This program counts to 10. Line 1 gives the program name.
Line 3 declares the variable COUNT as an integer. Line 5
initializes the loop by setting COUNT = 0. Line 6
establishes the condition to be met for the loop to continue, that is, as long
as COUNT <> 10 continues to execute the statements (lines 7
through 9). When the count reaches 10, however, the condition
becomes false and the program is terminated. Line 8
increments the variable count by 1 each time the program
passes through the loop.

## EXERCISE 8-1

1. Enter the program shown on page 140 (WHILECOUNT) and run it several times.

### WHILE–DO LOOP EXECUTION ANALYSIS

| | LOOP EXECUTION | CONTROL VARIABLE (COUNT) STATUS | DISPLAY | REFERENCE |
|---|---|---|---|---|
| | `PROGRAM WHILECOUNT:` | | | 1 |
| | `VAR` | | | 2 |
| | `COUNT:INTEGER;` | | | 3 |
| | `BEGIN` | | | 4 |
| Initialize | `COUNT:=0;` | 0 | | 5 |
| First Pass | `WHILE COUNT <> 3 DO` | | | 6 |
| | `BEGIN` | | | 7 |
| Increment | `COUNT:=COUNT+1;` | 1 = 0 + 1 | | 8 |
| | `WRITE(COUNT);` | | 1 | 9 |
| | `READLN` | | | 10 |
| | `END;` | | | 11 |
| Second Pass | `WHILE COUNT <> 3 DO` | | | 6 |
| | `BEGIN` | | | 7 |
| Increment | `COUNT:=COUNT+1;` | 2 = 1 + 1 | | 8 |
| | `WRITE(COUNT);` | | 2 | 9 |
| | `READLN` | | | 10 |
| | `END;` | | | 11 |
| Third Pass | `WHILE COUNT<> 3 DO` | | | 6 |
| | `BEGIN` | | | 7 |
| Increment | `COUNT:=COUNT+1;` | 3 = 2 + 1 | | 8 |
| | `WRITE(COUNT);` | | 3 | 9 |
| | `READLN` | | | 10 |
| | `END;` | | | 11 |
| | `END.` | | | 12 |

Line 5 initializes the loop; that is, it sets COUNT: = 0. (Think of the little plastic counters you use in the supermarket for keeping track of purchases.)

The first time the program reaches line 8 (COUNT: = COUNT + 1), 1 is added to COUNT, which was originally set = 0.

Line 9 outputs results to the display.

Line 10 was added to stop the program execution by requiring you to press [RETURN] to continue. This was used to help you see the program execution in steps.

After the first pass through the loop, the variable (COUNT) is tested to see if it has reached 3 yet (line 6). If not, it will continue to execute the loop.

After the third pass (COUNT = 3), the program exits the loop.

### The REPEAT–UNTIL *Loop Statement*

If the loop is to be executed until some condition is met, the **REPEAT-UNTIL** statement can be used. The format for **REPEAT-UNTIL** is:

```
REPEAT
        <STATEMENT>
UNTIL   <CONDITION>
```

Execute the <STATEMENT> or <SEQUENCE OF STATEMENTS> until the condition is met. This <CONDITION> is usually a Boolean value which can be evaluated as being either TRUE or FALSE. (See Fig. 8–2.)

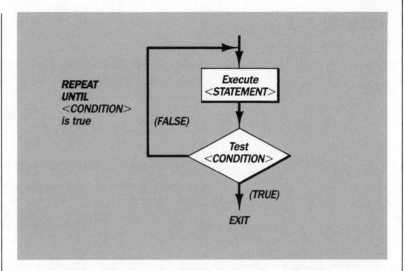

*Fig. 8–2 Execution of the REPEAT–UNTIL loop statement.*

The following is an example of a **REPEAT-UNTIL** program:

REFERENCE

```
1    PROGRAM REPCOUNT;

2      VAR
3        COUNT:INTEGER;

4      BEGIN
5        COUNT:=0;
6        REPEAT
7          COUNT:=COUNT+1;
8          WRITELN(COUNT);
9        UNTIL COUNT=10
10     END.
```

This program also counts to 10. Line 1 gives the program
name and line 3 declares the variable. Line 5 initializes the
counter (loop) by setting count = 0. Line 6 starts the **REPEAT**
loop. Line 7 increments the variable count by 1. Remember,
you set COUNT = 0 in line 5; therefore, the first pass
through this line will set COUNT = 1 (that is, 1 = 0 + 1).
Line 8 outputs the value of COUNT to the screen. Line 9
determines if COUNT = 10 (evaluates the condition), and, if
not, the process continues. When COUNT reaches 10, the
program is terminated (line 10).

## EXERCISE 8–2

1. Enter the program shown on page 143 (REPCOUNT) and run it several times.

**REPEAT—UNTIL *LOOP EXECUTION ANALYSIS***

| | *LOOP EXECUTION* | *CONTROL VARIABLE (COUNT) STATUS* | *DISPLAY* | *REFERENCE* |
|---|---|---|---|---|
| | BEGIN | | | 1 |
| First Pass Initialize | COUNT:=0; | 0 | | 2 |
| | REPEAT | | | 3 |
| Increment | COUNT:=COUNT+1; | 1 = 0 + 1 | | 4 |
| Output | WRITELN(COUNT); | | 1 | 5 |
| Test | UNTIL COUNT = 3 | | | 6 |
| Second Pass | REPEAT | | | 3 |
| Increment | COUNT:=COUNT+1; | 2 = 1 + 1 | | 4 |
| Output | WRITELN(COUNT); | | 2 | 5 |
| Test | UNTIL COUNT = 3 | | | 6 |
| Third Pass | REPEAT | | | 3 |
| Increment | COUNT:=COUNT+1; | 3 = 2 + 1 | | 4 |
| Output | WRITELN(COUNT); | | 3 | 5 |
| Test | UNTIL COUNT = 3 | | | 6 |
| Count = 3 | END. | | | 7 |

The **REPEAT-UNTIL** loop works very much like the **WHILE-DO** loop. The following should be noted.

The **REPEAT-UNTIL** loop was executed at least once (line 5) before the condition to be met is tested (line 6).

Note the cycle that proceeds after the loop is initialized in line 2. That is: INCREMENT, OUTPUT, and TEST until a condition is met.

When COUNT = 3, the loop is exited.

## WHILE-DO *Versus* REPEAT-UNTIL

WHILE-DO

```
BEGIN
   COUNT:=0;

   WHILE COUNT <> 10 DO

   BEGIN
      COUNT:=COUNT+1;

      WRITELN(COUNT);
   END; (*WHILE*)
END.
```

REPEAT-UNTIL

```
BEGIN
   COUNT:=0;
   REPEAT
      COUNT:=COUNT+1;
      WRITELN(COUNT);


   UNTIL COUNT = 10
END.
```

Essentially, the difference between the **WHILE-DO** loop and the **REPEAT-UNTIL** loop is that the **WHILE-DO** loop's <condition> is evaluated at the start of the loop and the **REPEAT-UNTIL** <condition> is evaluated at the end of the loop.

Note that the **REPEAT-UNTIL** statement is executed at least once before the first evaluation or before the condition is tested to be true. The **WHILE-DO** loop, however, may not be executed at all since the condition is evaluated first. Care must be exercised when selecting the conditions to be evaluated for either loop. If values for the conditions to be met are indeterminate or misleading, a programming error will result, which you may or may not be able to detect in time.

### The FOR–DO *Loop Statement*

The **WHILE-DO** and **REPEAT-UNTIL** statements are the primary statements used for repetitive situations in Pascal, especially when the number of times the program is to be repeated is *not* known. However, the **FOR-DO** statement is useful if you know how many times you want a statement executed to obtain the required result.

The format for the **FOR-DO** statement is as follows:

```
(1) FOR <control variable>:= <initial value> TO <final value> DO
         <statement>
```
    or
```
(2) FOR <control variable>:= <initial value> DOWNTO <final value> DO
         <statement>
```

The **FOR-DO** statement essentially tells the computer to "do something" (that is, execute a statement or several statements) *for* as long as the <control variable> is set to a value in a range that starts with the <initial value> and ends with the <final value>. You assign a value to the <control variable>; the value can be any simple type (that is, integer or scalar) except type REAL.

Here is how the **FOR-DO** loop works:

First, the value of the <control variable> is set equal to the <initial value>.

Next, the computer tests the statement to see whether the <control variable> has already exceeded the <final value>. If so, nothing happens and the loop is exited. Otherwise, the <statement> after the word **DO** is executed once.

Then, the <control variable> is either increased by one (if **TO** is used in the statement) or decreased by one (if **DOWNTO** is used in the statement).

Finally, the program loops back to the top and starts over, and checks to see whether the <control variable> has yet exceeded the <final value>. If the <control variable> has exceeded the <final value> the loop program exits; if not, the program continues.

The following is an example of a **FOR-DO** program:

*REFERENCE*

```
1   PROGRAM FORCOUNT;

2     VAR
3       COUNT:INTEGER;

4     BEGIN
5       FOR COUNT := 1 TO 10 DO
6         WRITELN(COUNT)
7     END.
```

First, the program sets the value of the control variable (COUNT=1) in line 5. Next, the program tests to see whether the control variable (COUNT) has already exceeded the final value (10). Since this is a first pass, the program has not exceeded the final value (10); therefore, it executes line 6. That is, it causes the computer to display 1 on the screen. Then 1 is added to the control variable COUNT (COUNT=2 now), and the program loops back to the top. This process continues until COUNT = 10; then the program exits the loop.

## EXERCISE 8–3

1. Enter the above program and run it several times.

## Summary

**COMPARISON OF WHILE–DO, REPEAT–UNTIL, *AND* FOR–DO *PROGRAM LOOPS***

| REFERENCE | | | |
|---|---|---|---|
| 1 | A. WHILE-DO | B. REPEAT-UNTIL | C. FOR-DO |
| 2 | BEGIN | BEGIN | BEGIN |
| 3 | COUNT:=0; | COUNT:=0; | FOR COUNT := 1 TO 10 DO |
| 4 | WHILE COUNT <> 10 DO | | |
| 5 | BEGIN | REPEAT | |
| 6 | COUNT:=COUNT+1; | COUNT:=COUNT+1; | |
| 7 | WRITELN(COUNT); | WRITELN COUNT; | WRITELN(COUNT) |
| 8 | END; (*WHILE*) | UNTIL COUNT = 10 | |
| 9 | END. | END. | END. |

Each of the above program loops counts to 10. But there are some differences:

A **BEGIN-END** pair (ref. lines 5 and 8) is required within the main program block for the WHILE-DO loop when more than one statement (lines 6 and 7) is used in the loop.

A **BEGIN-END** pair is not required in the **REPEAT-UNTIL** loop even though there is more than one statement (lines 6 and 7) because **REPEAT-UNTIL** serves the same purpose.

If there were more than one statement (line 7) in the **FOR-DO** loop, then a **BEGIN-END** pair would be required around the statements.

The **FOR-DO** loop statement contains the least number of statements because a separate statement is not required to update the loop control variable.

Remember that **BEGIN-END** are not statements but are reserved words which bracket program statements.

## PRACTICE 8–1

a. Using a **FOR-DO** loop, write a program to print numbers from 1 to 20.

b. Using the **REPEAT-UNTIL** loop, write a program that prints the numbers from 1 to 20.

c. Using the **WHILE-DO** loop, write a program that prints the numbers from 1 to 20.

## PRACTICE 8–2

a. Modify Exercise 8–1(b) to count from 2 to 20 by two's.

b Modify Exercise 8–2(c) to count from 2 to 20 by two's.

## PRACTICE 8–3

a. Using a **FOR-DO** loop, write a program that prints the numbers from 20 down to 1.

b. Using a **REPEAT-UNTIL** loop, write a program that prints the numbers from 20 down to 1.

c. Using a **WHILE-DO** loop, write a program that prints the numbers from 20 down to 1.

# Chapter 9

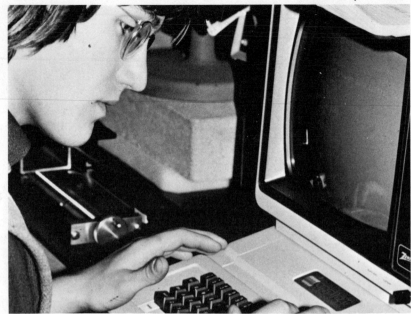

# Arrays

**What You Will Learn**

- To understand structured and unstructured data types.
- To explain the purpose of using arrays.
- To become familiar with the reserved word **ARRAY**.
- To set up one- and two-dimensional numeric arrays.
- To develop, enter, and run programs using numeric arrays.

## Data Types

### Unstructured Data Types

Pascal offers a variety of standard data types, and even allows you to define new data types (which you will learn later). Up until now, you have been introduced to five standard data types that are unstructured and predefined in Apple Pascal, namely: integer, real, Boolean, character, and string.

A data type defines a set of values, and Pascal requires that every data item in a program must have a type associated with it; that is, the type of every variable used in Pascal must be declared. Here is why.

The data type of a variable tells the computer what kind of data may be stored in the variable, and the operations that may be performed on it. (Table 9–1 summarizes the standard data types covered so far.)

The data type of a variable will help you (the programmer) to structure your program properly and to use the operators with the declared type. This is especially useful when you use the **TYPE** definition part of the declaration block, as you will see later.

### Structured Data Types

In addition to the unstructured data types (that is, standard and user-defined), Pascal provides four structured data types: array, record, set, and files. Structured data types are actually constructed from the unstructured types. We will introduce an array data type in this chapter. The other structured types, with the exception of files, will be covered in subsequent chapters of this book.

**TABLE 9–1. STANDARD DATA TYPES PREDECLARED IN APPLE PASCAL**

| TYPE | KIND OF DATA USED | OPERATIONS* |
|---|---|---|
| INTEGER | A set of whole numbers.<br>– Very useful for counting. | Read/Write<br>Arithmetic<br>$(+, -, *, \text{DIV}, \text{MOD})$ |
| REAL | A set of real numbers.<br>– Used with variables that require fractional parts or decimals. | Read/Write<br>Arithmetic<br>$(+, -, *, /)$ |
| CHAR | A set of characters available on the Apple.<br>– Used with variables that require processing of a single character at a time. | Read/Write<br>Comparison: with another character using its ordinal value (order number). (This will be covered in Chapter 12.) |
| BOOLEAN | True or False value.<br>– Very useful for variables that are compared and in operations that require a TRUE/FALSE response to make a decision. | Read/Write *not* permitted.<br>Assignment example:<br>   VAR RESPONSE:BOOLEAN<br>     RESPONSE: = TRUE<br>Logical comparison (And, Or, Not)<br>Relational Operators<br>$(=, <, >, < >, < =, \text{ and } > =)$ |
| STRING (UCSD) | A maximum length of 80 characters is permitted unless otherwise specified (declared).<br>– A predeclared data type that permits easy manipulation of a sequence of characters. | Read/Write<br>Assignment: letters, words, numbers, and/or a combination of letters and numbers.<br>Comparison: to a constant or another string variable. |

*Operations covered in this book only.

**Arrays**

An array is a lineup, an arrangement, or an orderly grouping of things. It is a collection of items, all of the same type, which is grouped together and indexed so that each item of the array can be accessed through a single label with a unique subscript or index.

An array allows you to assign many more values to one variable name, and thereby permitting you to work with more information at one time.

It is sometimes necessary to keep track of a large number of data items so that these items can be manipulated by the program. Although you could use a larger number of independent variables to assign to each of the data items, programming would become more cumbersome and more tedious as the number of variables increased. The array allows you to arrange your data items so that they can be stored and retrieved easier.

### Dimension of an Array

All array variables have a property that simple Pascal variables don't have—dimension. The dimension of the array tells the legal range of value for the array's subscripts. It must be declared before you can use it. Pascal allows arrays to be declared with more than one dimension.

Arrays can be singly subscripted (one-dimensional) or doubly subscripted (two-dimensional). Like all other variables, an array variable has a name, a type, and a value. The name and type must be declared *before* use. This is usually done in the **VAR** part of the declaration block. Value is usually assigned by means of an assignment statement (as with all other variables).

### The One-Dimensional Array

```
VAR
  <NAME>: ARRAY [DIMENSION] OF <ELEMENT TYPE>;
```

You must include the reserved words **ARRAY** and **OF** together with the square brackets [ ]. The label you assign to the array is <NAME>. The dimension is often a range of integers but need not be so (as you will see later in this book). An array dimension is specified by its bounds (or subscript range). For example:

```
<NAME>: ARRAY [0..N] OF <ELEMENT TYPE>;
```

Here the bounds, inside the brackets, are separated by two dots—which means that the subscripts of this array range from 0 to N inclusive.

The upper and lower bounds of each array dimension specify the size of the array. That is, they determine the number of elements that the array will hold. If an array has only one pair of bounds, as in the above example, it is called a *one-dimensional array*.

The <ELEMENT TYPE> defines the type of each element in the array. All elements in the array must be of the same type. Element types may be one of the standard data types (REAL, CHAR, BOOLEAN, INTEGER, STRING), or a user-defined data type (to be discussed later).

The following are types of one-dimensional arrays:

```
VAR

    GRADE  : ARRAY [0..100] OF REAL;
    NAME   : ARRAY [1..50] OF STRING;
    NUMBER : ARRAY [0..100] OF INTEGER;
```

NAME OF ARRAY

TYPE OF ELEMENTS THE ARRAY MAY CONTAIN

SUBSCRIPT RANGE OR DIMENSION (NOTE THE TWO PERIODS)

"GRADE" is an array of type REAL with integer subscripts that can have any value from 0 to 100. This array declaration tells the computer to set aside 101 memory locations (array elements) with the name "GRADE." Each element of this array may contain a single real value.

"NAME" is a string array with integer subscripts that can have any value from 1 to 50. This array declaration tells the computer to set aside 50 memory locations with the name "NAME." Each element of this array may contain a single string value.

"NUMBER" is an array of type INTEGER with integer subscripts that can have any value from 0 to 100. This array tells the computer to set aside 101 memory locations with the name "NUMBER." Each element of this array may contain a single integer value.

Individual elements of an array are stored and retrieved by using the subscripts or indexes to the array to reference each individual element. The value of each of the subscripts above is used to select one of the array elements for manipulation. For example, a typical indexing operation is as follows:

GRADE [2] refers to the third element of the array GRADE.

NAME [45] refers to the forty-fifth element of the array NAME.

NUMBER [5] refers to the fifth element of the array NUMBER.

A one-dimensional array is diagrammed in Fig. 9–1. Note that A and B are optional names. Any valid variable name can be used to name an array; for example, A1, B1, BB, CHECK, words, names, numbers, and so on. Although one side of the illustration shows a vertical arrangement while the other shows a horizontal arrangement, both are addressed the same way (that is, NAME (location) or A SUB 3 or B SUB 5).

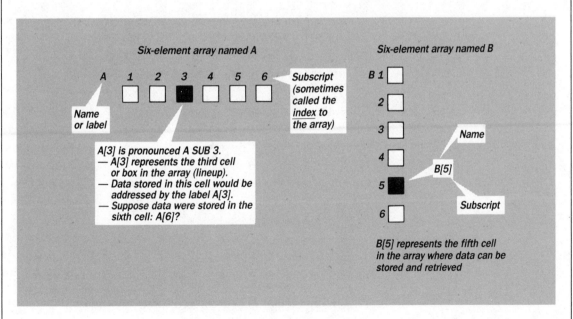

*Fig. 9–1 A one-dimensional array.*

## EXERCISE 9–1

**One-Dimensional
Array
(Reading Integers)**

1. Boot the system and clear the workfile. Note: To type the left bracket ([), press [CTRL] [K]; to type the right bracket (]), press [SHIFT] [M].

2. Enter this program.

```
PROGRAM READINT;

(* READ INTEGERS INTO AN ARRAY *)

  VAR
    A:ARRAY [1..6] OF INTEGER;
    LOOP:INTEGER;

  BEGIN
    WRITELN('ENTER SIX NUMBERS');
    WRITELN;
    FOR LOOP := 1 TO 6 DO
      BEGIN
        WRITE('NUMBER ',LOOP,' ');
        READLN(A[LOOP])
      END; (* FOR DO *)

    WRITELN;
    WRITELN('YOUR SIX NUMBERS');
    WRITELN;
    FOR LOOP := 1 TO 6 DO
      WRITELN(LOOP,'    ',A[LOOP])
  END. (* READINT *)
```

3. Press [Q], [U], and [R] (Quit, Update, and Run).

4. For your first pass, enter these six numbers:
     100
     200
     300
     400
     500
     600

5. What happened after you entered these six numbers?

An illustration of what happens after data are entered from the keyboard and stored in array A[LOOP] follows.

### ARRAY CONTENTS

```
A[LOOP]
A[1] ----> 100
A[2] ----> 200
A[3] ----> 300
A[4] ----> 400
A[5] ----> 500
A[6] ----> 600
```

Note that in location A[1], the first number [100] is stored. In location A[2], the second number [200] is stored, and so on until the sixth number entered is stored in location A[6].

Note that a **FOR-DO** loop was used to load the array with data. The loop control variable (LOOP) was used as the subscript for the array. Note, also, that the initial value (1) and the final value (6) of the **FOR-DO** loop corresponds to the subscripts of the array [1..6]. As you can see, **FOR-DO** loops are very useful for storing and retrieving data in arrays.

To access the contents of an array, you simply list the array's name followed by the element's subscript (for example, A[1]).

## EXERCISE 9–2

***One-Dimensional
Array
(Reading String
Variables)***

1. If the previous program "READINT" is still in your
   workfile, you can modify it to match the program that
   follows. (You also can clear the workfile and type in the
   program if you wish.)

```
PROGRAM READSTRING;

(* READ A STRING INTO AN ARRAY *)

  VAR
    A:ARRAY [1..6] OF STRING;
    LOOP:INTEGER;

  BEGIN
    WRITELN('ENTER SIX NAMES');
    WRITELN;
    FOR LOOP := 1 TO 6 DO
      BEGIN
        WRITE('NAME ',LOOP,' ');
        READLN(A[LOOP])
      END; (* FOR DO *)

    WRITELN;
    WRITELN('YOUR SIX NAMES');
    WRITELN;
    FOR LOOP := 1 TO 6 DO
      WRITELN(LOOP,'   ',A[LOOP])
  END. (* READSTRING *)
```

2. After you have entered the program, press [Q], [U], and [R].

3. For your first pass, enter six names. For example:
   AUBREY
   ALYCE
   ADRIENNE
   SHAWN
   TONY
   TONYA

4. What happened?

An illustration of what happens after data are entered from the keyboard and stored in array A[LOOP] follows.

**ARRAY CONTENTS**

```
A[LOOP]
A[1] ----> AUBREY
A[2] ----> ALYCE
A[3] ----> ADRIENNE
A[4] ----> SHAWN
A[5] ----> TONY
A[6] ----> TONYA
```

The difference between this array and the previous one is that this array stores strings (names) and the other stored numbers. Otherwise, everything else works just as described earlier.

## Two-Dimensional Array

**NOTE:** *Values go in two directions, down (row) and across (column). This is called a two-dimension array. Each row and column is numbered. A two-dimensional array is also called a matrix. (See Fig. 9–2.)*

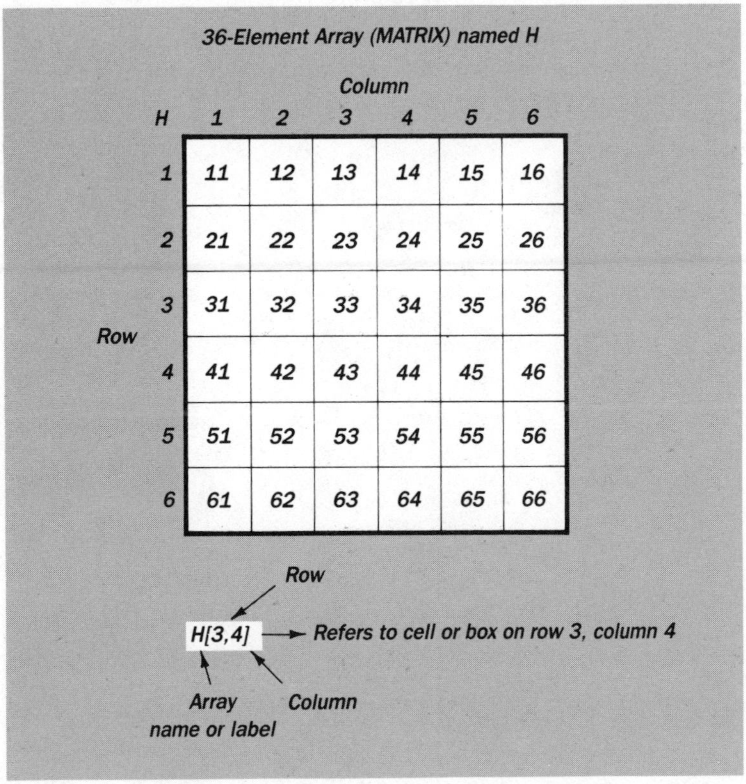

**36-Element Array (MATRIX) named H**

| H | 1 | 2 | 3 | 4 | 5 | 6 |
|---|---|---|---|---|---|---|
| 1 | 11 | 12 | 13 | 14 | 15 | 16 |
| 2 | 21 | 22 | 23 | 24 | 25 | 26 |
| 3 | 31 | 32 | 33 | 34 | 35 | 36 |
| 4 | 41 | 42 | 43 | 44 | 45 | 46 |
| 5 | 51 | 52 | 53 | 54 | 55 | 56 |
| 6 | 61 | 62 | 63 | 64 | 65 | 66 |

Column (across top); Row (down side)

H[3,4] → Refers to cell or box on row 3, column 4

Row; Array name or label; Column

*Fig. 9–2 A two-dimensional array.*

## EXERCISE 9–3

Fill in the remaining blanks in the following table, using the matrix shown in Fig. 9–2.

| LABEL | ROW | COLUMN | CONTENTS |
|-------|-----|--------|----------|
| H[1,1] | —— | —— | —— |
| H[4,5] | —— | —— | —— |
| H[3,3] | —— | —— | —— |
| H[2,3] | —— | —— | —— |
| H[6,6] | —— | —— | —— |
| H[1,6] | —— | —— | —— |
| H[2,4] | —— | —— | —— |
| H[4,4] | —— | —— | —— |

## A Two-Dimensional Array Format

```
VAR
<NAME> : ARRAY [0..N, 0..N] OF <ELEMENT TYPE>
```

In this format, <NAME> is the name or label you assign to the array and <ELEMENT TYPE> defines the type of array (just like the one-dimensional array).

The major difference between this format and the one-dimensional format is that inside the brackets are two sets of values which declare the range double-subscripted values used with the variable <NAME>. The two periods are still required, and a comma is used between the two range of values for the subscripts 0 to N.

Envision the above format as representing a matrix with rows and columns. Then you would have:

```
<NAME> : ARRAY [ROW,COL] OF <ELEMENT TYPE>
```

where ROW and COL would each represent subscripted values in the range 0 to N. (See Fig. 9–3.)

```
VAR
   CHECKS : ARRAY [1..6, 1..3] OF REAL;
   NAME   : ARRAY [1..25, 1..10] OF STRING;
```

*SETS THE DIMENSIONS OF THE ROW*

*SETS THE DIMENSIONS OF THE COLUMN*

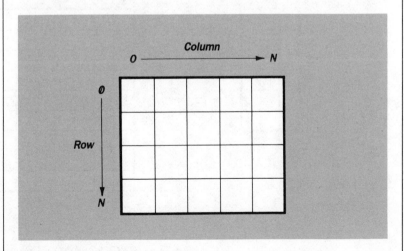

*Fig. 9–3 A matrix of rows and columns.*

Envision the CHECKS array as follows:

```
CHECKS: ARRAY [ROW,COL] OF REAL
```

where ROW represents a subscript value in the range of 1 to 6, and COL has a value in the range of 1 to 3.

"CHECKS" is an array of type REAL with integer subscripts for both the ROW and COL dimension. "NAME" is a string array with integer subscripts that have a range of values of 1 to 25 (ROW) and 1 to 10 (COL). (See Fig. 9–4.)

So far, all of the subscripts used in the examples have been integers. But a subscript doesn't have to be an integer constant; it can be any variable or any expression that yields a value within the declared range of the subscript. For example:

**NOTE** *that this is the same array described earlier. By declaring ROWMAX and COLMAX as constants, it is a simple matter to change the subscripts or the size of the array or matrix.*

```
PROGRAM CHECKBAL;
    CONST
        ROWMAX=6;
        COLMAX=3;

VAR
    CHECKS:ARRAY [1..ROWMAX,1..COLMAX] OF REAL;
```

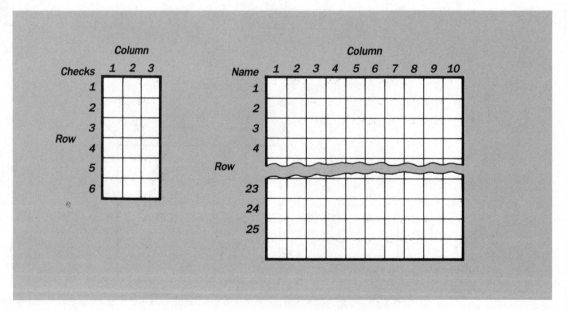

*Fig. 9–4 The CHECKS and NAMES arrays.*

## EXERCISE 9–4

### *Checkbook Array*

Consider the following table of checkbook information:

| CHECK # | DATE WRITTEN | AMOUNT |
|---------|--------------|--------|
| 100 | 6/5/84 | $ 15.50 |
| 101 | 6/7/84 | 25.00 |
| 102 | 6/15/84 | 145.00 |
| 103 | 6/22/84 | 65.00 |
| 104 | 6/30/84 | 211.00 |
| 105 | 6/30/84 | 79.50 |

Note that every item in the table may be specified by reference to two numbers: the row number and the column number. For example, Row 3, Column 3 refers to the amount $145.00.

This table can be set up in a 6 × 3 array or matrix.

### *Note*

The checks were arranged in this order for the purpose of illustrating arrays. This arrangement goes in two directions, down (row) and across (columns), and could therefore be placed in a 6 × 3 matrix (see Table 9–2). Compare this table with the data given in the table above.

**NOTE:** *Data recorded in form mmddyy where mm = month number, dd = day, and yy = last two digits of the year. Since CHECKS is a numeric array, alphanumerical characters such as dashes cannot be stored.*

**Table 9–2. A CHECKBOOK ARRAY NAMED CHECKS**

| CHECKS | 1 | 2 | 3 |
|--------|-----|-------|--------|
| 1 | 100 | 60584 | $15.50 |
| 2 | 101 | 60784 | 25.00 |
| 3 | 102 | 61584 | 145.00 |
| 4 | 103 | 62284 | 65.00 |
| 5 | 104 | 63084 | 211.00 |
| 6 | 105 | 63084 | 79.50 |

---

**EXERCISE 9–4 *(continued)***

---

***Checkbook Array
Program: Setting Up
The Array***

1. Type in the following lines.

```
PROGRAM CHECKBOOK;

  VAR
    CHECK:ARRAY [1..6,1..3] OF REAL;
    ROW,COL:INTEGER;
    DATE,SUM:REAL;


BEGIN

  (* INITIALIZES SUM *)
  SUM := 0;

  (* LOADS THE CHECK ARRAY *)
  WRITELN('INPUT DATA:');
  FOR ROW := 1 TO 6 DO
    BEGIN
      WRITELN;
      FOR COL := 1 TO 3 DO
        BEGIN
          CASE COL OF
            1:WRITE('CHECK NUMBER ');
            2:WRITE('CHECK DATE ');
            3:WRITE('CHECK AMOUNT ')
          END; (* CASE *)
          READLN(CHECK[ROW,COL])
        END; (* COL *)
    END; (* ROW *)

  (* SUMS THE THIRD COLUMN *)
  FOR ROW := 1 TO 6 DO
    SUM := SUM + CHECK[ROW,3];
  WRITELN;
  WRITELN('TOTAL OF CHECKS WRITTEN $',SUM :8:2);

  (* SEARCHES THE SECOND COLUMN FOR CHECKS *)
  (* WRITTEN ON THE SPECIFIC DATE *)
  WRITE('LIST CHECKS WRITTEN ON (MM DD YY) ');
  READLN(DATE);
  WRITELN;
  WRITELN('CHECKS WRITTEN ON',DATE:5:1,' ARE LISTED BELOW:');
  WRITELN;
  WRITELN('CHECK #        AMOUNT');
  FOR ROW := 1 TO 6 DO
    IF CHECK[ROW,2] = DATE THEN
        WRITELN(CHECK[ROW,1]:3:1,'          ',CHECK[ROW,3]:3:2)
END.
```

2. Trace the program (manually) and predict the output.

3. Run the program.

```
TOTAL OF CHECKS WRITTEN $   541.00
```

**Explanation of the Checkbook Program**

In Pascal, you must define the array before the program is run. Therefore, you (or the programmer) should know how large any data array will become before the program is written. If you make your array too big for the computer's memory, a program error will result. Here we defined "CHECK" at the beginning of the program as an array type that has the dimensions of 6 rows by 3 columns. That is, row subscript values range from 1 to 6, and column subscript values range from 1 to 3.

As usual, all variables must be declared at the beginning of the program. Here we have CHECK as an array type, ROW/COL as integer types, and DATE/SUM as real types. If an integer value occurs where a real value is required, it is automatically converted to the equivalent real value. For example, 63084 will be converted to 6.30840E4.

It is important to initialize the variable SUM at the beginning of the program to ensure that SUM = 0 each time the program is run. If you don't set SUM = 0, you will get a surprise answer.

The part of the program in the first box loads the data from the keyboard into the array. Note that the first WRITELN statement within this box is just a prompt statement for the user. The two **FOR-DO** loops, one **CASE** statement, and one READLN statement are used to load the array. Here is how it works: Data are read into row 1 and columns 1 to 3 first, then row 2 and columns 1 to 3, and so on until all six rows are read (refer to Table 9–2 and note that after row 1 and columns 1 to 3 are read, the computer has loaded the data 100, 60584, and 15.50). Note also that the loop statement **FOR** COL: 1 **TO** 3 **DO** is used in conjunction with the **CASE** statement to prompt the user for each input.

As indicated by the comment statement, the program lines in the second dotted box add each row in the third column of the array. The check values are stored in the third column. Here is how this part of the program works:

| CHECK [ROW, 3] | SUM = SUM + CHECK [ROW, 3] |
|---|---|
| **INITIALIZE** | $\boxed{0}$ |
| **CHECK [1,3]** | $\boxed{15.50}$ = 0 + 15.50 |
| **CHECK [2,3]** | $\boxed{40.50}$ = 15.50 + 25.00 |
| **CHECK [3,3]** | $\boxed{185.50}$ = 40.50 + 145.00 |
| **CHECK [4,3]** | $\boxed{250.50}$ = 185.50 + 65.00 |
| **CHECK [5,3]** | $\boxed{461.50}$ = 250.50 + 211.00 |
| **CHECK [6,3]** | $\boxed{541.00}$ = 461.50 + 79.50 |

Note that column 3 is held fixed and the row is changed for each pass (row, 3). This is because column 3 of the matrix has all the dollar amounts we wish to add. So by starting with row (1,3), $15.50, and adding it to row (2,3), $25.00, we have the sum of the first two rows—$40.50. Now if we take this sum ($40.50) and add it to row (3,3), $145.00, we will have the sum of the first three rows ($185.50), and so on. (Note that we set SUM = 0 at the start of the program.)

Finally, the expression SUM :8:2 specifies the maximum number of characters to be written (8) and the number of digits to be written after the decimal point (2).

## EXERCISE 9–4 (continued)

**Checkbook Array Program: Manipulating the Array**

4. Add these lines to your program. Be sure to delete the last reserved word **END** and add a semicolon at the end of the line preceding this **END** statement.

```
WRITELN;
WRITELN('TOTAL OF CHECKS WRITTEN $',SUM :8:2);

(* SEARCHES THE SECOND COLUMN FOR CHECKS *)
(* WRITTEN ON THE SPECIFIC DATE *)
WRITE('LIST CHECKS WRITTEN ON (MM DD YY) ');
READLN(DATE);
WRITELN;
WRITELN('CHECKS WRITTEN ON',DATE:5:1,' ARE LISTED BELOW:');
WRITELN;
WRITELN('CHECK #        AMOUNT');
FOR ROW := 1 TO 6 DO
   IF CHECK[ROW,2] = DATE THEN
       WRITELN(CHECK[ROW,1]:3:1,'          ',CHECK[ROW,3]:3:2)
END.
```

5. Trace the program (manually) to make certain you understand it.

6. Run the program again and enter 63084 for input.

```
TOTAL OF CHECKS WRITTEN $   541.00
LIST CHECKS WRITTEN ON (MM DD YY)
CHECKS WRITTEN ON 63084.0 ARE LISTED BELOW:


CHECK #    AMOUNT
104.0     211.00
105.0      79.50
```

### Notes:

The comments in the last blocks explain the purpose of this part of the program. First, note that the first WRITE statement prompts the user on how to enter the date (MM DD YY). The next WRITELN statements are used to format and label to output. The **FOR** *ROW:=1* **TO** *6* **DO** *loop searches for checks written on the specific date entered. READLN (DATE) inputs the date.*

Column 2 is held constant because it contains the dates of checks written. Each row (1 to 6) is compared with the date you inputted. If the date is found, the check number and amount of check written on that date are printed out. The elements of an array must all be of the same type; therefore, the check number is of type REAL, and the check number will print out 104.0 instead of 104. If we could use a different type for each element, we would declare the variables as follows:

```
VAR
  CHECKNUMBER, DATE:INTEGER;
  CHECKAMOUNT:REAL;
```

As you will see later, there is another data type called **RECORD** which will permit you to have data items of different data types.

A2 is not the same as A[2]. A2 is an ordinary variable, and A[2] is a subscripted variable.

The one-dimensional array element A[3] is pronounced A SUB 3.

NAME    SUBSCRIPT

The one-dimensional **ARRAY** format is as follows:

```
VAR
  <NAME> : ARRAY [0..N] OF <ELEMENT TYPE>
```

ROW

The two-dimensional array (matrix) element H[3,4] refers to the cell or box on row 3 and column 4.

NAME    COLUMN

The two-dimensional **ARRAY** format is as follows:

```
VAR
  <NAME> : ARRAY [0..N,0..N] OF <ELEMENT TYPE>
```

*Summary*

## PRACTICE 9–1

1. Using an array, write a program to find the sum and average of the following ten numbers:

676 150 175 188 190 277 876 976 912 544

a. Make certain that you prompt the user for each number.
b. Label the answer as follows:
The sum is _____ and the average is _____.

## PRACTICE 9–2

### One-Dimensional Array

1. Suppose we had the following results of a quiz given to a class of 10 students:

| Student # | 1 | 2 | 3 | 4 | 5 | 6 | 7 | 8 | 9 | 10 |
|---|---|---|---|---|---|---|---|---|---|---|
| Student's grade | 75 | 85 | 95 | 87 | 100 | 77 | 83 | 69 | 98 | 88 |

**Hint:** *Modify the program used in Practice 9–1. Set the lowest and the highest grades equal to the first number in the array. That is:*

```
LOWEST:=A[1]
HIGHEST:=A[1]
```

a. Using a one-dimensional array, write a program to find the class average.
b. Add the necessary program lines to find the highest grade and the lowest grade.
c. Have the program print on separate lines: CLASS AVERAGE IS _____, HIGHEST GRADE IS _____, and LOWEST GRADE IS _____.
d. Enter and run each of these programs several times.

## PRACTICE 9–3

### Two-Dimensional Array

1. Using a two-dimensional array, read ten names into an array.

2. Add program lines to permit you to search for a specific name that was entered into the array.
Hints:
a. Enter the name into the array that you are searching for.
b. Compare the name entered with names in the array.
c. If the name is in the array, print out the name; if the name is not found, print out NOT FOUND.

# Chapter 10

## Procedures and Functions

**What You Will Learn**

- To understand and learn how to use the various procedures used in Pascal.

- To understand and learn how to use the various functions used in Pascal.

- To use the reserved words **PROCEDURE** and **FUNCTION**.

- To understand and learn how to use the APPLESTUFF package. More specifically you will learn about the:
  RANDOM and RANDOMIZE procedure.
  KEYPRESS function.
  PADDLE and BUTTON function.

## Procedure

A procedure is a routine or a block of program code that is executed by simply referencing or calling its name in the main program (or in another procedure later in the program).

Procedures are used to break a large and complex program into its component parts, each of which performs some fairly simple tasks. There are times when you need to perform the same tasks in several different places in your program, but instead of retyping the statements needed for this task each time, you can write a procedure to perform the needed task no matter how many times it's called and run. The use of procedures is a very powerful programming feature of Pascal. Also, programs that make good use of procedures are generally easier to follow, understand, and change.

To call a procedure, a separate **PROCEDURE** statement (in the calling program) is used. A procedure is called by its name. If information is to be passed from the calling program to the procedure when it is called, special data items called *parameters* are used in the procedure's heading together with the procedure's name.

## Parameters

A parameter is similar to a variable in that it can hold or represent a value. But unlike a variable, a parameter can hold or represent a variable itself.

Parameters are used as the vehicle to permit the passing of values and information between a procedure and a calling program (main program block). The features of calling procedures and passing values make Pascal a very useful and powerful tool.

There are several types of parameters used in Pascal: formal, actual, value, and variable. Formal parameters define a set of dummy quantities that represent the data to be manipulated by a procedure. Actual parameters, which are specified in the procedure statement of the calling program, replace the corresponding formal parameters when the procedure is called. Value parameters are formal parameters whose values *do not* change by the execution of the procedure. They receive information only from the calling program. Variable parameters are formal parameters whose values may change by execution of the procedure. They are used by the procedure to receive and return information to the calling program. The reserved word **VAR** is used to indicate a variable parameter in the formal parameter list.

## Procedure Structure

In structure, a procedure looks much like a small Pascal program. It has its own name, a declaration section, and a block of statements that are executed whenever the procedure is called. More details on procedure structure follow.

```
PROCEDURE <PROCEDURE NAME> (FORMAL PARAMETER LIST);
CONST
      <LOCAL CONSTANT DECLARATIONS>;
TYPE
      <LOCAL TYPE DECLARATIONS>;           LOCAL DECLARATIONS
VAR
      <LOCAL VARIABLE DECLARATIONS>;
BEGIN
      <PROCEDURE STATEMENTS OR INSTRUCTIONS>;
END;
```

The major differences between a procedure block and a main program block are as follows:

A procedure heading line begins with the word **PROCEDURE** instead of the word **PROGRAM**.

The <procedure name> is followed by a formal parameter list enclosed in parentheses. Note: A procedure can send or receive special data items called *parameters*. A parameter must be defined as a particular type when the procedure is called. Only these types of data must pass when the procedure is executed. If there are no parameters, the "formal parameter list" and the parentheses should be omitted.

Variables, and other declarations within the procedure itself, are said to be *local* to the procedure since they can be used only within that procedure and have no meaning once they leave that procedure. That is, the value of the variables and even their names are defined only when the program is executing the procedure.

Finally, a semicolon (;) is used after the word **END** instead of a period (.), as is used in the main program block.

The following is an example of a procedure program (without parameters).

PROGRAM NAME

PROCEDURE BLOCK

MAIN PROGRAM BLOCK

```
PROGRAM EXAMPLE1;

PROCEDURE SKIPLINES;
(*SKIPS 3 LINES*)
  BEGIN
      WRITELN;
      WRITELN;
      WRITELN

  END;

BEGIN
  WRITE ('THIS IS AN EXAMPLE ');
  WRITELN ('OF CALLING A PROCEDURE');
  (*CALL SKIPLINES PROCEDURES*)
  SKIPLINES;
  WRITE ('THIS PROCEDURE CAUSES ');
  WRITE ('THE CONSOLE TO SKIP');
  WRITELN ('3 LINES EACH TIME');
  WRITELN ('IT IS CALLED')
END.
```

In the Pascal program structure, a procedure must be declared at the start of the program. The procedure is called by its name (SKIPLINES), and control passes to the procedure block until the procedure has completed its execution. Then control is given back to the main program.

The following program is an example of calling more than one procedure (without parameters).

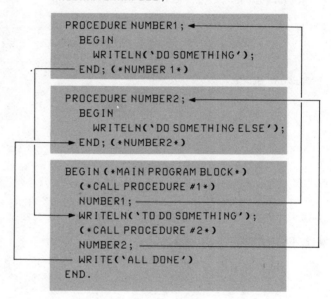

```
PROGRAM EXAMPLE2;

   PROCEDURE NUMBER1;
      BEGIN
         WRITELN('DO SOMETHING');
      END; (*NUMBER 1*)

   PROCEDURE NUMBER2;
      BEGIN
         WRITELN('DO SOMETHING ELSE');
      END; (*NUMBER2*)

   BEGIN (*MAIN PROGRAM BLOCK*)
      (*CALL PROCEDURE #1*)
      NUMBER1;
      WRITELN('TO DO SOMETHING');
      (*CALL PROCEDURE #2*)
      NUMBER2;
      WRITE('ALL DONE')
   END.
```

### Notes

1. A separate procedure statement in the calling program is used to call a procedure (for example, NUMBER1 is used to call procedure #1 above).

2. Each time the procedure is called, program control is passed to it. When the procedure completes its execution, control is given back to the main program.

3. Procedures are always placed ahead of the main program block.

4. Procedure NUMBER2 could call procedure NUMBER1 if you wanted it to do so because NUMBER1 precedes NUMBER2.

## The PAGE Procedure

PAGE is a built-in procedure in Apple Pascal that permits a new page output to be started. That is, the screen can be cleared and the next output placed on the top line of the screen. Since it is built-in, the PAGE procedure does not have to be defined in a **PROCEDURE** structure. PAGE is very useful in clearing the screen before displaying a message.

An example of a program using procedures follows:

```
PROGRAM TEMPCONVERSION;

  VAR
    ANSWER1,ANSWER2:CHAR;


  PROCEDURE CELSIUS;

  (* FAHRENHEIT TO CELSIUS *)

    VAR
      CELS,FAHR:REAL;

  BEGIN
    PAGE(OUTPUT);
    WRITE('ENTER DEGREES FAHRENHEIT ');
    READLN(FAHR);
    CELS := (FAHR-32) * (5/9);
    WRITELN;
    WRITELN;
    WRITELN(FAHR:3:1,' DEGREES FAHRENHEIT');
    WRITELN(CELS:3:1,' DEGREES CELSIUS')
  END; (* CELSIUS *)


  PROCEDURE FAHRENHEIT;

  (* CELSIUS TO FAHRENHEIT *)

    VAR
      CELS,FAHR:REAL;

  BEGIN
    PAGE(OUTPUT);
    WRITE('ENTER DEGREES CENTIGRADE ');
    READLN(CELS);
    FAHR := (9/5) * CELS + 32;
    WRITELN;
    WRITELN;
    WRITELN(CELS:3:1,' DEGREES CELSIUS');
    WRITELN(FAHR:3:1,' DEGREES FAHRENHEIT')
  END; (* FAHRENHEIT *)
```

*(*program continued on next page*)*

*(\*program continued from previous page\*)*

```
(* MAIN PROGRAM *)


BEGIN
  REPEAT
    PAGE(OUTPUT);
    WRITELN('ENTER WHAT YOU WISH TO CONVERT');
    WRITE('(CELSIUS OR FAHRENHEIT) ');
    READ(ANSWER1);
    CASE ANSWER1 OF
     'C':CELSIUS;
     'F':FAHRENHEIT
     END; (* CASE *)
    WRITELN;
    WRITE('HAVE YOU FINISHED (YES OR NO) ');
    READ(ANSWER2);
  UNTIL ANSWER2 = 'Y'
END. (* TEMPCONVERSION *)
```

### Explanation of the Tempconversion Program

Note that this program is divided essentially into four parts:

1. Program heading and variable declaration part.

2. A procedure for converting Fahrenheit to Celsius (first box).

3. A procedure for converting Celsius to Fahrenheit (second box).

4. The main program (last box).

To trace a Pascal program's operation, always start with the main program. Note the following in the main program block:

The program prompts the user by asking the question using WRITE/WRITELN statements.

Next, the READLN statement was used to accept the response from the keyboard and to store the response in a variable (ANSWER1). Since the answer was declared as a CHAR variable at the top of the program, the program will look only at the first character of the Celsius or Fahrenheit response.

Then, the **CASE** statement is used to evaluate the answer to determine if it is a C (for Celsius) or an F (for Fahrenheit).

If C is the response, the program calls the procedure to convert Fahrenheit to Celsius (that is, procedure CELSIUS).

If F is the response, the program calls the procedure to convert Celsius to Fahrenheit (that is, procedure FAHRENHEIT).

Finally, the program asks the user if he/she is finished, and the response is placed in the variable ANSWER2, which was also declared at the top of the program in the **VAR** block.

Note that the procedures are themselves small programs that do something when called. When the procedure is finished converting C to F or F to C, control is passed back to the main program.

## EXERCISE 10–1

1. Type and enter the Temperature Conversion program.
2. Run the program several times until you understand it.

### Format for Procedures that Require Parameters

```
PROGRAM EXAMPLE3;

  <GLOBAL DECLARATIONS PART>

  PROCEDURE <PROCEDURE NAME> (FORMAL PARAMETER LIST);
    <LOCAL DECLARATION PART>
    BEGIN
    <PROCEDURE BODY>
    END;

  BEGIN (*MAIN PROGRAM BLOCK*)
    <PROGRAM STATEMENT>;
    <PROCEDURE NAME> (ACTUAL PARAMETER LIST);
    <ANOTHER PROGRAM STATEMENT>
  END. (*MAIN PROGRAM BLOCK*)
```

### Notes

1. A formal parameter list consists of a list of names or identifiers separated by commas and their data types.

2. An actual parameter list is a list of constants, variables, or expressions separated by commas.

3. There must be the same number of actual parameters in the actual parameter list as there are formal parameters in the formal parameter list.

The following is a procedure example (with parameters).

```
PROGRAM EXAMPLE 4;
```

```
    PROCEDURE SKIPLINE (NUMLINE:INTEGER);
      VAR
        N:INTEGER;
      BEGIN
        FOR N:=1 TO NUMLINE DO
              WRITELN
      END; (*SKIP LINE*)
```

FORMAL PARAMETER    TYPE

PROCEDURE CALL

ACTUAL PARAMETER

```
    BEGIN
      PAGE (OUTPUT);
      SKIPLINE (3);
      WRITELN ('THIS IS AN EXAMPLE OF');
      SKIPLINE(2);
      WRITELN ('A PROGRAM THAT PASSES');
      SKIPLINE(2);
      WRITELN ('VALUES TO THE PROCEDURE');
      SKIPLINE(2);
      WRITELN ('SO THAT THE NUMBER OF LINES');
      SKIPLINE(2);
      WRITELN ('SKIPPED CAN BE VARIED BY');
      SKIPLINE(2);
      WRITELN ('USING DIFFERENT PARAMETERS')
    END. (*MAIN PROGRAM BLOCK*)
```

*The value of the corresponding actual parameter (3 or 2) at the time of the call is assigned to the formal parameter (NUMLINE).*

---

## EXERCISE 10–2

### Using a Procedure that Requires a Value Parameter

1. Type and enter the program as shown.

```
PROGRAM MAILLIST;

  VAR
    NAME,ADDRESS:STRING;

  PROCEDURE FORMAT (DATA:STRING);

    BEGIN
      WRITELN;
      WRITELN;
      WRITELN('                    ',DATA)
    END;

  (* MAIN PROGRAM *)

  BEGIN
    WRITE('ENTER YOUR NAME: ');
    READLN(NAME);
    WRITE('   YOUR ADDRESS: ');
    READLN(ADDRESS);
    FORMAT(NAME);
    FORMAT(ADDRESS)
  END. (* MAILLIST *)
```

2. Trace the program and predict the output.

3. Run the program.

There was one actual parameter (NAME) to correspond with the formal parameter (DATA) the first time the procedure FORMAT was called. The actual parameter (ADDRESS) used the same formal parameter (DATA) when the procedure was called the second time.

DATA is a value parameter in the formal parameter list. It can receive information only from the calling program and its value *does not* change by the execution of procedure (that is, when passed to the procedure, NAME and ADDRESS will not be changed by the execution of the procedure).

## EXERCISE 10–3

### Using a Procedure that Requires a Variable Parameter

1. Enter the program EXPONENT as shown.

```
PROGRAM EXPONENT;

  VAR
    NUMBER,EXPN:INTEGER;

  PROCEDURE RAISE(VAR NUM:INTEGER; X:INTEGER);

    VAR
      POWER,I:INTEGER;

    BEGIN
      POWER:=1;
      FOR I := 1 TO X DO
        POWER := POWER * NUM;
      NUM:=POWER
    END; (* RAISE *)


  (* MAIN PROGRAM *)


  BEGIN
    WRITELN('THIS PROGRAM WILL RAISE A');
    WRITELN('NUMBER TO A SPECIFIC POWER');
    WRITELN;
    WRITE('ENTER A NUMBER: ');
    READLN(NUMBER);
    WRITE('         POWER: ');
    READLN(EXPN);
    WRITELN;
    WRITELN('NUMBER = ',NUMBER,' POWER = ',EXPN);
    RAISE(NUMBER,EXPN);
    WRITELN;
    WRITELN('THE NUMBER RAISED IS ',NUMBER)
  END. (* EXPONENT *)
```

2. Trace the program manually.

3. Run the program.

There are two parameters in the formal parameter list, NUM and X. NUM is a variable parameter because it is preceded by the reserved word **VAR.** Since NUM is a variable parameter, its value may be changed by execution on the procedure. In contrast, X is a value parameter, which means its value will not change during program execution.

There are two actual parameters (NUMBER and EXPN) that correspond with the formal parameter list (NUM and X). There is a corresponding relationship between the actual parameter list and the formal parameter list. That is, the actual parameter NUMBER passes information to the formal parameter NUM, and the actual parameter EXPN passes information to the formal parameter X. After the procedure is executed, it passes the new value of the variable parameter (NUM) back to the actual parameter (NUMBER) in the main program.

The following diagram shows a procedure with a variable parameter passing values between formal and actual parameters.

```
PROGRAM EXPONENT;
  VAR NUMBER, EXPN: INTEGER;

PROCEDURE RAISE (VAR NUM: INTEGER; X: INTEGER);

  VAR
    <VARIABLES : TYPE>

BEGIN

  <PROCEDURE BODY>

END; (*RAISE*)


(*MAIN PROGRAM*)

BEGIN
  .
  .
  .
  .
  .
  RAISE(NUMBER, EXP);
  .
  .
  .
END. (*EXPONENT*)
```

PROCEDURE CALL

There is a corresponding link between the actual and formal parameters. The value of a number is changed by the execution of the procedure. A value is first passed from the actual parameter (NUMBER) to the variable parameter (NUM), and then a new value is passed back to NUMBER from NUM.

## How to Use the Mathematical Functions Package*

If you are interested in using mathematical functions such as sine, cosine, logarithm, and square root, then you should become familiar with TRANSCEND. TRANSCEND is a package of mathematical functions included as a special unit in Apple Pascal. It is saved in the file SYSTEM.LIBRARY on APPLE1: diskette. To use any of the mathematical functions, you must include TRANSCEND in a USES declaration block as shown below.

```
USES
   TRANSCEND
```

Here are some of the mathematical functions:

| FUNCTION | MEANING |
|---|---|
| SIN (X) | Takes the sine of the angle(X). X is a real parameter and is in radians. |
| COS (X) | Takes the cosine of the angle(X). X is a real parameter and is in radians. |
| EXP (X) | Returns a real value equal to $e^x$, where e is the base of natural logarithms raised to the power X. |
| ATAN (X) | Returns the arctangent of (X). X is a real number and is in radians. |
| LN (X) | Takes the natural logarithm of (X). Both X and LN (X) are real. X must be a positive number. |
| LOG (X) | Returns the logarithm of (X) to base ten. Both X and LOG (X) are real numbers. X must be a positive number. |
| SQRT (X) | Returns the square root of (X). Both X and SQRT (X) are real numbers. X must be a positive number. |

---

*Skip this section if you are not familiar with the mathematical functions discussed here. You don't need to know them to continue this course.

## Defining Your Own Functions

Sometimes the functions provided by Pascal are not sufficient for the solution of a particular problem, and, therefore, you may wish to write your own. Fortunately, Pascal provides a means to write your own functions in a way that is very similar to writing your own procedure. That is, in structure, a user-defined function (as it is sometimes called) looks very much like a user-defined procedure.

A function may be thought of as a formula or a set of rules used to calculate values. Like a formula, after the appropriate value is plugged in, a function produces a result. You may use the standard Pascal functions, such as the mathematical functions discussed in the previous pages, or you may define your own functions.

### Function Structure

A function structure looks much like a procedure structure. It has its own name, a declaration section, and a block of statements that are executed whenever the function is called. Essentially, the difference between a function and a procedure is that a function always returns a value to the calling program; a procedure does not return a value unless a variable parameter is declared in the formal parameter list. The format for a function structure follows:

```
FUNCTION <FUNCTION NAME> (FORMAL PARAMETER LIST): <FUNCTION TYPE>;
   CONST
   <LOCAL CONSTANT DECLARATION>;
   VAR                                    LOCAL DECLARATIONS
   <LOCAL VARIABLE DECLARATION>;
   BEGIN
   <FUNCTION STATEMENTS TO DO SOMETHING>;
   END;
```

The major differences between a function and a procedure are as follows:

- A function heading line begins with the word **FUNCTION** instead of the word **PROCEDURE**.

- A <function type> is included after the <formal parameter list>. This <function type> or <result type> is required for the function and not the procedure because a function returns a value (or result) to the calling program and a procedure does not.

- The remainder of the format and the parameter requirements are the same as for the procedure.

An example of a function follows.

```
PROGRAM ADDING;

  VAR
    ANSWER,NUM1,NUM2:INTEGER;

FUNCTION ADD(NUM1,NUM2:INTERGER):INTEGER;

  BEGIN
    ADD := NUM1 + NUM2
  END;  (*ADD*)

(*MAIN PROGRAM*)

BEGIN
  PAGE(OUTPUT);
  WRITELN('THIS PROGRAM ADDS TWO NUMBERS');
  WRITELN;
  WRITE('ENTER FIRST NUMBER: ');
  READLN(NUM1);
  WRITE('      SECOND NUMBER: ');
  READLN(NUM2);
  ANSWER := ADD(NUM1,NUM2);
  WRITELN;
  WRITELN(NUM1, ' + ',NUM2, ' = ',ANSWER)
END.  (*ADDING*)
```

FUNCTION NAME

RESULT TYPE

PARAMETERS TYPE

FORMAL PARAMETERS

ACTUAL PARAMETERS

FUNCTION CALL

**Notes**

1. This is an example of a simple function that adds two integer numbers when called and returns the value (result) to the calling program. The result is stored in the variable ANSWER.

2. The actual parameters are separated by commas. There is an equal number of actual parameters (2) as there are formal parameters.

3. The value of each parameter is assigned to the corresponding formal parameter when called (that is, NUM1 to NUM1 and NUM2 to NUM2). The actual parameters must be integers in this example since the formal parameters are integers. That is, each parameter must be compatible with the formal parameters in type and number.

## EXERCISE 10—4

### Simple Calculator

1. Enter the program as shown.

```
PROGRAM CALCULATOR;

  VAR
    ANSWER,OPERATION:CHAR;
    NUM1,NUM2:REAL;


  FUNCTION ADD(NUM1,NUM2:REAL):REAL;

   BEGIN
     ADD := NUM1 + NUM2
   END; (* ADD *)


  FUNCTION DIVIDE(NUM1,NUM2:REAL):REAL;

   BEGIN
     DIVIDE := NUM1 / NUM2
   END; (* DIVIDE *)


  FUNCTION MULTIPLY(NUM1,NUM2:REAL):REAL;

   BEGIN
     MULTIPLY := NUM1 * NUM2
   END; (* MULTIPLY *)
```

```
FUNCTION SUBTRACT(NUM1,NUM2:REAL):REAL;

  BEGIN
    SUBTRACT := NUM1 - NUM2
  END; (* SUBTRACT *)


(* MAIN PROGRAM *)


BEGIN
  REPEAT
    PAGE(OUTPUT);
    WRITE('A)DD, D)IVIDE, M)ULTIY, S)UBTRACT ');
    READ(OPERATION);
    PAGE(OUTPUT);
    WRITE('ENTER YOUR FIRST NUMBER:  ');
    READLN(NUM1);
    WRITE('          SECOND NUMBER:  ');
    READLN(NUM2);
    WRITELN;
    CASE OPERATION OF
      'A':WRITELN(NUM1:4:1,' + ',NUM2:4:1,' = ',ADD(NUM1,NUM2):4:1);
      'D':WRITELN(NUM1:4:1,' / ',NUM2:4:1,' = ',DIVIDE(NUM1,NUM2):4:1);
      'M':WRITELN(NUM1:4:1,' X ',NUM2:4:1,' = ',MULTIPLY(NUM1,NUM2):4:1);
      'S':WRITELN(NUM1:4:1,' - ',NUM2:4:1,' = ',SUBTRACT(NUM1,NUM2):4:1)
    END; (* CASE *)
    WRITELN;
    WRITELN;
    WRITELN;
    WRITE('DO YOU WISH TO CONTINUE (YES OR NO) ');
    READ(ANSWER);
  UNTIL ANSWER = 'N'
END. (* CALCULATOR *)
```

2. Trace the program and predict the output.

3. Run the program.

4. Do the results of the program run match your predictions?

## TRUNC *(X)*, ROUND *(X)*, and ABS *(X)* Functions

TRUNC (X), or the truncate function, produces a value of X without its fractional part. That is, it chops off the fractional part of a real number and leaves the whole number or integer. For example:

TRUNC (2.345) returns 2

TRUNC (2.545) returns 2

The ROUND (X) function rounds off any real number, positive or negative, into a whole number (or integer). For example:

ROUND (2.545) returns 3

ROUND (2.345) returns 2

ABS (X), or the absolute function, produces the absolute value or magnitude of X. For example:

ABS ($-12$) returns 12

ABS ($-357$) returns 357

## EXERCISE 10–5

### ABS Function

1. Type and enter the program as shown.

```
PROGRAM ORDER;
  BEGIN
    WRITELN(ABS(38))
  END.
```

2. Run the program.

3. What happened?

4. Change the program and run it again.

```
PROGRAM ORDER;

  BEGIN

    WRITELN(ABS(-251))

  END.
```

5. Change the program as shown.

```
PROGRAM ORDER;

  VAR
    X:REAL;

  BEGIN

    X:=-4.256;
    WRITELN(ABS(X))

  END. (* ORDER *)
```

6. Run the program once again.

ABS ignores the sign of the number; that is, ABS $(-5)$ is 5, ABS $(-14)$ is 14, and so on.

The type of value of the function is determined by the type of the parameter. If the parameter is real, the value of ABS is real; if the parameter is an integer, the value of ABS is an integer.

---

## EXERCISE 10–6

### ABS (X)

1. Enter the program as shown.

```
PROGRAM NEGATIVE;

(* ABSOLUTE VALUE EXAMPLE *)

  VAR
    NUM:INTEGER;

  BEGIN
    WRITE('ENTER A NEGATIVE NUMBER ');
    READLN(NUM);
    WRITELN;
    WRITELN;
    WRITELN('ABSOLUTE VALUE OF YOUR NUMBER IS ',ABS(NUM))
  END. (* NEGATIVE *)
```

2. Run the program several times and observe the results.

## EXERCISE 10–7

Fill in the blanks in the following table.

**COMPARISON OF ROUND (X) AND TRUNC (X)**

| x | ROUND (X) | TRUNC (X) |
|---|---|---|
| 0.4 | 0 | 0 |
| 0.5 | 1 | 0 |
| 0.7 | 1 | 0 |
| −1.7 | −2 | −1 |
| 2.345 | 2 | 2 |
| 2.545 | 3 | 2 |
| −.7 | _____ | _____ |
| −.1 | _____ | _____ |
| 10.56 | _____ | _____ |
| 7.45 | _____ | _____ |
| 125.3 | _____ | _____ |

**NOTES:** *Trunc (X) chops off the fractional part. Round (X) rounds to the next highest integer, if the fractional part is = > 0.5.*

## EXERCISE 10–8

**Round (X) and Trunc (X)**

1. Enter the program as shown.

```
PROGRAM ROUNDING;

(* ROUND(X) AND TRUNC(X) EXERCISE *)

  VAR
    NUM:REAL;

  BEGIN
    WRITE('ENTER A DECIMAL NUMBER ');
    READLN(NUM);
    WRITELN;
    WRITELN;
    WRITELN('YOUR NUMBER IS ',NUM:2:2);
    WRITELN;
    WRITELN('YOUR NUMBER ROUNDED IS ',ROUND(NUM));
    WRITELN;
    WRITELN('YOUR NUMBER TRUNCATED IS ',TRUNC(NUM))
  END. (* ROUNDING *)
```

2. Run the program several times and observe the results.

## The APPLESTUFF Package

APPLESTUFF is a collection of special functions and procedures. This package permits you to use special Apple Pascal features to generate random numbers, to use the game paddles and button inputs, to read the cassette audio input, to switch the game control's outputs, and to generate sounds on the Apple speaker.

The APPLESTUFF package is stored on the APPLE1: diskette in the SYSTEM.LIBRARY. (Therefore, APPLE1: diskette should be in your disk drive unit when you execute APPLESTUFF.)

To use the features of APPLESTUFF, you must declare it in the **USES** part of the declaration block immediately after the program heading. For example:

```
PROGRAM SPECIALFEATURES

  USES

    APPLESTUFF;
```

When the program is compiled, the computer introduces APPLESTUFF into the program. If the program does not use any of the special procedures and functions, there is no need for the APPLESTUFF declaration.

## The Random Function

The RANDOM function causes the computer to give you a "surprise" number, as if the computer were pulling a number out of a hat. In Apple Pascal, RANDOM is an integer function with no parameters. It returns a positive value from 0 to 32767. It is a built-in function that is included with APPLESTUFF procedures. Therefore, APPLESTUFF must be declared in the USES part of the declaration block if you wish to use the RANDOM function.

To generate a RANDOM number within a certain range, use the **MOD** function plus a constant. Since RANDOM is an integer, you must use the special operators **DIV** and **MOD** if you wish to divide two numbers. For example, 7 **MOD** 3 gives you the remainder of 7 divided by 3, which is 1. We will use this property of integers with random numbers. Let's look at some examples of using the RANDOM function for a range of values.

| FUNCTION | PRODUCES A NUMBER (N) IN A RANGE |
| --- | --- |
| N: = RANDOM | 0 to 32767 |
| N: = RANDOM **MOD** 10 | 0 to 9 |
| N: = (RANDOM **MOD** 10) + 1 | 1 to 10 |
| N: = (RANDOM **MOD** 100) + 1 | 1 to 100 |
| N: = RANDOM **MOD** 2 | 0 to 1 |
| N: = RANDOM **MOD** 0 | ERROR (division by 0 is illegal) |

The general form for the RANDOM number function's range for values of N from 0 to $(X - 1)$ is:

N: = (RANDOM **MOD** X) + 1

X = Any integer between 1 and 32767

If you have a problem understanding how **MOD** works, review the following material.

`N:=RANDOM MOD 3`

where RANDOM can be any number between 0 and 32,767.

| IF RANDOM = | N = (REMAINDER) | MOD 3 |
|---|---|---|
| 99 | 0 | |

$$3\,\overline{)99}$$ gives 33, remainder 0:

```
      33
  3 )99
     9
     9
     9
     0
```

| 1000 | 1 | |

```
     333
  3 )1000
     9
     10
      9
     10
      9
      1
```

| 569 | 2 | |

```
     189
  3 )569
     3
     26
     24
     29
     27
      2
```

1. When an integer is divided by 3, the remainder can be only 0, 1, or 2.

2. RANDOM **MOD** 3 is the remainder of RANDOM when divided by 3. Therefore, RANDOM **MOD** 3 can attain values of only 0, 1, or 2.

3. Try dividing any integer in the range 0 to 32767 by 3 and see what value the remainder (RANDOM **MOD** 3) has.

4. Similarly, RANDOM **MOD** X will generate integers from 0 to X − 1.

## EXERCISE 10–9

### Random Number Program

1. Boot up Pascal, enter the Editor, and type in the program as shown.

```
PROGRAM CHANCE;

  USES
    APPLESTUFF;

  VAR
    COUNT,SURPRISE:INTEGER;

  BEGIN
    WRITELN('HERE ARE 10 RANDOM NUMBERS');
    FOR COUNT := 1 TO 10 DO
      BEGIN
        SURPRISE:=RANDOM;
        WRITELN(COUNT,'    ',SURPRISE)
      END; (* COUNT *)
END. (* CHANCE *)
```

2. Check your program for errors.

3. Run the program. There should be two columns of integers on your screen. The first column should be a list of numbers that increases from 1 to 10, and a second column should be a list of random numbers in the range from 0 to 32,766. If the program does not run, correct the errors and then try again. Repeat the process until the program runs without any errors.

4. The first column of numbers represents the value of the **FOR-DO** LOOP variable COUNT.

5. Run the program several times; notice that you get the same sequence of numbers in the second column of your screen.

6. The next section introduces a procedure that will help generate different random numbers each time a program utilizing RANDOM is run.

## The RANDOMIZE Procedure

RANDOMIZE is a procedure with no parameters that "reseeds" the RANDOM number generator. Each time you run a given program using RANDOM, you will get the same random sequence unless you use RANDOMIZE.

Since random numbers are unpredictable and computers are not, we get pseudorandom numbers (that is, not the real thing). Each time you use the RANDOM function, the computer uses an internal seed number to produce the desired random number. Therefore, it is a good idea to set the seed number (reseed) to an unpredictable value when you are running game programs or programs that require random numbers.

## EXERCISE 10–10

1. Type in the following program.

```
PROGRAM COINTOSS;

   USES
     APPLESTUFF;

   VAR
     HEADS,FLIPS,LOOP,NUMBER,TAILS:INTEGER;

   BEGIN
     HEADS := 0;
     TAILS := 0;
     WRITE('HOW MANY TIMES SHALL I FLIP THE COIN ');
     READLN(FLIPS);
     PAGE(OUTPUT);
     WRITELN('IM FLIPPING THE COIN ... STANDBY');
     RANDOMIZE;
     FOR LOOP := 1 TO FLIPS DO
       BEGIN
         NUMBER := 1 + RANDOM MOD 2;
         CASE NUMBER OF
             1:HEADS:=HEADS + 1;
             2:TAILS:=TAILS + 1
             END; (* CASE *)
       END; (* FOR DO LOOP *)
     WRITELN;
     WRITELN;
     WRITELN;
     WRITELN;
     WRITELN('HEADS = ',HEADS);
     WRITELN('TAILS = ',TAILS);
     WRITELN('TOTAL NUMBERS OF FLIPS ARE ',FLIPS);
     WRITELN;
     WRITELN('% OF HEADS ',HEADS/FLIPS*100:2:2);
     WRITELN('% OF TAILS ',TAILS/FLIPS*100:2:2)
   END.
```

2. Trace the program.
   a. Why was RANDOMIZE used in this program?
   b. What is the range of values for the NUMBER assignment statement "NUMBER := 1 + RANDOM **MOD** 2;"?
   c. What happens if NUMBER := 1?
   d. What happens if NUMBER := 2?

3. Run the program several times and discuss the results.

## The KEYPRESS Function

The KEYPRESS function has no parameters. It returns True if a key has been pressed on the keyboard since the program started or since the last time the keyboard was read (whichever is most recent).

Once KEYPRESS becomes True, it remains True until you READ (or READLN) the keyboard again. Then it becomes False. KEYPRESS is usually False.

The following statement has the effect of detecting the last character typed on the keyboard. This would be useful for retrieving a character typed when the program was doing something else, such as displaying graphics.

```
IF KEYPRESS THEN READ (KEYBOARD,CH)
```

where CH is a CHAR variable.

Note that KEYPRESS does not have any other effect on Input/Output; it simply detects any activity on the Apple keyboard.

## The PADDLE and BUTTON Functions

The Apple computer comes equipped with a game paddle port. A paddle is connected to the port and might have a button. You can test if the button is pressed with the BUTTON function, and you can determine the position of the selected paddle with the PADDLE function.

The PADDLE function has the form:

```
PADDLE (SELECT)
```

where SELECT is an integer from 0 to 3 which selects one of the four paddle inputs numbered 0, 1, 2, and 3. PADDLE returns an integer in the range of 0 to 255, which represents the positions of the selected paddle.

The BUTTON function has the form:

```
BUTTON (SELECT)
```

where SELECT is an integer from 0 to 3 which selects one of the three button inputs numbered 0, 1, and 2 or the audio cassette input numbered 3.

BUTTON returns a Boolean value of True if the selected game-control button is pressed; otherwise, a value of False is returned. When the BUTTON input number 3 is selected to read the audio cassette input, it samples the cassette input— which changes from True to False and vice versa at each zero crossing on the input signal.

## Summary

| | |
|---|---|
| **ABS (X)** | Returns the absolute value of X regardless of the number you input (that is, X is that same number without the sign). |
| **ROUND (X)** | Produces a value of X rounded to the nearest (highest) integer. |
| **TRUNC (X)** | Produces a value of X without its fractional part (that is, it returns an integer). |
| **RANDOM** | An integer function with no parameters. It returns a value from 0 through 32767. |
| **RANDOMIZE** | A procedure with no parameters. Each time you run a given program using RANDOM, you will get the same random sequence, unless you use RANDOMIZE. |

## PRACTICE 10–1

1. Trace the following program manually, and predict the output.

```
PROGRAM MESSAGE;

 PROCEDURE A;

   BEGIN
     WRITE('AN EXAMPLE ')
   END; (* A *)
```

*(*program continued on next page*)*

*(\*program continued from previous page\*)*

```
    PROCEDURE B;

      BEGIN
        WRITE('THIS IS ');
        A
      END; (* B *)

    PROCEDURE C;

      BEGIN
        WRITELN('OF HOW ')
      END; (* C *)

    PROCEDURE D;

      BEGIN
        WRITE('WORKS')
      END; (* D *)

    (* MAIN PROGRAM *)

    BEGIN
      B;
      C;
      WRITE('A PROCEDURE ');
      D
    END. (* MESSAGE *)
```

2. Enter and run the program.

3. Compare your predicted output with the computer's output.

---

## PRACTICE 10–2

---

### Part A

1. Using procedures, write a program that calculates the area and the perimeter of a rectangle.

   *Hints:*
   a. Use a separate procedure to calculate the area and perimeter.
   b. Use formal parameters in each procedure for length and width.
   c. Use real numbers.
   d. Use the main program block to enter actual parameters (length and width).
   e. Use comments and indentation for clarity.

### Part B

1. Using functions, modify the program in Part A of this section to calculate the area and perimeter of a rectangle.

2. Compare the program in Part A with the program in Part B. What are the major differences?

## PRACTICE 10–3

1. Type in the following program.

```
PROGRAM PICKNUMBER1;

  USES
    APPLESTUFF;

  VAR
    X,TRIES,NUMBER:INTEGER;

  BEGIN
    RANDOMIZE;
    X := 1 + RANDOM MOD 10;
    WRITE('ENTER A NUMBER BETWEEN 1 & 10 ');
    READLN(NUMBER);
    TRIES := 1;
    WHILE X <> NUMBER DO
      BEGIN
        IF X < NUMBER THEN WRITELN('PICK A NUMBER LOWER')
        ELSE
          WRITELN('PICK A NUMBER HIGHER');
        WRITE('ENTER ANOTHER NUMBER BETWEEN 1 & 10 ');
        READLN(NUMBER);
        TRIES := TRIES + 1
      END; (* WHILE *)
    WRITELN;
    WRITELN;
    WRITELN('YOU GUESSED THE RIGHT NUMBER');
    WRITELN;
    WRITELN('YOU MADE ',TRIES,' ATTEMPTS TO GUESS THE NUMBER')
  END. (* PICKNUMBER1 *)
```

2. Run this program several times.

3. Modify the program so that it will pick a random number from 1 to 100.

# Chapter 11

# Graphics and Sounds

***What You Will Learn***

- To become familiar with the layout of the graphic display of Apple Pascal and to learn how to use the TURTLEGRAPHICS package.

- To understand and use MOVE, MOVETO, TURNTO, TURN, and VIEWPORT procedures.

- To draw pictures on the screen.

- To understand how to make sounds and music using the APPLESTUFF package and the NOTE procedure.

- To write and run programs using all of the concepts covered in this lesson.

**The
TURTLEGRAPHICS
Package**

The Apple Pascal graphics package provides you with an
unlimited number of possibilities of graphic application. You
should experiment with graphics. This lesson will introduce
you to some of the basic features of graphics used with Apple
Pascal, but we will only scratch the surface. You will find out
by yourself what other kinds of things can be done with
graphics using the TURTLEGRAPHICS package on your
Apple Pascal system.

TURTLEGRAPHICS is a graphics package based on the turtle
devised by Seymore Papert and his co-workers at the
Massachusetts Institute of Technology. Papert and his co-
workers invented the "turtle," an invisible animal, to make
graphics easy for children who might have difficulty
understanding Cartesian coordinates.

The "turtle" is envisioned as being able to walk a given
distance and turn through a specified angle while dragging
along a pen. The color of the ink in the imaginary pen can be
changed to any of the colors available on the Apple. The
"turtle" is used to draw lines and figures on the display.

Before any graphics can be used, the TURTLEGRAPHICS
package must be declared immediately after the program
heading. For example:

```
PROGRAM DRAW;
  USES
    TURTLEGRAHPICS;
```

The TURTLEGRAPHICS unit contains a special package of
graphic routines stored on APPLE1: in the
SYSTEM.LIBRARY file. Once TURTLEGRAPHICS is
declared, the graphics procedures and functions contained in
the package can be used. Some of the procedures included are:

INITTURTLE

MOVE and MOVETO

TURN and TURNTO

PENCOLOR, VIEWPORT, and FILLSCREEN

GRAFMODE and TEXTMODE

Each of these procedures will be discussed in more detail later
in this chapter.

The display screen has 280 horizontal points by 192 vertical points. (See Fig. 11–1.) The center of the display (140,96) is the point where the turtle is positioned when the INITTURTLE command is used. INITTURTLE is a procedure that initializes the graphics screen.

To draw lines on the screen, you must give special commands (to be described later) that move the turtle to a point that is distance X from the left edge of the screen and distance Y from the bottom edge. The (X,Y) coordinate describes the MOVETO points.

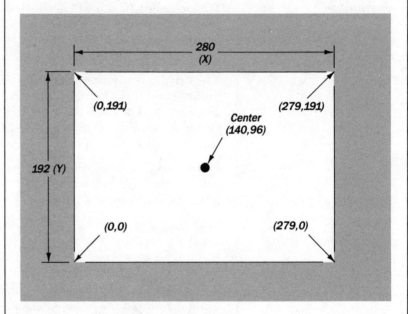

*Fig. 11–1 A video display layout.*

## INITTURTLE Procedure

The INITTURTLE procedure clears the screen and allows the screen to be used for graphics instead of text. This procedure has no parameters, and is found in the TURTLEGRAPHICS unit. Use this procedure before starting any graphics.

INITTURTLE does a few other things as well. These things will be discussed later but are summarized below:

- Sets the boundaries of the screen to a maximum (that is, the VIEWPORT or WINDOW is set to the full width of the screen).

- Sets the PENCOLOR to none or off (that is, so you can move the turtle without drawing lines). PENCOLOR tells the turtle what pencolor to use.

- Positions the turtle at the center of the screen facing right (that is, the turtle's angle is set to zero).

The following format shows how this procedure is called:

```
PROGRAM DRAW;
   USES
      TURTLEGRAPHICS;
BEGIN
      INITTURTLE;

         .
         .            CALLS INITTURTLE
         .
         .
         .
```

## The MOVE Procedure

The MOVE procedure has the effect of moving the turtle forward a distance equal to a specified number of screen units in whatever direction the turtle is headed. (There are 280 horizontal screen units and 192 vertical screen units.) The MOVE procedure has the form:

```
MOVE (DISTANCE)
```

where distance is any positive integer and represents the relative number of screen units the turtle will move.

MOVE does *not* affect the heading of the turtle—only the distance it travels. If the pencolor is set to some color other than none, MOVE causes the turtle to leave a trail in the current pencolor. (See Fig. 11–2.)

| EXAMPLE | COMMENT |
|---|---|
| ```
INITTURTLE
PENCOLOR (WHITE)
MOVE(30)
``` | Move the turtle a relative distance of 30 screen units; that is, move from point (140, 96) to point (170,96). |

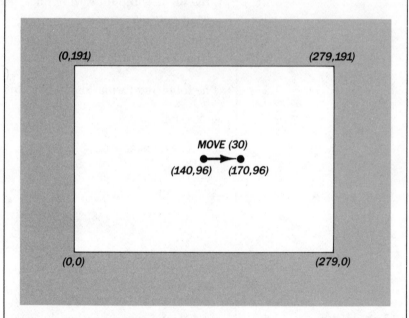

*Fig. 11–2 The MOVE procedure.*

**The MOVETO Procedure**

The MOVETO procedure is used to plot a line from the current position of the turtle to a new X and Y coordinate. The MOVETO procedure has the form:

```
MOVETO (X,Y)
```

where X and Y are screen coordinates.
```

MOVETO moves the turtle to the point (X,Y). This creates a line in the current pencolor from the turtle's last position to the point (X,Y). The direction of the turtle is not changed by MOVETO. MOVETO can also be used to position the turtle before drawing a line. This is done by first setting the pencolor to none so that when you move the turtle, the line will not be visible. (See Fig. 11–3.)

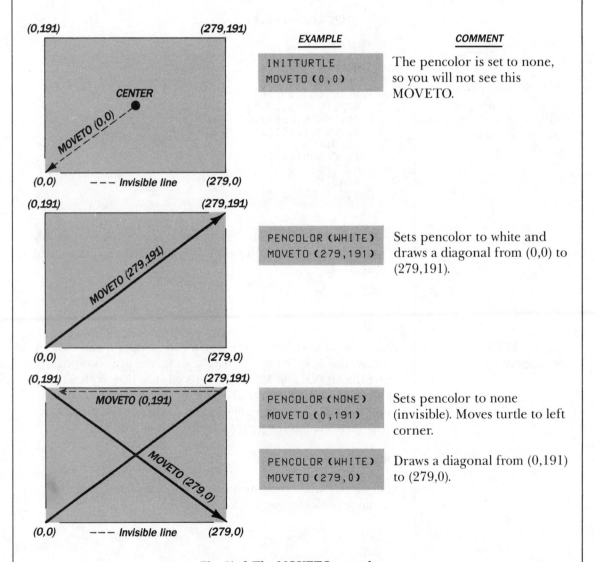

| EXAMPLE | COMMENT |
|---|---|
| `INITTURTLE`<br>`MOVETO (0,0)` | The pencolor is set to none, so you will not see this MOVETO. |
| `PENCOLOR (WHITE)`<br>`MOVETO (279,191)` | Sets pencolor to white and draws a diagonal from (0,0) to (279,191). |
| `PENCOLOR (NONE)`<br>`MOVETO (0,191)` | Sets pencolor to none (invisible). Moves turtle to left corner. |
| `PENCOLOR (WHITE)`<br>`MOVETO (279,0)` | Draws a diagonal from (0,191) to (279,0). |

*Fig. 11–3 The MOVETO procedure.*

## EXERCISE 11–1

### Using MOVETO to Draw an "X"

1. Type and enter the program shown.

```
PROGRAM DRAWX;

  USES
    TURTLEGRAPHICS;

  BEGIN
    INITTURTLE;
    MOVETO(0,0);
    READLN;
    PENCOLOR(WHITE);
    MOVETO(279,191);
    PENCOLOR(NONE);
    MOVETO(0,191);
    READLN;
    PENCOLOR(WHITE);
    MOVETO(279,0);
    READLN
  END. (* DRAWX *)
```

**NOTE:** *Press* RETURN *once to draw the first line of the "X"; then press* RETURN *again to draw the second line; press* RETURN *a third time to end the program.*

2. Trace the program and draw an output on a piece of graph paper. Label the graph paper with coordinates as shown in Fig. 11–1.

3. Run the program.

### The TURNTO Procedure

The turtle can do only two things: it can turn, or it can walk in the direction it is facing. We have seen on the previous pages, using the MOVE and MOVETO procedures, that as the turtle walks, it leaves behind a trail of ink in the current pen color. The TURNTO procedure allows you to change the direction of the turtle. It has the general form:

TURNTO (DEGREES)

where DEGREES is an integer that has an effective value in the range −359 through 359.

The TURNTO procedure is an *absolute turn* to a specific heading. When this procedure is invoked, it causes the turtle to turn from its present angle to the indicated angle. Zero degrees is exactly to the right. The counterclockwise rotation represents increasing angles. The TURNTO procedure never causes any change to the image on the screen.

The following is an example of the TURNTO procedure. The program uses TURTLEGRAPHICS.

**PROGRAM**              **DISPLAY**

```
PROGRAM TURNTOEX;

  USES
    TURTLEGRAPHICS;

BEGIN
  INITTURTLE;
  PENCOLOR(WHITE);
  TURNTO(90);
  MOVE(40);
  READLN
END. (* TURNTOEX *)
```

### Notes

1. The INITTURTLE procedure clears the screen and positions the turtle at the center of the screen heading to the right.

2. The PENCOLOR procedure is set to white.

3. The TURNTO (90) procedure points the turtle in a direction of 90 degrees which is toward the top of the screen.

4. The MOVE (40) procedure causes the turtle to move 40 screen units in the direction it is headed.

5. The READLN procedure is added to the program so that the screen will not clear until the [RETURN] key is pressed.

Fig. 11–4 shows the turtle heading from the center of the screen to the indicated angle. The INITTURTLE is used to position the turtle at the center of the screen each time.

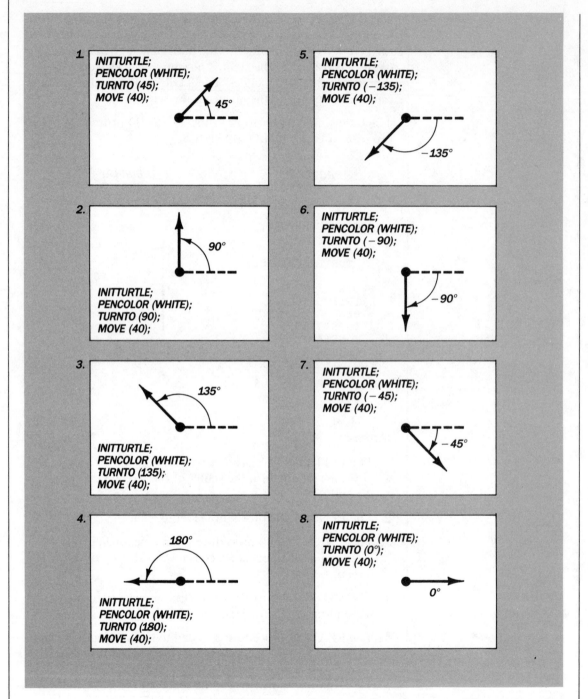

**Fig. 11–4 Movement of the turtle from the center of the screen to the indicated angle.**

## EXERCISE 11–2

### Understanding TURNTO

1. Type and enter the program TURNTOEX shown in the TURNTO example on page 207.

2. Run the program.

3. Does the output match the illustration shown in the example?

4. Refer to Fig. 11–4. Modify the TURNTOEX program to include several of the TURNTO angles shown in Fig. 11–4.

5. Run the program several times and compare the results with the illustrations in Fig. 11–4.

## EXERCISE 11–3

### Drawing a Square

1. Enter this program.

```
PROGRAM TURNSQUARE;

  USES
    TURTLEGRAPHICS;

  BEGIN
    INITTURTLE;
    PENCOLOR(WHITE);
    READLN;
    MOVE(40);
    READLN;
    TURNTO(90);
    MOVE(40);
    READLN;
    TURNTO(180);
    MOVE(40);
    READLN;
    TURNTO(270);
    MOVE(40);
    READLN
  END. (* TURNSQUARE *)
```

2. Trace the program and draw the output on a piece of graph paper.

3. Run the program.

## The TURN Procedure

The TURN procedure, like the TURNTO procedure, also permits the turtle to change direction. The TURN procedure has the form:

```
TURN (DEGREES)
```

where degrees is again an integer that has an effective value in the range −359 through 359. This procedure causes the turtle to rotate counterclockwise *from its current direction* through the specified angle. It causes no change to the image on the screen. Fig. 11–5 shows an example of the TURN procedure.

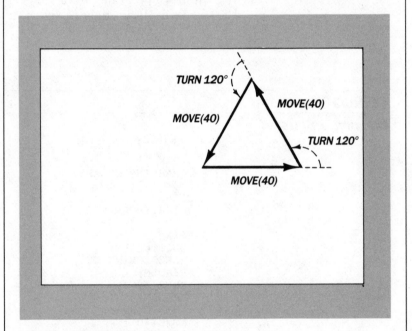

*Fig. 11–5 The TURN procedure.*

| PROGRAM | COMMENT |
|---------|---------|
| PROGRAM TRIANGLE; | |
| USES<br>  TURTLEGRAPHICS; | Initializes graphics. |
| BEGIN | |
|   INITTURTLE; | |
|   PENCOLOR(WHITE); | The PENCOLOR procedure is set to white. |
|   READLN; | |
|   MOVE(40); | Moves the turtle to the right 40 screen units. |
|   READLN; | |
|   TURN(120); | Turns the turtle's direction 120 degrees. |
|   MOVE(40); | Moves turtle a distance equal to 40 screen units. |
|   READLN; | |
|   TURN(120); | Turns the turtle's direction another 120 degrees. |
|   MOVE(40); | Moves the turtle's direction 40 more units (or back to origin). |
|   READLN | Keeps the image on the screen until RETURN is pressed. |
| END. (*  TRIANGLE    *) | |

---

## EXERCISE 11–4

### Drawing a Triangle Using MOVE and TURN Procedures

1. Enter the program TRIANGLE used in the previous TURN procedure example.

2. Run the program several times and observe the results.

3. READLN statements after each MOVE (40) permit you to stop the program after each line is drawn.

4. Run the program again. (Remember, you must press [ RETURN ] each time to continue because the program will stop at each READLN statement.)

## The VIEWPORT Procedure

The VIEWPORT procedure, which is included in the TURTLEGRAPHICS package, creates a "window" or viewport on the screen for graphics displays. If you don't use this procedure, Apple Pascal assumes that you want to use the entire screen for your graphics.

INITTURTLE sets the viewport to the maximum screen width. A program can contain more than one viewport statement, although there can be only one viewport in effect at a time. This procedure has the form:

```
VIEWPORT (LEFT,RIGHT,BOTTOM,TOP)
```

where LEFT, RIGHT, BOTTOM, and TOP are the parameters that give the boundaries of the viewport.

Once a viewport is set, no graphic output will occur outside the rectangle or viewport until it is changed. When a line is drawn using any of the graphic commands, it is automatically clipped so that only the portion that lies within the current viewport is displayed. Points whose coordinates are not in the current viewport (even those points that would not be on the screen at all) are legal but are ignored. (See Fig. 11–6.)

The following is an example of a program that sets up a "window" or viewport 80 units square. The full dimension of the display is: viewport (0,279,0,191).

```
PROGRAM WINDOW;
  USES
    TURTLEGRAPHICS;

  BEGIN
    INITTURTLE;
    VIEWPORT (100,180,56,136);
    FILLSCREEN (WHITE);
    READLN
  END.
```

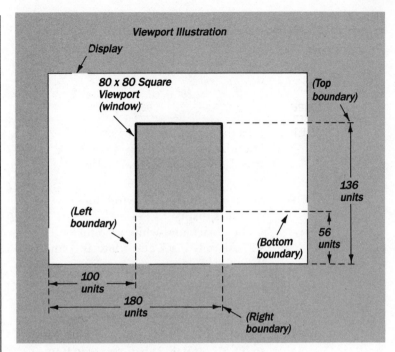

**Fig. 11–6 The VIEWPORT procedure.**

## EXERCISE 11–5

### Creating a Viewport

1. Type and enter the program shown.

```
PROGRAM WINDOW;

(* SETTING A WINDOW IN THE DISPLAY *)

  USES
    TURTLEGRAPHICS;

BEGIN
  INITTURTLE;
  VIEWPORT(100,180,56,136);
  FILLSCREEN(WHITE);
  READLN
END. (* WINDOW *)
```

2. Trace the program and predict the output.

3. Run the program.

4. Make the viewport larger and run the program again.

## Other
## TURTLEGRAPHICS
## Procedures

| PROCEDURE | USE | FORMAT |
|---|---|---|
| FILLSCREEN | Fills the screen between certain boundaries with whatever color is specified as a parameter in the procedure. | `FILLSCREEN(COLOR)` <br> `EXAMPLE:` <br> `  FILLSCREEN (BLACK);` |
| PENCOLOR | Selects a color for drawing lines on the graphics display. <br> – On a black-and-white monitor or TV set, use only black and white as colors. | `PENCOLOR(COLOR)` <br> `EXAMPLE:` <br> `  PENCOLOR(WHITE);` |
| GRAFMODE | Switches the display to show the graphics screen without the other intialization that INITTURTLE does. <br> – This procedure has no parameters. | `GRAFMODE` |
| TEXTMODE | Switches the display from graphics mode to TEXTMODE. When you switch to TEXTMODE, the image you saw in GRAFMODE is not lost but will still be there when you use GRAFMODE to go into graphics mode again (unless you change it). <br> – Upon termination of any program that uses graphics, the system automatically goes back to TEXTMODE. This procedure has no parameters. | `TEXTMODE` |

## Making Music Using the Note Procedure

To create a tone on the Apple speaker, use the NOTE procedure, which has the form:

```
NOTE (PITCH,DURATION)
```

where PITCH is an integer in the range of 0 to 50 and DURATION is an integer in the range of 0 to 255.

A pitch of 0 is used for rest, and a pitch of 2 through 48 provides tones that are a rough approximation of a chromatic scale. Duration is arbitrary units of time, and bears no relation to real time, although a duration of 200 lasts about a second.

The NOTE procedure is included in the APPLESTUFF package; therefore, APPLESTUFF must be declared under USES in the declaration block if you wish to use the NOTE procedure. For example:

```
PROGRAM TONE;
  USES
    APPLESTUFF;
  BEGIN
    NOTE(30,150)
  END.
```

PITCH and DURATION can also be declared as variables; in this case the above program would take the form shown in the example that follows.

**NOTE:** *PITCH and DURATION were declared as integer variables in the VAR block. The program allows you to change the PITCH and DURATION from the keyboard.*

```
PROGRAM TONES;

  USES
    APPLESTUFF;

  VAR
    PITCH,DURATION:INTEGER;

  BEGIN
    WRITE('ENTER PITCH ');
    READLN(PITCH);
    WRITE('ENTER DURATION ');
    READLN(DURATION);
    NOTE(PITCH,DURATION)
  END. (* TONES *)
```

## EXERCISE 11–6

1. Enter the above program and experiment with it.

## EXERCISE 11–7

### Chromatic Scale

1. Boot your system and enter this program.

```
PROGRAM SCALE;

  USES
    APPLESTUFF;

  VAR
    PITCH,DURATION:INTEGER;

  BEGIN
    DURATION:=100;
    FOR PITCH := 1 TO 25 DO
      NOTE(PITCH,DURATION)
  END. (* SCALE *)
```

2. Run the program. (This program should play a chromatic scale.)

3. Enter the Editor and change the DURATION to 200; leaving the rest of the program the same.

4. Now run the program again. What happened?

5. Experiment with the values for DURATION and PITCH until you understand the concept.

## EXERCISE 11–8

### Keyboard

1. Type and enter the program SOUND1.

```
PROGRAM SOUND1;

  USES
    APPLESTUFF;

  TYPE
    CHARSET = SET OF CHAR;

  VAR
    PITCH:INTEGER;
    BADNOTES:CHARSET;
    ANSWER,PITCH1:CHAR;
```

```
PROCEDURE KEYBOARD;

BEGIN
  WRITELN('TYPE B TO BEGIN');
  WRITE('     X TO STOP');
  READ(ANSWER);
  IF ANSWER = 'B' THEN
      BEGIN
        PAGE(OUTPUT);
        WRITELN('PRESS KEYS A,W,S,E,D,F,T,G,Y,H,U,J,K');
        READ(PITCH1);
        REPEAT
          PAGE(OUTPUT);
          CASE PITCH1 OF
            'A':PITCH := 20;
            'W':PITCH := 21;
            'S':PITCH := 22;
            'E':PITCH := 23;
            'D':PITCH := 24;
            'F':PITCH := 25;
            'T':PITCH := 26;
            'G':PITCH := 27;
            'Y':PITCH := 28;
            'H':PITCH := 29;
            'U':PITCH := 30;
            'J':PITCH := 31;
            'K':PITCH := 32
            END; (* CASE *)
          NOTE(PITCH,20);
          READ(PITCH1);
          IF PITCH1 IN BADNOTES THEN
            PITCH := 0;
        UNTIL PITCH1 = 'X'
      END; (* IF *)
  PAGE(OUTPUT)
END; (* KEYBOARD *)


(* MAIN PROGRAM *)

BEGIN
  BADNOTES:=['Q','R','I','O','L','P',';','Z'
           ,'/','C','V','B','N','M',',','.'];
  PAGE(OUTPUT);
  KEYBOARD
END. (* SOUND1 *)
```

2. Trace the program manually and predict the output.

3. Run the program several times.

### Notes

The program shown in Exercise 11–8 permits you to use the Apple keyboard as a musical keyboard by pressing certain keys. Here is how it works.

1. Notice that there is a variable called BADNOTES. It is a new data type called CHARSET. CHARSET is defined in the **TYPE** block to be a **SET** OF CHAR. **SET** is a reserved word that you have not seen before. It means that the variable BADNOTES can have as a value any of the particular set of characters assigned in the main program block. The first line of the main program block assigns some characters to the variable BADNOTES. (We will discuss sets in more detail in Chapter 13.)

2. When the procedure KEYBOARD is called by the main program, control is passed to the procedure.

3. Note that in the procedure, a **CASE** statement is used within the **REPEAT-UNTIL** loop. First, a character is entered from the keyboard via the READ (PITCH1) statement and is evaluated. Next, a match is looked for between the values of PITCH1 (the input character) and one of the values in the **CASE** statement (that is, A, W, S, and so forth). If a match is found, then PITCH is assigned the corresponding value. This value is used in the NOTE procedure to provide an output (sound).

4. If one of the characters entered from the keyboard happens to be one of the characters defined in BADNOTES, no output is produced (PITCH : = 0).

5. The procedure will continue until you type in the character X **REPEAT-UNTIL** PITCH1 : = X).

## EXERCISE 11–9

### Random Sounds

1. Type and enter the simple program SOUND2.

```
PROGRAM SOUND2;

  USES
    APPLESTUFF;

  VAR
    PITCH,DURATION,COUNT:INTEGER;

 PROCEDURE RANDOMS;

  BEGIN
    FOR COUNT := 1 TO 100 DO
      BEGIN
        PITCH := 1 + RANDOM MOD 49;
        DURATION := 20;
        NOTE(PITCH,DURATION)
      END; (* FOR *)
  END; (* RANDOMS *)


  (* MAIN PROGRAM *)


  BEGIN
    RANDOMS
  END. (* SOUND2 *)
```

2. Run the program several times.

### Notes

The program shown in Exercise 11–9 produces random sounds when executed. Here is how it works.

1. Note that the variables used in the program are PITCH and DURATION, which are integers used as parameters for the procedure NOTE (PITCH,DURATION).

2. When the procedure RANDOMS is called by the main program block, control is passed to the procedure.

3. The procedure simply uses a **FOR-DO** loop that counts from 1 to 100; then it produces random sounds using the procedure NOTE (PITCH,DURATION); it then passes control back to the main program.

## EXERCISE 11–10
### Scale

1. Type and enter the simple program SOUND3.

```
PROGRAM SOUND3;

  USES
    APPLESTUFF;

  VAR
    PITCH,DURATION,COUNT:INTEGER;

  PROCEDURE SCALE;

  BEGIN
    FOR COUNT := 1 TO 49 DO
      BEGIN
        PITCH := COUNT;
        DURATION := COUNT;
        NOTE(PITCH,DURATION)
      END; (* FOR *)
    FOR COUNT := 49 DOWNTO 1 DO
      BEGIN
        PITCH := COUNT;
        DURATION := COUNT;
        NOTE(PITCH,DURATION)
      END; (* FOR *)
  END; (* SCALE *)


(* MAIN PROGRAM *)


  BEGIN
    SCALE
  END. (* SOUND3 *)
```

2. Trace the program manually.

3. Run the program several times.

### Notes

The program shown in Exercise 11–10 produces a musical scale as its output when executed. Here is how it works.

1. Note that the variables used in this program are PITCH, DURATION, and COUNT.

2. When the SCALE procedure is called by the main program block, control is passed to the procedure.

3. The procedure uses **FOR-DO** loops. One loop counts from 1 to 49, and the other counts from 49 **DOWNTO** 1. The value of the variable count is assigned to the variables PITCH and DURATION. As the value of count varies, the value of PITCH and DURATION will vary accordingly. Finally, by varying PITCH and DURATION, the computer output is varied (that is, each note has a different duration and pitch).

**Summary**

You have been introduced to some of the basic procedures used in TURTLEGRAPHICS and APPLESTUFF packages. For graphics, you used the TURTLEGRAPHICS package, which provides the tools for you to draw pictures and other graphics. You were introduced to the APPLESTUFF package earlier in this book when you learned about random numbers, and Game Paddle and Button inputs. Here you learned that APPLESTUFF permits you to develop programs to make music using the NOTE procedure.

You are not expected to use every application of the computer (unless you really want to), but you can see from the lessons in this chapter that the APPLESTUFF and TURTLEGRAPHICS packages are very powerful. Essentially, you are only limited by your imagination on what you can do with these packages. So if you enjoy making graphics and sounds, continue to experiment and have fun doing it.

---

## PRACTICE 11–1

---

1. Type and enter the program PICTURES.

```
PROGRAM PICTURES;

  USES
    TURTLEGRAPHICS;

  VAR
    POINT,POINT2,SIDES,DEGREES,DISTANCE,LOOP1,LOOP2:INTEGER;

  BEGIN
    WRITE('TYPE IN NUMBER OF SIDES ');
    READLN(SIDES);
    WRITE('TYPE IN DEGREES OF OBJECT ');
    READLN(DEGREES);
    INITTURTLE;
    FILLSCREEN(WHITE);
    POINT := 80;
    POINT2 := 36;
    DISTANCE := 100;
    FOR LOOP1 := 1 TO 9 DO

      BEGIN
        POINT := POINT + 5;
        POINT2 := POINT2 + 5;
        DISTANCE := DISTANCE - 10;
        PENCOLOR(NONE);
        MOVETO(POINT+10,POINT2+10);
        FOR LOOP2 := 1 TO SIDES DO

          BEGIN
            PENCOLOR(BLACK);
            MOVE(DISTANCE);
            TURN(DEGREES)
          END (* DO LOOP2 *)

      END; (* DO LOOP1 *)
    READLN

END. (* PICTURES *)
```

2. Trace the program manually using the following inputs. Predict the outputs.
   - a. Four sides and 90 degrees.
   - b. Three sides and 120 degrees.
   - c. Five sides and 72 degrees.

3. Run the program with each of the inputs in 2a, 2b, and 2c above, and discuss the results.

4. Experiment with this program by using different inputs for sides and degrees.

## PRACTICE 11–2

1. Program SOUNDDEMO, shown on page 224, is really a composite of the programs in Exercises 11–8, 11–9, and 11–10 with a few modifications. When you first look at program SOUNDDEMO, it might look complicated, but after you break it down into manageable pieces, it will look easy. Here is how to do that.

   a. First, scan the program and notice that three procedures are used: KEYBOARD, RANDOMS, and SCALE. These are the same procedures used in Exercises 11–8, 11–9, and 11–10, respectively.

   b. Next, look at the main program block and notice that we added a pause and a **CASE** statement. The **FOR-DO** PAUSE loop is a programming technique for inserting a delay in your program. We placed a delay so that you would have time to read the **WRITELN** statement ('THIS IS A SOUND DEMO') when the program is executed. If you wish for a longer or shorter time, just change the value in the **FOR-DO** statement from "2000" to the desired value. Since PAUSE is not a reserved word, we could have used any words of our choice, such as DELAY, HOLD, and so on.

   c. The **CASE** statement in the main program block is used to call the procedures. That is,

   ```
   CASE ANSWER OF
        'K': KEYBOARD;
        'R': RANDOMS;
        'S': SCALE;
   ```

   The **CASE** statement is used inside a **REPEAT-UNTIL** loop. This loop receives an input from the keyboard via READ (ANSWER). The **CASE** statement evaluates this input and matches it with the value assigned to one of the three procedures (that is, K, R, or S). Once a procedure is selected, control is passed to it and the procedure is executed.

   d. Notice that there is a variable called BADNOTES. It is a new type called CHARSET, and is defined in the **TYPE** block to be a **SET** OF CHAR. **SET** is a reserved word that was explained in Exercise 11–8.

Also notice that the first line of the main program block assigns some characters to BADNOTES. Now the program will restrict the input to only the keys we will use on the keyboard. BADNOTES will produce no outputs.

2. Type and enter the program SOUNDDEMO.

```
PROGRAM SOUNDDEMO;

  USES
    APPLESTUFF;

  TYPE
    CHARSET = SET OF CHAR;

  VAR
    PAUSE,PITCH,DURATION,COUNT:INTEGER;
    BADNOTES:CHARSET;
    ANSWER,PITCH1:CHAR;

  PROCEDURE KEYBOARD;
  BEGIN
    WRITELN('TYPE B TO BEGIN');
    WRITE('      X TO STOP');
    READ(ANSWER);
    IF ANSWER = 'B' THEN
      BEGIN
        PAGE(OUTPUT);
        WRITELN('PRESS KEYS A,W,S,E,D,F,T,G,Y,H,U,J,K');
        READ(PITCH1);
        REPEAT
          PAGE(OUTPUT);
          CASE PITCH1 OF
             'A':PITCH := 20;
             'W':PITCH := 21;
             'S':PITCH := 22;
             'E':PITCH := 23;
             'D':PITCH := 24;
             'F':PITCH := 25;
             'T':PITCH := 26;
             'G':PITCH := 27;
             'Y':PITCH := 28;
             'H':PITCH := 29;
             'U':PITCH := 30;
             'J':PITCH := 31;
             'K':PITCH := 32
          END; (* CASE *)
          NOTE(PITCH,20);
          READ(PITCH1);
          IF PITCH1 IN BADNOTES THEN
             PITCH := 0;
        UNTIL PITCH1 = 'X'
      END; (* IF *)
    PAGE(OUTPUT)
  END; (* KEYBOARD *)
```

```
      PROCEDURE RANDOMS;
       BEGIN
         FOR COUNT := 1 TO 100 DO
           BEGIN
             PITCH := 1 + RANDOM MOD 49;
             DURATION := 20;
             NOTE(PITCH,DURATION)
           END; (* FOR *)
       END; (* RANDOMS *)


      PROCEDURE SCALE;
       BEGIN
         FOR COUNT := 1 TO 49 DO
           BEGIN
             PITCH := COUNT;
             DURATION := COUNT;
             NOTE(PITCH,DURATION)
           END; (* FOR *)
         FOR COUNT := 49 DOWNTO 1 DO
           BEGIN
             PITCH := COUNT;
             DURATION := COUNT;
             NOTE(PITCH,DURATION)
           END; (* FOR *)
       END; (* SCALE *)

    (* MAIN PROGRAM *)
     BEGIN
       BADNOTES:=['Q','R','I','O','L','P',';','Z'
                 ,'/','C','V','B','N','M',',','.'];
       PAGE(OUTPUT);
       WRITELN('THIS A SOUND DEMO');
       FOR PAUSE := 1 TO 2000 DO
         PAUSE := PAUSE;
       REPEAT
         PAGE(OUTPUT);
         WRITELN('TYPE K FOR KEYBOARD SOUND');
         WRITELN('     R FOR RANDOM SOUND');
         WRITE('      S FOR SCALED SOUND');
         READ(ANSWER);
         PAGE(OUTPUT);
         CASE ANSWER OF
           'K':KEYBOARD;
           'R':RANDOMS;
           'S':SCALE
         END; (* CASE *)
         WRITE('DO YOU WISH TO PLAY AGAIN (Y OR N) ');
         READ(ANSWER);
       UNTIL ANSWER = 'N'
     END. (* SOUNDDEMO *)
```

3. Trace the program manually, starting with the main program block. Compare this program with the programs in Exercises 11–8, 11–9, and 11–10.

4. Run the program several times.

# Chapter 12

# Scalar and Subrange Data Types

**What You Will Learn**

- To understand how to use the **TYPE** definition part of the declaration block.

- To understand and learn how to use scalar data types used in Pascal.

- To understand and learn how to use the functions ORD(X), PRED(X), and SUCC(X).

- To understand and learn how to use subrange data types.

**The TYPE Definition Part of the Declaration Block**

Before we discuss scalar and subrange data types, let's review the declaration block. So far, you have been introduced to two parts of the declaration block of a Pascal program: **CONST** and **VAR**. There is a third part of the declaration block called **TYPE**. When used, the type definitions should be placed between the constant definitions (if any) and the variable declarations as shown below:

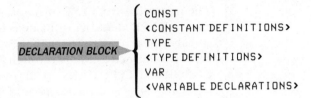

```
         ⎧ CONST
         ⎪ <CONSTANT DEFINITIONS>
DECLARATION BLOCK ⎨ TYPE
         ⎪ <TYPE DEFINITIONS>
         ⎪ VAR
         ⎩ <VARIABLE DECLARATIONS>
```

In most Pascal programs, you will find that it is not necessary to have a type declaration part at all. That is because standard data types (BOOLEAN, INTEGER, CHAR, REAL) are predefined data types in Apple Pascal and may be used without being defined in a **TYPE** block. Until now, you simply declared the data type along with the variable declarations. For example,

```
VAR
   LETTER  :CHAR;
   NUMBER  :INTEGER;        TYPE
   AVERAGE :REAL;
   NAME    :STRING;
```

There are times, however, when you need a **TYPE** part. Here are some reasons for using a **TYPE** block.

- All new or user-defined data types must be declared in the **TYPE** part of the definition block. (We will discuss user-defined data types in more detail later in this chapter.)

- A separate **TYPE** part of the declaration block in your program will make your program easier to read and easier to understand. That is, you will have a single place to go to find out all information about the data types used in your program.

Here is an example of **TYPE** definitions:

```
TYPE

  WEEK = (MON,TUE,WED,THU,FRI,SAT,SUN);
  COLOR = (RED,BLU,GRN,ORG,WHT);
  CARS = (CADILLAC,MERCEDES,DATSUN, FIREBIRD);
```

The reserved word **TYPE** introduces the **TYPE** definition part. A **TYPE** identifier or name is followed by an equal sign (=) and the type definition. In the above example, **TYPE** WEEK is defined as MON through SUN. Likewise, **TYPE** COLOR and **TYPE** CARS are defined as shown. These data types are called *scalar data types* and must be defined in a **TYPE** block before they can be used throughout a program.

## Scalar Data Types

A scalar data type is any data type whose values may be enumerated (counted) or listed. The standard data types INTEGER, BOOLEAN, and CHAR are considered to be scalar types since each of these types may be listed.

### User-Defined Scalar Types

Pascal permits you to define a new scalar type. This gives you the flexibility to either define a specific value that can be taken, or to specify a whole range of values. This scalar type should be declared in the **TYPE** section of the declaration box. It takes the form:

```
TYPE
  SCALAR NAME = (LIST OF SCALAR VALUES)
```

For example:

```
TYPE
  WEEK = (MON, TUE, WED, THUR, FRI, SAT, SUN);
VAR
  WORKDAY: WEEK;
```

In the above example, the only values that can be assigned to a variable "WORKDAY" are specified in the list of scalar values for **TYPE** WEEK. (That is, only the value MON, TUE, WED, and so on can be assigned to the variable "WORKDAY.")

The list of scalar values must be enclosed in parentheses, and each value in the list must be separated by commas. Each scalar value in the list must start with a letter followed by letters or digits only. Essentially, any name can be used in the list of scalar values except a Pascal reserved word.

A user-defined scalar type is usually declared in a **TYPE** block in the declaration section of a program, a procedure, and/or a function. A **TYPE** is known globally if declared in the main program **TYPE** block, and is known locally if declared in a procedure or function's **TYPE** block. If a user-defined scalar type is not declared in a **TYPE** block, other variables cannot use that type. That is, it is legal to declare the variable WORKDAY as follows:

```
VAR
WORKDAY:(MON,TUE,WED,THU,FRI);
```

But because the data type has not been formally declared with a specific name, other variables cannot be defined as belonging to that type.

Sometimes you may wish to use more descriptive values in problems. Suppose you were designing a program that, for one reason or another, had to deal with the days of the week. You could represent the days by using numbers. For example, MONDAY becomes 1, TUESDAY becomes 2, and so on. Numbering the days of the week is convenient but is not always the most desirable approach. You could, however, define the days of the week as a scalar type, and then declare variables of that **TYPE** as shown below:

```
TYPE
   WEEK = (MON,TUE,WED,THUR,FRI,SAT,SUN);
VAR
   DAY: WEEK;
```

In the above example, a new scalar type (WEEK) is defined, and then a variable (DAY) of **TYPE** WEEK is declared.

There are other kinds of user-defined scalar types. Some other examples are:

```
TYPE
   SUIT      = (CLUB,DIAMOND,HEART,SPADE);
   SCALE     = (DOE,RE,MI,FA,SO,LA,TI);
   BRAND     = (PEPSI,COKE,SEVENUP, SPRITE);
   SHIRTSIZE = (SMALL,MEDIUM,LARGE,XLARGE);
```

The **TYPE** declarations above define four scalar types: SUIT, SCALE, BRAND, and SHIRTSIZE. Each declaration specifies the name of a new data type and a list of scalar values for that type. Once you define new scalar types and their associated scalar values, you can then declare them as variables of the types defined in the **TYPE** block (that is, SUIT, SCALE, BRAND, or SHIRTSIZE) as shown below:

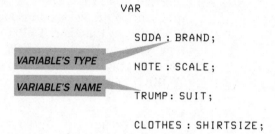

```
VAR

    SODA : BRAND;

    NOTE : SCALE;

    TRUMP: SUIT;

    CLOTHES : SHIRTSIZE;
```

### Comparing Scalar Types Using Relational Operators

Scalars can be compared using the relational operators ( = , <>, >, <, > = , < = ). The order in which the values of scalar types are listed also defines their ordering for purposes of applying relational operators. For example, the order of the names in parentheses below for **TYPE** WEEK establishes the ordinal number (or order number) of the days. These ordinal numbers for **TYPE** WEEK can be used for comparison. Thus:

```
TYPE
   WEEK =          (MON,TUE,WED,THUR,FRI,SAT,SUN);
```

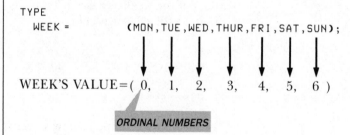

WEEK'S VALUE = ( 0,   1,   2,   3,   4,   5,   6 )

From above, if we compared the values, we would get:

MON < TUE          is true since $0 < 1$

TUE > THUR         is false since $1 < 3$

FRI > WED          is true since $4 > 2$

Note that the relative position of the scalar name determines its value.

All enumerated types are defined to be ordinal types. That is, the order in which their values are listed also defines the ordering for purposes of comparison. Here are some examples:

```
                SUIT = (CLUB,DIAMOND,HEART,SPADE);
SUIT'S VALUE = (  0,       1,       2,        3  )
```

```
                SCALE = (DOE,RE,MI,FA,SO,LA,TI)
SCALE'S VALUE = ( 0,  1,  2,  3,  4,  5,  6 )
```

```
                BRAND = (PEPSI,COKE,SEVENUP,SPRITE);
BRAND'S VALUE = (  0,     1,       2,        3  )
```

**NOTE:** *Since* DO *is a reserved word, we use* DOE *as the first SCALE value. The ordinal value of these scalar types starts with 0.*

To take advantage of the above relationships, we next introduce the functions ORD, PRED, and SUCC.

The following table lists some functions you should know how to use: ORD(X), PRED(X), and SUCC(X).

| FUNCTION | MEANING | EXAMPLES |
|---|---|---|
| ORD(X) | Means the ordinal value of X. It returns the ordinal number of X.<br>– The ordinal number (or order number) indicates the relative position of the scalar value of X.<br>– X can be of type BOOLEAN, CHAR, INTEGER, or SCALAR. | Each character has a unique "ordinal" value. For example:<br>ORD('A') = 65<br>ORD('B') = 66<br>ORD('C') = 67<br>ORD('1') = 49<br>ORD('2') = 50<br>ORD('3') = 51<br>(The above values are built into the Apple Pascal system.) |
| PRED(X) | Means predecessor of X; that is, the number that preceeds X.<br>– PRED returns the value whose ordinal number is one less than the ordinal number of X. | From above, you saw that character values have a predefined order. Therefore:<br>PRED('B') = 'A'<br>and<br>PRED('2') = '1' |
| SUCC(X) | Means the successor of X or the number that succeeds or follows X.<br>– SUCC(X) returns the value whose ordinal number is one more than the ordinal number of X. | SUCC('B') = 'C'<br>and<br>SUCC('2') = '3' |

The following table lists some examples of ORD(X), PRED(X), and SUCC(X):

| X | PRED(X) | SUCC(X) | ORD(X) |
|---|---------|---------|--------|
| A | @ | B | 65 |
| B | A | C | 66 |
| C | B | D | 67 |
| D | C | E | 68 |
| E | D | F | 69 |
| F | E | G | 70 |
| 0 | / | 1 | 48 |
| 1 | 0 | 2 | 49 |
| 2 | 1 | 3 | 50 |
| 3 | 2 | 4 | 51 |
| 4 | 3 | 5 | 52 |

### Notes

1. The ORD function returns a unique integer for each character value. It gives the order number of the character value represented by X.

2. The order number for the CHAR data type varies between 0 and 255 for Apple Pascal.

3. PRED('B') = 'A' means the character 'A' (note the quotes) preceeds the character 'B'.

4. SUCC('B') = 'C' means the character 'C' succeeds or follows the character 'B'.

## EXERCISE 12–1

### PRED(X), SUCC(X), ORD(X) Functions

1. Fill in the blanks in the table below.
   Given:

```
TYPE
   DAYS =  (MON,TUE,WED,THUR,FRI,SAT,SUN);
   SCALE = (DOE,RE,MI,FA,SO,LA,TI);
   BRAND = (PEPSI,COKE,SEVENUP,SPRITE);
   MONTHS = (JAN,FEB,MAR,APR,MAY,JUN,JUL,AUG,SEPT,OCT,NOV,DEC);
```

|     | X | PRED(X) | SUCC(X) | ORD(X) |
|-----|------|---------|---------|--------|
| 1.  | WED  | TUE     | THUR    | 2      |
| 2.  | MI   |         |         |        |
| 3.  | COKE |         |         |        |
| 4.  | FA   |         |         |        |
| 5.  | THUR |         |         |        |
| 6.  | MAY  |         |         |        |
| 7.  | OCT  |         |         |        |
| 8.  | RE   |         |         |        |
| 9.  | FEB  |         |         |        |
| 10. | APR  |         |         |        |

### Some Things You Should Know about Scalar Types

Scalar values can be used to control the execution of **FOR-DO** loops and **CASE** statements. For example,

```
TYPE
   WEEK = (MON,TUE,WED,THU,FRI,SAT,SUN);
VAR
   DAY,CHURCH,PAYDAY,HOLIDAY:WEEK;
```

Using the scalar declarations above, you can write a **FOR-DO** loop to be executed MON through FRI. That is:

```
FOR DAY:=MON TO FRI DO
<SOMETHING>
```

You can also use scalars to select **CASE** alternatives. For example, using the variable DAY of **TYPE** WEEK, we have:

```
CASE DAY OF
    MON:WRITELN ('BLUE MONDAY');
    WED:WRITELN ('HALF WAY THERE');
    FRI:WRITELN ('TGIF')
END; (*CASE*)
```

Scalars can be assigned for use directly in the program. From the above declaration of type week, you could assign the following:

```
BEGIN
  CHURCH:= SUN;
  PAYDAY:= FRI;
  HOLIDAY:= TUE;
  .
  .
  .
  .
END.
```

Scalar values are restricted in use. You can use this feature to let the computer help catch errors in your programs. That is, if you inadvertently try to assign a value to a scalar variable that is not of the same type, the computer (compiler) would catch the error. For example:

```
TYPE
  WEEK = (MON,TUE,WED,THU,FRI,SAT,SUN);

VAR
  DAY,SCHOOLDAY,OFFDAY:WEEK;
```

|               *RIGHT*               |               *WRONG*              |
| ----------------------------------- | ---------------------------------- |
| ```                                 | ```                                |
| BEGIN                               | BEGIN                              |
|   SCHOOLDAY:=MON;                   |   SCHOOLDAY:=OCT;                  |
|     OFFDAY:=SAT;                    |     OFFDAY:=10;                    |
|   .                                 |   .                                |
|   .                                 |   .                                |
|   .                                 |   .                                |
| END.                                | END.                               |
| ```                                 | ```                                |

Note: Neither OCT nor 10 are legal scalar values for the type WEEK. The compiler should catch this type of error.

No value of a scalar type can belong to more than one type.

| **RIGHT** | **WRONG** |
|---|---|

```
TYPE                                    TYPE
  WEEK = (MON,TUE,WED,THU,FRI,SAT,SUN);   SCHOOLDAY = (MON,TUE,WED,THU, FRI);
                                          WEEKEND = (FRI,SAT,SUN);


  VAR
    SCHOOLDAY,WEEKEND:WEEK;
```

Note: The declaration in the right column is confusing. Is FRI the last value of type SCHOOLDAY or the first value of WEEKEND? Or to put it another way, is the ordinal value of FRI = 0 (which it would be for WEEKEND) or is it 4 (which it would be for SCHOOLDAY)? Care should be taken in writing your programs to avoid confusion in type declarations.

## EXERCISE 12–2

### Scalar Program

1. Type and enter the program SCALAR.

```
PROGRAM SCALAR;

(* FINDS AVERAGE ATTENDANCE FOR A WEEK *)

  TYPE
    WEEKDAY=(MON,TUE,WED,THUR,FRI);

  VAR
    A:ARRAY[MON..FRI] OF INTEGER;
    DAY:WEEKDAY;
    TOTAL:INTEGER;


BEGIN
  WRITELN('ENTER NUMBER OF STUDENTS PRESENT');
  WRITELN;
  FOR DAY:=MON TO FRI DO
    BEGIN
      WRITE('DAY ',ORD(DAY)+1,' ');
      READLN (A[DAY])
    END;
  WRITELN;
  WRITELN;
  TOTAL:=0;
  FOR DAY:=MON TO FRI DO
    TOTAL:=TOTAL+A[DAY];
  WRITELN('AVERAGE ATTENDANCE',' ',ROUND(TOTAL/5))
END. (* SCALAR *)
```

2. Trace the program manually.

3. Run the program several times.

### Notes

The program shown in Exercise 12–2 was developed to demonstrate the use of scalars without regard to the best programming technique. The important things to note are:

1. The scalar type WEEKDAY was defined in the **TYPE** declaration block.

2. Scalar values [MON..FRI] were used to index an array, although the actual values to be stored in the array are of type INTEGER.

3. The variable DAY was declared as the scalar type WEEKDAY in the **VAR** block.

4. Since a scalar value cannot be read or printed, we made use of the ordinal value of the scalar to write the day number. If we had not added 1 to ORD(DAY), the ordinal value for the first day would be 0 (by the rules of order for scalar values). But we wanted the first day to be DAY 1, the second day to be DAY 2, and so on. That is, when the program is executed, you get the following prompts:

```
DAY 1
DAY 2
DAY 3
```

**Reading and Printing Scalar Data Types**

Pascal does not allow the direct reading or printing of scalar values. However, you can read or print the corresponding ordinal number instead of the scalar value. For example:

```
PROGRAM WHATDAY;

  TYPE
    DAY=(MON,TUE,WED,THU,FRI,SAT,SUN);

  VAR
    DAYNUM :INTEGER;
    TODAY  :DAY;

BEGIN
  WRITE('ENTER ORDINAL NUM 0-6: ');
  READLN(DAYNUM);
  CASE DAYNUM OF
      0:TODAY:= MON;
      1:TODAY:= TUE;
      2:TODAY:= WED;
      3:TODAY:= THU;
      4:TODAY:= FRI;
      5:TODAY:= SAT;
      6:TODAY:= SUN
    END; (*CASE*)
  IF (TODAY=SUN) OR (TODAY=SAT) THEN
      WRITELN('NO SCHOOL TODAY')
  ELSE
      WRITELN('IT''S A SCHOOL DAY')
END.
```

This simple program illustrates how the ordinal value of a scalar can be used to read data from the keyboard. The **CASE** statement is used to convert the ordinal number of the day (0 through 6) to its corresponding scalar value (MON through SUN). If the value of DAYNUM (the **CASE** selector) matches the number listed to the left of the colon, the assignment statement on that line is executed. That is, the variable TODAY is assigned the corresponding scalar value that matches the ordinal number.

There are two apostrophes in the last WRITELN statement so that the actual apostrophe will print out in the statement.

IT'S A SCHOOLDAY.

---

## EXERCISE 12–3

### The Program WHATDAY

1. Type and enter the program WHATDAY.

```
PROGRAM WHATDAY;

  TYPE
    DAY=(MON,TUE,WED,THU,FRI,SAT,SUN);
    NUMRANGE=0..6;

  VAR
    DAYNUM :NUMRANGE;
    TODAY  :DAY;
    NUMBER:INTEGER;


BEGIN
  WRITELN('PROGRAM DETERMINES IF IT''S A SCHOOLDAY');
  WRITE('ENTER A NUMBER 0-6: ');
  READLN(NUMBER);
  DAYNUM := NUMBER;
  CASE DAYNUM OF
      0:TODAY:= MON;
      1:TODAY:= TUE;
      2:TODAY:= WED;
      3:TODAY:= THU;
      4:TODAY:= FRI;
      5:TODAY:= SAT;
      6:TODAY:= SUN
      END; (*CASE*)
  IF (TODAY=SUN) OR (TODAY=SAT) THEN
      WRITELN('NO SCHOOL TODAY')
  ELSE
      WRITELN('IT''S A SCHOOL DAY')
END. (* WHATDAY *)
```

2. Trace the program manually.

3. Run the program several times.

**SUMMARY**

You can write programs without creating new scalar types. But sometimes, by defining new scalar types, you can make your programs easier to understand and to follow. For example, compare the following program statements:

| *OK* | *BETTER* |
|---|---|
| FOR-DO loop | FOR-DO loop |

```
FOR MONTH:=1 TO 12 DO
```
```
FOR MONTH:=JAN TO DEC DO
```

Assignment           Assignment

```
MONTH:=2;
```
```
MONTH:=FEB;
```

Case               Case

```
CASE DAY OF
   1:WRITELN('---');
   2:WRITELN('---');
   3:WRITELN('---')

END;(*CASE*)
```
```
CASE DAY OF
   MON:WRITELN('---');
   TUE:WRITELN('---');
   WED:WRITELN('---')

END;(*CASE*)
```

Index to an array     Index to an array

```
VAR
  A:ARRAY[1..5]OF STRING;
BEGIN
  FOR J:=1 TO 5 DO
    READLN(A[J]);
      .
      .
  END;
```
```
VAR
  A:ARRAY[MON..FRI]OF STRING;
BEGIN
  FOR DAY:=MON TO FRI DO
      READLN(A[DAY]);
      .
      .
  END;
```

From this list, you or anyone else reading your program would know immediately that you are dealing with months or days. It is better to use scalar data types rather than having to translate that a "2" means "FEB" or that a "1" means "MON."

## Subrange Data Types

When writing a program, you often know beforehand that certain variables will have a particular limited set of values. For example, if in one of your programs you declared "year" as a variable of type INTEGER, but you know that the only values the variable will hold range from 1984 to 1990, then you could say 1984 to 1990 is a "subrange" of type INTEGER. That is, 1984 to 1990 is only part of the complete range of integers that range from − 32768 to + 32767 for the Apple computer. In Pascal, you would write 1984 to 1990 as the subrange 1984..1990. (The two periods can be read as "to," and mean 1984 to 1990 inclusive.)

To define a subrange data type, you simply choose the limiting values (upper and lower) of the subrange type and separate them with two periods or dots as shown below.

```
TYPE
   SUBRANGE TYPE NAME = LOWER VALUE..UPPER VALUE
```

**TWO PERIODS ARE A MUST!**

LOWER VALUE is the smallest value that may be assigned to a variable of this subrange type. UPPER VALUE is the largest value that may be assigned. Some examples of subrange types follow.

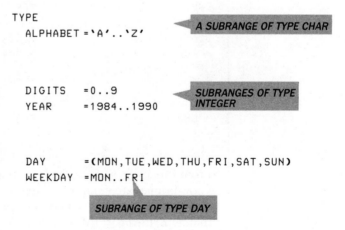

```
TYPE
   ALPHABET = 'A'..'Z'
```
**A SUBRANGE OF TYPE CHAR**

```
   DIGITS   = 0..9
   YEAR     = 1984..1990
```
**SUBRANGES OF TYPE INTEGER**

```
   DAY      = (MON,TUE,WED,THU,FRI,SAT,SUN)
   WEEKDAY  = MON..FRI
```
**SUBRANGE OF TYPE DAY**

*A subrange type declaration should be preceded by the word **TYPE,** and any scalar type declaration defining lower value and upper value must be preceded by **TYPE.** Although you do not have to declare a **TYPE** block for subranges of predefined data types (that is, INTEGER), it is a good practice to do so. It makes your program clearer and easier to follow and to debug.*

### Some Things You Can Do with Subrange Types

Pascal allows subranges of previously declared scalar types to be defined. For example:

```
TYPE
   DAY = (MON,TUE,WED,THU,FRI,SAT,SUN);
   WORKDAY = MON..FRI;
VAR
   PAYDAY,VACATION,HOLIDAY:WORKDAY;
```

These declarations define WORKDAY as a subrange of the scalar type DAY. A variable type WORKDAY can assume any scalar values MON through FRI.

Subranges may overlap. Overlapping subrange types are legal, and is an important feature in Pascal programming. Here is an example:

```
TYPE
   MONTH=(JAN,FEB,MAR,APR,MAY,JUN,JUL,AUG,SEP,OCT,NOV,DEC);

   YEAR=JAN..DEC;
   QTR1=JAN..MAR;
   QTR2=APR..JUN;
   QTR3=JUL..SEP;
   QTR4=OCT..DEC;

   FIRSTHALF=JAN..JUN;
   SECONDHALF=JUL..DEC;
```

A scalar value may appear in more than one subrange, as shown above. When declaring subranges of scalar type, you must be certain that the ordinal number of the lower limit is less than the ordinal number of the upper limit. For example, since ORD (JAN) = 0 AND ORD (MAR) = 2, then the subrange "JAN..MAR" is legal because the lower limit (JAN) is less than the upper limit (MAR).

You can use the subrange feature to specify limits on variable values. For example:

```
TYPE
  NUMRANGE = 0..100;
  ALPHARANGE = 'A'..'F';

VAR
  NUMGRADE   : NUMRANGE;
  LETTERGRADE: ALPHARANGE;
```

The declarations above define a subrange of the integers named NUMRANGE and a subrange of the characters named ALPHARANGE. Any attempt to assign a value to these variables outside of their range would result in an error. For example:

```
BEGIN
  NUMGRADE:=150;
  LETTERGRADE:='Z';
  .
  .
  .
END.
```

would result in a value range error at run time since the values of 150 and Z are outside the range of their declared subrange.

## *USING SUBRANGE DATA TYPES FOR PROGRAM CLARITY*

| *GOOD* | *BETTER* | *BEST* |
|---|---|---|

```
VAR
  AGE,MONTH,YEAR:INTEGER;
```

1. The above declaration is legal and should be used if you do not know beforehand the limits of range of values for the variables.

```
VAR
  AGE:8..80;
  MONTH:1..12;
  YEAR:1984..1990;
```

1. This approach is better if you know beforehand that you will use a limited set of values.

2. This tells you or anyone reading this program a lot about the variables without looking beyond the **VAR** declaration block.

```
TYPE
  AGERANGE=8..80;
  MONTHRANGE=1..12;
  YEARSPAN=1984..1990;
VAR
  AGE:AGERANGE;
  MONTH:MONTHRANGE;
  YEAR:YEARSPAN;
```

1. It is best to use a **TYPE** declaration block in your program so that your program will be easier to read and to understand.

2. If used properly, the **TYPE** block will make it easier for you or anyone else reading your program to determine at a glance what data types are used in your program.

**Summary**

1. Subrange types are useful for detecting assignment errors during program execution. You can use the computer to help you locate errors. For example, the following declaration

```
VAR
  AGE:8..80;
```

means that the legal values that can be assigned to the variable AGE are in the range between 8 and 80. If an assignment such as

```
BEGIN
  AGE:=90;
  .
  .
  .
END.
```

was made *accidentally,* the computer would print a "value range error" message during program execution.

2. For program clarity, subrange types should be defined in the **TYPE** declaration block. However, a scalar type declaration defining the lower and upper value of a subrange type *must* be declared in a **TYPE** block.

3. LOWER VALUE is the smallest value that may be assigned to a subrange type, and UPPER VALUE is the largest value that may be assigned. Upper and lower limiting values must be scalar values of the same type. They can either be standard-data type or user-defined data type.

4. Apostrophes are used to enclose characters in the subrange if we are interested in the character values themselves. Remember that a character value consists of a single printable character (letter, digit, punctuation mark, etc.) enclosed in apostrophes.

5. You should be careful when specifying subranges to be certain that they are adequate for the data to be expected. If you are not careful, you will cause your program execution to be interrupted—and this can be a nuisance.

## PRACTICE 12–1

1. Type and enter the program MUSIC.

```
PROGRAM MUSIC;

  USES
    APPLESTUFF;

  TYPE
    MUSICNOTES = (LC,LCS,LD,LDS,LE,LF,LFS,LG,LGS,LA,LBF,LB,
                  C,CS,D,DS,E,F,FS,G,GS,A,BF,B,
                  HC,HCS,HD,HDS,HE,HF,HFS,HG,HGS,HA,HBF,HB,HHC);


  (* GLOBAL VARIABLES *)

  VAR
    KEY:MUSICNOTES;
    PAUSE:INTEGER;
    PLAYER:BOOLEAN;


  (* PROCEDURE BLOCK *)

  PROCEDURE PLAY(ONENOTE:MUSICNOTES;DURATION:INTEGER);

    BEGIN
      NOTE(10+ORD(ONENOTE),DURATION)
    END; (* PLAY *)


  PROCEDURE SUPERPLAY(KEY:MUSICNOTES;DURATION:INTEGER);

    (* LOCAL VARIABLE *)

    VAR
      LENGTH:INTEGER;

    BEGIN
      IF PLAYER THEN
        BEGIN
          FOR LENGTH := 1 TO 10 DO
            PLAY(KEY,DURATION DIV 10);
        END (* IF PLAYER *)
      ELSE
        PLAY(KEY,DURATION)
    END; (* SUPERPLAY *)
```

*(\*program continued on next page\*)*

*(*program continued from previous page*)*

```
PROCEDURE PRACTICE;

  BEGIN
    WRITELN('THE ORCHESTRA IS TUNING');
    FOR KEY := LC TO HHC DO
      PLAY(KEY,10);

    FOR KEY := HHC DOWNTO LC DO
      PLAY(KEY,10);

    FOR KEY := LD TO HBF DO
      BEGIN
        PLAY(PRED(KEY),10);
        PLAY(PRED(PRED(KEY)),10);
        PLAY(SUCC(KEY),10);
        PLAY(SUCC(SUCC(KEY)),10);
      END;
  END; (* PRACTICE *)


PROCEDURE ROCKIT;

  BEGIN
    IF (NOT PLAYER) THEN
      BEGIN
        WRITELN;
        WRITELN;
        WRITELN('AND NOW FOR THE CONCERT');
        WRITELN;
        WRITELN;
        WRITELN('             ROCK IT');
        WRITELN('        BY HERBIE HANCOCK');
      END; (* IF PLAYER *)
    FOR PAUSE := 1 TO 1000 DO;
    SUPERPLAY(A,60);
    SUPERPLAY(B,90);
    SUPERPLAY(E,60);
    SUPERPLAY(HC,90);
    SUPERPLAY(E,100);
    SUPERPLAY(HDS,60);
    SUPERPLAY(HD,70);
    SUPERPLAY(HC,90);
    SUPERPLAY(A,50);
    SUPERPLAY(E,30);
    SUPERPLAY(G,80);
    SUPERPLAY(HD,70);
    SUPERPLAY(HC,60);
    SUPERPLAY(G,50);
    SUPERPLAY(G,50);
    SUPERPLAY(A,90);
  END; (* ROCKIT *)
```

```
(* MAIN PROGRAM *)


BEGIN
  PLAYER:=FALSE;
  PRACTICE;
  ROCKIT;
  PLAYER:=TRUE;
  ROCKIT;
END. (* MUSIC *)
```

2. Trace the program manually and answer the following
   questions.
   a. Refer to MUSICNOTES in the **TYPE** block and fill in
      the blanks.

| X | ORD(X) | PRED(X) | PRED(PRED(X)) | SUCC(X) | SUCC(SUCC(X)) |
|---|--------|---------|---------------|---------|---------------|
| LF | _____ | _____ | _____ | _____ | _____ |
| LA | _____ | _____ | _____ | _____ | _____ |
| E | _____ | _____ | _____ | _____ | _____ |
| G | _____ | _____ | _____ | _____ | _____ |
| HDS | _____ | _____ | _____ | _____ | _____ |
| HA | _____ | _____ | _____ | _____ | _____ |

   b. What is the purpose of the procedure PLAY?
   c. What is the purpose of the procedure SUPERPLAY?
   d. What is the data type of the variable PLAYER? How is it
      used in this program?
   e. What is the purpose of the procedure PRACTICE?
   f. What is the purpose of the procedure ROCKIT?

3. Run the program several times.
   a. Try to modify the program to play a tune of your choice.

## PRACTICE 12–2

1. Type and enter the program PAYDAY.

```
PROGRAM PAYDAY;

  CONST
    HOURLYRATE = 3.35;

  TYPE
    DAY = (MON,TUE,WED,THU,FRI,SAT,SUN);

  VAR
    WORKDAY:DAY;
    HOURSWORKED,PAYHOURS,TOTALWAGES:REAL;
    THEDAY:STRING;


  PROCEDURE GIVEDAY(WHATDAY:DAY);

    BEGIN
      CASE WHATDAY OF
           MON:WRITE('    MONDAY: ');
           TUE:WRITE('   TUESDAY: ');
           WED:WRITE('WEDNESDAY: ');
           THU:WRITE(' THURSDAY: ');
           FRI:WRITE('    FRIDAY: ');
           SAT:WRITE('  SATURDAY: ');
           SUN:WRITE('    SUNDAY: ')
           END (* CASE WHATDAY *)
    END; (* GIVEDAY *)


  (* MAIN PROGRAM *)


BEGIN

  (* INITIALIZE SUM VARIABLE *)

  TOTALWAGES:=0.0;
  WRITELN('ENTER HOURS WORKED EACH DAY');
  FOR WORKDAY := MON TO SUN DO
    BEGIN
      GIVEDAY(WORKDAY);
      READLN(HOURSWORKED);
      CASE  WORKDAY OF
            MON,TUE,WED,THU,FRI:PAYHOURS:=HOURSWORKED;
            SAT:PAYHOURS:=1.5*HOURSWORKED;
            SUN:PAYHOURS:=2.0*HOURSWORKED
            END; (* CASE WORKDAY *)
      TOTALWAGES:=TOTALWAGES+(PAYHOURS*HOURLYRATE)
    END; (* FOR WORKDAY *)
  WRITELN;
  WRITELN('YOUR GROSS PAY FOR THE WEEK IS $',TOTALWAGES:4:2,'.')
END. (* PAYDAY *)
```

```
(* MAIN PROGRAM *)


BEGIN
  PLAYER:=FALSE;
  PRACTICE;
  ROCKIT;
  PLAYER:=TRUE;
  ROCKIT;
END. (* MUSIC *)
```

2. Trace the program manually and answer the following
   questions.
   a. Refer to MUSICNOTES in the **TYPE** block and fill in
      the blanks.

| X | ORD(X) | PRED(X) | PRED(PRED(X)) | SUCC(X) | SUCC(SUCC(X)) |
|---|--------|---------|---------------|---------|---------------|
| LF | _____ | _____ | _____ | _____ | _____ |
| LA | _____ | _____ | _____ | _____ | _____ |
| E | _____ | _____ | _____ | _____ | _____ |
| G | _____ | _____ | _____ | _____ | _____ |
| HDS | _____ | _____ | _____ | _____ | _____ |
| HA | _____ | _____ | _____ | _____ | _____ |

   b. What is the purpose of the procedure PLAY?
   c. What is the purpose of the procedure SUPERPLAY?
   d. What is the data type of the variable PLAYER? How is it
      used in this program?
   e. What is the purpose of the procedure PRACTICE?
   f. What is the purpose of the procedure ROCKIT?

3. Run the program several times.
   a. Try to modify the program to play a tune of your choice.

---

## PRACTICE 12–2

---

1. Type and enter the program PAYDAY.

```
PROGRAM PAYDAY;

  CONST
    HOURLYRATE = 3.35;

  TYPE
    DAY = (MON,TUE,WED,THU,FRI,SAT,SUN);

  VAR
    WORKDAY:DAY;
    HOURSWORKED,PAYHOURS,TOTALWAGES:REAL;
    THEDAY:STRING;


  PROCEDURE GIVEDAY(WHATDAY:DAY);

    BEGIN
      CASE WHATDAY OF
            MON:WRITE('   MONDAY: ');
            TUE:WRITE('  TUESDAY: ');
            WED:WRITE('WEDNESDAY: ');
            THU:WRITE(' THURSDAY: ');
            FRI:WRITE('   FRIDAY: ');
            SAT:WRITE(' SATURDAY: ');
            SUN:WRITE('   SUNDAY: ')
            END (* CASE WHATDAY *)
    END; (* GIVEDAY *)


  (* MAIN PROGRAM *)


BEGIN

  (* INITIALIZE SUM VARIABLE *)

  TOTALWAGES:=0.0;
  WRITELN('ENTER HOURS WORKED EACH DAY');
  FOR WORKDAY := MON TO SUN DO
    BEGIN
      GIVEDAY(WORKDAY);
      READLN(HOURSWORKED);
      CASE  WORKDAY OF
            MON,TUE,WED,THU,FRI:PAYHOURS:=HOURSWORKED;
            SAT:PAYHOURS:=1.5*HOURSWORKED;
            SUN:PAYHOURS:=2.0*HOURSWORKED
            END; (* CASE WORKDAY *)
      TOTALWAGES:=TOTALWAGES+(PAYHOURS*HOURLYRATE)
    END; (* FOR WORKDAY *)
  WRITELN;
  WRITELN('YOUR GROSS PAY FOR THE WEEK IS $',TOTALWAGES:4:2,'.')
END. (* PAYDAY *)
```

```
(* MAIN PROGRAM *)


BEGIN
  PLAYER:=FALSE;
  PRACTICE;
  ROCKIT;
  PLAYER:=TRUE;
  ROCKIT;
END. (* MUSIC *)
```

2. Trace the program manually and answer the following questions.

   a. Refer to MUSICNOTES in the **TYPE** block and fill in the blanks.

| X | ORD(X) | PRED(X) | PRED(PRED(X)) | SUCC(X) | SUCC(SUCC(X)) |
|---|--------|---------|---------------|---------|---------------|
| LF | _____ | _____ | _____ | _____ | _____ |
| LA | _____ | _____ | _____ | _____ | _____ |
| E | _____ | _____ | _____ | _____ | _____ |
| G | _____ | _____ | _____ | _____ | _____ |
| HDS | _____ | _____ | _____ | _____ | _____ |
| HA | _____ | _____ | _____ | _____ | _____ |

   b. What is the purpose of the procedure PLAY?
   c. What is the purpose of the procedure SUPERPLAY?
   d. What is the data type of the variable PLAYER? How is it used in this program?
   e. What is the purpose of the procedure PRACTICE?
   f. What is the purpose of the procedure ROCKIT?

3. Run the program several times.
   a. Try to modify the program to play a tune of your choice.

## PRACTICE 12–2

1. Type and enter the program PAYDAY.

```
PROGRAM PAYDAY;

  CONST
    HOURLYRATE = 3.35;

  TYPE
    DAY = (MON,TUE,WED,THU,FRI,SAT,SUN);

  VAR
    WORKDAY:DAY;
    HOURSWORKED,PAYHOURS,TOTALWAGES:REAL;
    THEDAY:STRING;


  PROCEDURE GIVEDAY(WHATDAY:DAY);

    BEGIN
      CASE WHATDAY OF
          MON:WRITE('   MONDAY: ');
          TUE:WRITE('  TUESDAY: ');
          WED:WRITE('WEDNESDAY: ');
          THU:WRITE(' THURSDAY: ');
          FRI:WRITE('   FRIDAY: ');
          SAT:WRITE(' SATURDAY: ');
          SUN:WRITE('   SUNDAY: ')
          END (* CASE WHATDAY *)
    END; (* GIVEDAY *)


  (* MAIN PROGRAM *)


BEGIN

  (* INITIALIZE SUM VARIABLE *)

  TOTALWAGES:=0.0;
  WRITELN('ENTER HOURS WORKED EACH DAY');
  FOR WORKDAY := MON TO SUN DO
    BEGIN
      GIVEDAY(WORKDAY);
      READLN(HOURSWORKED);
      CASE  WORKDAY OF
          MON,TUE,WED,THU,FRI:PAYHOURS:=HOURSWORKED;
          SAT:PAYHOURS:=1.5*HOURSWORKED;
          SUN:PAYHOURS:=2.0*HOURSWORKED
          END; (* CASE WORKDAY *)
      TOTALWAGES:=TOTALWAGES+(PAYHOURS*HOURLYRATE)
    END; (* FOR WORKDAY *)
  WRITELN;
  WRITELN('YOUR GROSS PAY FOR THE WEEK IS $',TOTALWAGES:4:2,'.')
END. (* PAYDAY *)
```

2. Trace the program manually, and answer the following questions.
   a. What is the purpose of the procedure GIVEDAY?
   b. When the procedure GIVEDAY is called by the main program, what is the "actual" parameter passed to the procedure?
   c. What is the standard hourly rate?
   d. What is the hourly rate for working on Saturday?
   e. What is the purpose of the statement "TOTALWAGES: = TOTALWAGES + (PAYHOURS*HOURLYRATE)"?

3. Run the program several times.

## PRACTICE 12–3

### ORD(X), SUCC(X), PRED(X)

Fill in the blanks below.

```
TYPE
    NETWORK =       (ABC,CBS,NBC);
    CARS     =      (AMC,CHRYSLER,FORD,GM);
    SCHOOLDAYS =    (MONDAY,TUESDAY,WEDNESDAY,THURSDAY,FRIDAY);
    COMPLANGUAGE =(BASIC,COBOL,PASCAL,FORTRAN,APL);
```

| $\underline{X}$ | PRED(X) | SUCC(X) | ORD(X) |
|---|---|---|---|
| 1. FORD | _____ | _____ | _____ |
| 2. CBS | _____ | _____ | _____ |
| 3. TUESDAY | _____ | _____ | _____ |
| 4. CHRYSLER | _____ | _____ | _____ |
| 5. PASCAL | _____ | _____ | _____ |
| 6. THURSDAY | _____ | _____ | _____ |
| 7. COBOL | _____ | _____ | _____ |
| 8. WEDNESDAY | _____ | _____ | _____ |
| 9. ABC | * | _____ | _____ |
| 10. FORTRAN | _____ | _____ | _____ |

*This is UNDEFINED since it is the first element.

**Chapter 13**

# Sets and Records

**What You Will Learn**

- How a set is defined.
- To use set type declarations.
- Set operators (union, intersection, and difference) and relational operators.
- How a record is defined.
- To use the "field selector" to reference individual fields of a record.
- To use the WITH statement.

## More on Sets

In Chapter 11, you were introduced to the reserved word **SET** when you ran Exercise 11–8 and Practice 11–2. Let's look at sets more closely.

Sets are collections of data items all of the same type. They are similar to arrays except that there are no subscripts (that is, A[1], A[2], and so on). The data type of the items that belong to a set is called the set's base type. Only scalar types may be specified as the base type of a set.

One of the things you can do with sets is to manipulate them. You can combine them in various ways using the set operators Union, Difference, and Intersection.

You can compare each set's contents using the set relational operators (as you will see soon), and you can test them to determine whether or not a data item is a member of a set.

As you saw in chapter 11, one of the most important uses of sets is to test character input (that is, **SET** OF CHAR) so that you can protect the user of a program from undesired results if the wrong key is pressed when entering data from the keyboard.

Refer to Exercise 11–8 on page 216 and note that BADNOTES was a **SET OF** CHAR that produced no output, even if one of the designated BADNOTES characters was entered from the keyboard.

## Examples of Set Construction

The simplest way to construct a set is to list its elements. Here are some examples of sets:

| SET (Base type) | MEANING |
|---|---|
| [ ] | An "empty set," or a set with no elements. |
| [RED,YEL,BLU] | A set of colors. |
| [1,3,5,7,9] | A set of odd integers. |
| [2,4,6,8] | A set of even integers. |
| ['A','E','I','O','U'] | A set of vowels. |
| [DOE,RE,MI,FA] | A set of notes. |
| ['A'..'Z'] | A set of type CHAR that includes all 26 letters. (This is also a subrange of type CHAR which may be used as a base type.) |
| ['0'..'9'] | A set of type INTEGER that includes all digits from 0 to 9 inclusive. (This is also a subrange of type INTEGER.) |

### Notes

1. The square brackets ([ ]) are used to denote that elements are members of the same set.

2. The elements in the bracket comprise the base type that specifies the range of values for the declared set type.

3. The base type must be a scalar type.

4. A subrange of INTEGERS or CHARACTERS may be a base type.

## Set Type Declarations

*Apple Pascal supports all of the standard Pascal constructs for sets with the following limitations: A set may not have more than 512 elements assigned to it. A set may not have any integers less than 0 or greater than 511 assigned to it.*

In most applications where a set is used, the type of the set is usually CHAR or a user-defined scalar type. The general form for set type declaration is shown below:

```
<SET TYPE> =      SET OF   <BASE TYPE>
```

NAME OR IDENTIFIER    RESERVED WORDS

SPECIFIES THE RANGE VALUES FOR <SET TYPE>.
– MUST BE A SCALAR TYPE.
– CAN BE A SUBRANGE OF INTEGERS OR CHARACTERS.

### Declarations and Assignment of Sets

When the base type is one of the standard predefined data types (that is, INTEGER, REAL, CHAR, STRING), you may declare a set as follows:

```
VAR
   VOWELS,UPPERCASE,LOWERCASE,DIGITS:SET OF CHAR;

BEGIN
   VOWELS:=['A','E','I'.'O','U'];
   UPPERCASE:=['A'..'Z'];
   LOWERCASE:=['a'..'z'];
   DIGITS:=['0'..'9'];
   .
   .
   .
END.
```

The following is an example of how declaration and assignments are made when the base type is a user-defined data type:

```
TYPE
   TVS=(RCA,ZENITH,SYLVANIA,SONY,HITACHI,PHILCO,GE,SANYO);
   BRAND=SET OF TVS;

VAR
   HOME,SCHOOL,LODGING,HEALTHCARE:BRAND;

BEGIN (*TOP 3 TV BRANDS IN EACH MARKET SEGMENT*)
   HOME:=[RCA,ZENITH,SONY];
   SCHOOL:=[SONY,HITACHI,GE];
   LODGING:=[RCA,ZENITH,GE];
   HEALTHCARE:=[SONY,SYLVANIA,RCA];
   .
   .
   .
END.
```

### Notes

- The initial element of a set must always be specified using a **SET** assignment statement before a set can be manipulated.

- Each assignment statement consists of a set variable on the left and a set value on the right separated by (:=).

- In the second example here, TVS is a user-defined scalar data type and BRAND is a **SET** data type. HOME, SCHOOL, LODGING, and HEALTH CARE are variables of type BRAND.

- An empty set, [ ], or a set with no elements may be used to initialize a set variable.

## Set Operators (Union, Intersection, and Difference)

There are three operators that have special meaning when applied to sets. These are:

| OPERATOR | MEANING |
|----------|--------------|
| + | UNION |
| * | INTERSECTION |
| – | DIFFERENCE |

The *union* of two sets is a new set that contains all the elements of the other two. For example,

| ORIGINAL SETS | NEW SETS |
|---------------|----------|
| [A,B,C] + [A,C,D] | [A,B,C,D] |
| [1,2,4,5] + [1,3,4,6] | [1,2,3,4,5,6] |

*If a set has no numbers at all, it is called an empty set.*

The *intersection* of two sets is a new set that contains all the elements common to both sets. For example,

| ORIGINAL SETS | NEW SETS |
|---------------|----------|
| ['A','E','I','O','U'] * ['A','B','C','I','J','K'] | ['A','I'] |
| [1,2,4,5] * [1,3,4,6] | [1,4] |
| [1,2,3,4] * [5,6,7,8] | [ ] |

The *difference* between set A and set B is a new set of elements that are in set A but not in set B. For example:

| SET A | SET B | NEW SET |
|-------|-------|---------|
| [1,2,4,6] − [1,3,4,6,] | | [2] |
| ['A','E','I','O','U'] | −['A','B','C','I','J','K'] | ['E','O','U'] |

## Set Relational Operators

Set relational operators allow a computer to compare the contents of two sets. The relational operators include: $=, <>, <=, <, >=, >$. In addition to the relational operators, there is an operator, **IN,** which is used to test set membership.

| SYMBOL | MEANING | EXAMPLES |
|--------|---------|----------|
| = | Set equality (A = B). | [2,5] = [2,5] is TRUE <br> [2,5] = [5,2] is TRUE |
| < > | Set inequality (A<>B). | [2,5]<>[1,7] is TRUE <br> [2,5]<>[2,5] is FALSE |
| < = | Subset, or "is contained in" A<=B means A is a subset of B if every element of set A is contained in set B. | [2,5]<=[1,2,5,6] is TRUE <br> [2,5]<=[2,5] is TRUE <br><br> [1,2,5,6]<=[2,5] is FALSE <br><br> [ ]<=[2,5] is TRUE |
| < | Proper subset (A<B) means A is a proper subset of B. That is, A is a subset of B if there is at least one element in B that is *not* in A. | [2,5]<[2,4,6,8] is TRUE <br> [2,5]<[2,5] is FALSE <br> [ ]<[2,5] is TRUE |
| > = | Superset, or "contains." A>=B means A is a superset of B if set A contains every element of set B. | [1,2,5,6]>=[2,5] is TRUE <br> [2,5]>=[2,5,6] is FALSE <br> [2]>=[ ] is TRUE |
| > | Proper Superset (A>B) means A is a superset of B. That is, A is a superset of B if there is at least one element of A *not* in B. | [2,4,6,8]>[2,4] is TRUE <br> [2,4]>[2,4] is FALSE <br> [2]>[ ] is TRUE |
| IN | Set membership test. Test to see if an element is a member of a set. | 5 IN [4,5,6] is TRUE <br> 1 IN [4,5,6] is FALSE <br> 'A' **IN** ['A','B','C'] is TRUE <br> 'D' IN ['A','B','C'] is FALSE |

> **NOTE:** Equality means that both sets contain exactly the same elements. The empty set, [ ], is a subset or "is contained in" every set. The order in which elements of a set are listed is not important, that is, [2,5] and [5,2] denote the same set.

## EXERCISE 13–1

### Using Sets to Test Keyboard Inputs

1. Enter the following program.

```
PROGRAM VOWELCK;

  TYPE
    LETTERSET = SET OF CHAR;

  VAR
    VOWELS,LETTERS:LETTERSET;
    CHARACTER:CHAR;

  BEGIN
    LETTERS:=['A'..'Z'];
    VOWELS:=['A','E','I','O','U'];
    WRITELN('TYPE IN ANY LETTER');
    WRITELN('TYPE A PERIOD TO QUIT');
    WRITELN;
    REPEAT
      WRITE('ENTER A LETTER, PLEASE? ');
      READ(CHARACTER);
      WRITELN;
      IF CHARACTER IN VOWELS THEN
          WRITELN(CHARACTER,' IS A VOWEL.')
      ELSE
          IF CHARACTER IN LETTERS THEN
              WRITELN(CHARACTER,' IS A CONSONANT.')
          ELSE
              WRITELN('I DO NOT KNOW WHAT IT IS?');
      WRITELN;
    UNTIL CHARACTER = '.'
  END. (* VOWELCK *)
```

2. Trace the program manually.

3. Run the program several times, or until you feel you understand it.

### Notes:

1. The variables VOWELS and LETTERS are of type LETTERSET.

2. LETTERSET is defined in the **TYPE** block with a **SET** OF CHAR specified as its base type. This means that a variable of type LETTERSET can have as a value any particular set of characters.

3. The first line of the main program block (**BEGIN/END**) assigns the 26 letters of the alphabet to the variable LETTERS, and the second line assigns the vowels ['A', 'E', 'I', 'O', 'U'] to the variable VOWELS.

4. The WRITELN statement prompts the user, then the **REPEAT-UNTIL** loop accepts input from the keyboard and tests the input to see if it is made up of vowels, consonants, or something else, and then prints the results on the display.

5. The program continues until the user types a period.

## EXERCISE 13–2

### Using Sets to Count Keyboard Inputs (CHARCOUNT)

1. Enter the program CHARCOUNT.

```
PROGRAM CHARCOUNT;

  VAR
    CH:CHAR;
    DIGITCOUNT,VOWELCOUNT:INTEGER;

BEGIN

  (* INITIALIZE COUNTERS *)
  DIGITCOUNT:=0;
  VOWELCOUNT:=0;

  WRITELN;
  WRITELN('ENTER ANY CHARACTER');
  WRITELN('TYPE A PERIOD TO QUIT');
  WRITELN;
  REPEAT
    READ(CH);
    IF CH IN ['A','E','I','O','U'
            ,'1','2','3','4','5','6','7','8','9','0'] THEN
      CASE CH OF
          '1','2','3','4','5','6','7','8','9','0':DIGITCOUNT:=DIGITCOUNT+1;
          'A','E','I','O','U':VOWELCOUNT:=VOWELCOUNT+1
        END; (* CASE CH *)
  UNTIL CH = '.';
  WRITELN;
  WRITELN;
  WRITELN('THE NUMBER OF DIGITS ARE ',DIGITCOUNT);
  WRITELN('THE NUMBER OF VOWELS ARE ',VOWELCOUNT)
END. (* CHARCOUNT *)
```

2. Trace the program manually and predict the output.

3. Run the program several times.

### Notes:

1. The elements of the set to be tested include vowels and digits.

2. DIGITCOUNT and VOWELCOUNT are simple variable counters which keep track of the number of vowels and digits.

3. If you enter a character from the keyboard that is not in the declared set, it is ignored or not counted.

## Summary of Sets

1. Sets are used as an easy means of identifying data values in a collection. Therefore, the set data type is one of the available alternatives that should be considered when devising an appropriate data structure.

2. A set variable must always be initialized before it can be manipulated.

3. The set membership operator **(IN)** makes it easy to search a set for a specific element.

4. The base type, specified in a declaration, indicates which values belong to a set.

## Records

A record is a collection of two or more related items. The data items in a record need not be of the same data type (and in most cases, are not). You can use records to store a variety of information about a person, a place, or a thing. A record is a type of data that is unique to Pascal.

The following is the format for a record.

```
TYPE

<NAME OF RECORD TYPE> = RECORD
                        <FIELD-NAME1> : <DATA-TYPE1>;
                        <FIELD-NAME2> : <DATA-TYPE1>;
                            .
                            .
                            .
                        <FIELD-NAMEn> : <DATA-TYPEn>
                        END;
```

### Notes:

1. A record type consists of the keywords **RECORD** and **END,** which enclose several lines that are called fields.

2. Each field has two properties, NAME and TYPE (much like a variable).

3. The fields of a record may be simple data types (that is, INTEGER, REAL, CHAR), or more complex types, such as ARRAYS, SETS, or even records themselves.

4. A null field list is illegal. That is, the construction
   **RECORD**
      **END;**
   will cause an error.

```
              TYPE                         RESERVED WORD

              STUDENT=RECORD                        FIELDS OF RECORDS
                      NAME:STRING [20];
NAME OF RECORD        IDNO:INTEGER;
                      SPORT:STRING [20];
                      GRADEPT:  REAL
                      END; (*STUDENT*)


              VAR
                  ATHLETE: STUDENT;


        NAME OF VARIABLE FOR THIS
        RECORD TYPE
```

To declare a record, you must specify the name of the record and the name and type of each field of the record.

The following example of a record shows a record named STUDENT and a record variable named ATHLETE. The record's field contains two strings (NAME and SPORT), an INTEGER (IDNO), and a REAL number (GRADEPT).

The following is an example of records with fields of simple data types:

```
TYPE
   STUDENT=RECORD
              NAME:STRING[20];
              IDNO:INTEGER;
              GRADEPT:REAL;
              CLASS:1984..1990
           END;
```

The following is an example of a record with fields of more complex data types:

```
TYPE
   MONTHTYPE=(JAN,FEB,MAR,APR,MAY,JUN,JUL,AUG,SEP,OCT,NOV,DEC);
   DATETYPE=RECORD
              DAY:1..31;
              MONTH:MONTHTYPE;
              YEAR:INTEGER
           END;

   STUDENT=RECORD
              NAME:STRING[20];
              IDNO:1000..9999;
              BIRTHDATE:DATETYPE;
              GRADEPT:ARRAY[1..5] OF REAL
           END;
```

**FIELD OF TYPE RECORD** →

**Notes:**

1. A record is a collection of fields that may be of different types. A field may be of a simple data type (that is, INTEGER, REAL, CHAR) or of a more complex data type (that is, an ARRAY, SET, or even another record).

2. Each field of a record has its own type and is subject to all the rules that apply to that type.

**Using the "Field Selector" to Reference Individual Fields of a Record**

In Pascal, you are able to reference each record field using a "field designator" or "field selector." A field selector consists of a record name followed by a period, and then a field name of the record to be accessed. The field selector format is as follows:

```
<RECORD NAME>.<FIELD NAME>
                ↑
              (period)
```

The following is an example of storing data in a record using assignment statements:

```
BEGIN
   ATHLETE.NAME    := SAM JONES;
   ATHLETE.IDNO    := 123456;
   ATHLETE.SPORT   := FOOTBALL;
   ATHLETE.GRADEPT:=3.5
END;
```

The following is an example of inputting data into a record via the keyboard:

```
BEGIN
   READLN(ATHLETE.NAME);
   READLN(ATHLETE.IDNO);
   READLN(ATHLETE.SPORT);
   READLN(ATHLETE.GRADEPT)
END;
```

The following is an example of outputting data from a record:

```
BEGIN
   WRITELN(ATHLETE.NAME);
   WRITELN(ATHLETE.IDNO);
   WRITELN(ATHLETE.SPORT);
   WRITELN(ATHLETE.GRADEPT)
END;
```

## The WITH Statement

Once data are stored in a record, they can be manipulated. As shown in the previous section, each field in a record can be accessed through its field selector. But it becomes tedious to write the complete field selector each time you wish to reference a field of a record. Pascal gives you a way to abbreviate the field selector through the use of the **WITH** statement. The format is as follows:

```
WITH <RECORD-NAME> DO

    <STATEMENT BODY>
```

Note the following:

1. **WITH** and **DO** are reserved words.

2. <RECORD-NAME> is the name of a variable of type RECORD.

3. The <STATEMENT BODY> is a single or compound statement. But in most cases, a compound statement is used, and, therefore, the statement must be bracketed by **BEGIN** and **END.** For example,

```
WITH <RECORD-NAME> DO

  BEGIN
    <STATEMENT1>;
    <STATEMENT2>;
      •
      •
      •

  END;
```

4. The **WITH** statement allows the <RECORD-NAME> to be specified only once, thereby eliminating the need to specify the <RECORD-NAME> every time.

The following is an example of reading data; a comparison is made between the field selector and the **WITH** statement.

### GOOD

```
BEGIN
  READLN (ATHLETE.NAME);
  READLN (ATHLETE.IDNO);
  READLN (ATHLETE.SPORT);
  READLN (ATHLETE.GRADEPT)
END;
```

Notes:

1. The complete field selector is written for each field.

2. The above approach would become very tedious if you had to type the complete field selector for many records.

### BETTER

```
WITH ATHLETE DO
  BEGIN
    READLN (NAME);
    READLN (IDNO);
    READLN (SPORT);
    READLN (GRADEPT)
  END; (*WITH*)
```

Notes:

1. It is not necessary to specify both the record variable and field names inside the **WITH** statement.

2. The **WITH** statement allows you to specify the record variable name (ATHLETE) only once, and then omit it inside the **WITH** statement.

3. The **WITH-DO** statement saves typing and provides a convenience to you.

## EXERCISE 13–3

**Student Eligibility
Program**
         1. Enter the program ELIGIBILITY.

```
PROGRAM ELIGIBILITY;

  CONST
    N = 5;

  TYPE
    STUDENTREC = RECORD
                   NAME:STRING[20];
                   IDNO:INTEGER;
                   SPORT:STRING[20];
                   GRADEPT:REAL
                 END; (* STUDENTREC *)

  VAR
    ATHLETE:ARRAY[1..N] OF STUDENTREC;
    I:INTEGER;


(* MAIN PROGRAM BLOCK *)

BEGIN
  WRITELN('ENTER DATA ON STUDENT');
  WRITELN;
  FOR I := 1 TO N DO
    BEGIN
      WITH ATHLETE[I] DO
        BEGIN
          WRITE('ENTER STUDENT #',I,' NAME: ');
          READLN(NAME);
          WRITE('          ID NUMBER: ');
          READLN(IDNO);
          WRITE('              SPORT: ');
          READLN(SPORT);
          WRITE('       GRADE PT AVG: ');
          READLN(GRADEPT)
        END; (* WITH ATHLETE *)
      WRITELN
    END; (* FOR I *)
  WRITELN;
  WRITELN('THE FOLLOWING STUDENTS ARE ELIGIBLE:');
  WRITELN('------------------------------------');
  FOR I := 1 TO N DO
    IF ATHLETE[I].GRADEPT >= 2.5 THEN
      WRITELN(ATHLETE[I].NAME,' IS ELIGIBLE FOR ',ATHLETE[I].SPORT)
END. (* ELIGIBILITY *)
```

         2. Trace the program manually and predict the output.

         3. Run the program several times.

### Analysis of the Program ELIGIBILITY

1. One way to look at the program is to envision the block structure using a conceptual block diagram.

2. The conceptual block diagram as shown below divides the main program block into the three steps of data processing: input, processing, and output. This was done to help you to visualize the structure from a data-processing perspective.

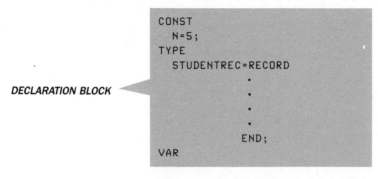

**DECLARATION BLOCK**

```
CONST
  N=5;
TYPE
  STUDENTREC=RECORD
              .
              .
              .
              .
              END;
VAR
```

**MAIN PROGRAM BLOCK**

```
BEGIN
  INPUT
  (ENTER DATA INTO RECORDS)

  PROCESSING
  (TEST FOR GRADEPT>=2.5)

  OUTPUT
  (WRITELN ELIGIBLE STUDENTS)
END. (*ELIGIBILITY*)
```

3. Note the spacing used in writing this program. For example, the fields are indented two spaces in the record declaration.

4. Note, also, the consistent use of spacing throughout the program. For example, spacing is used in the WRITE statements that are used for prompts. The spacing you use is up to you, but you should use spacing where possible to improve the clarity of your program.

5. If you wish to increase the number of records this program processes, simply change the value of **CONST** N to a larger number.

## EXERCISE 13–4

### Payroll Program

1. Enter the program PAYROLL.

```
PROGRAM PAYROLL;

  CONST
    N = 2;

  TYPE
    WORKREC = RECORD
                  NAME:STRING[20];
                  IDNO:INTEGER;
                  HOURS:INTEGER;
                  PAYRATE:REAL;
                  PAY:REAL
                END; (* WORKREC *)

  VAR
    WORKER:ARRAY[1..N] OF WORKREC;
    I,OTHOURS:INTEGER;
    OTRATE:REAL;


  BEGIN
    WRITELN('THIS PROGRAM PROCESSES A PAYROLL');
    WRITELN;

    (* READ WORKER'S INFORMATION *)

    FOR I := 1 TO N DO
      BEGIN
        WITH WORKER[I] DO
          BEGIN
            WRITE('ENTER WORKER #',I,' NAME: ');
            READLN(NAME);
            WRITE('          ID NUMBER: ');
            READLN(IDNO);
            WRITE('        HOURS WORKED: ');
            READLN(HOURS);
            WRITE('            PAYRATE: ');
            READLN(PAYRATE)
          END; (* WITH WORKER *)
```

```
(* CALCULATE WORKER'S PAY *)

    IF WORKER[I].HOURS <= 40 THEN
       WORKER[I].PAY:=WORKER[I].HOURS*WORKER[I].PAYRATE
    ELSE
       BEGIN
          OTHOURS:=WORKER[I].HOURS-40;
          OTRATE:=WORKER[I].PAYRATE*1.5;
          WORKER[I].PAY:=(OTHOURS*OTRATE)+(40*WORKER[I].PAYRATE)
       END; (* ELSE HOURS *)
    WRITELN
  END; (* FOR LCV *)
WRITELN;
WRITELN;


(* PRINT WORKER'S PAY *)

WRITELN('NAME              ID NO.  HOURS      PAY');
FOR I :=1 TO N DO
  BEGIN
    WITH WORKER[I] DO
       WRITELN(NAME,'      ',IDNO,'       ',HOURS,'      $',PAY:2:2);
  END(* FOR LCV *)
END. (* PAYROLL *)
```

2. Trace the program manually and predict the output.

3. Run the program several times.

4. Change the value of N and run the program again.

## Analysis of the Program PAYROLL

1. This program processes a payroll for two employees. If you wish to increase the number of employees from 2 to 10 or even 100, all you have to do is change the value of the **CONST** N to the desired number.

2. A conceptual block diagram of the program structure is shown below:

**DECLARATION BLOCK**

```
CONST
   N=2;
TYPE
   WORKREC=RECORD;
                .
                .
                .
                END;
VAR
```

**MAIN PROGRAM BLOCK**

```
BEGIN
    INPUT
    (*READ WORKER'S INFORMATION*)

    PROCESSING
    (*CALCULATE WORKER'S PAY*)

    OUTPUT
    (*PRINT WORKER'S PAY*)
END.
```

3. Note the formatting of the output. Specifically, note the following:
   a. The spacing used in the last WRITELN statement between the NAME, IDNO, HOURS, and PAY.
   b. The 2:2 specifies fieldwith:fractionlength, respectively. The fieldwith, 2, specifies the minimum number of characters to be written, and fractionlength specifies the number of digits (2) to be written after the decimal point.

4. Two key assumptions were made in developing this program:
   a. A standard work week of 40 hours.
   b. A worker receives time and a half for overtime (that is, 1.5 times the normal rate).

## EXERCISE 13–5

**The Program
PASSFAIL**

1. Enter the program PASSFAIL.

```
PROGRAM PASSFAIL;

  CONST
    N = 10;

  TYPE
    STUDENTREC = RECORD
                      NAME:STRING[20];
                      IDNO:1000..9999;
                      STATUS:CHAR
                    END;(* STUDENTREC *)

  VAR
    STUDENT,PASS,FAIL:ARRAY[1..N] OF STUDENTREC;
    I,P,F:INTEGER;

BEGIN
  WRITELN('THIS PROGRAM CREATES TWO RECORDS');
  WRITELN('ONE FOR PASS AND ONE FOR FAIL');
  WRITELN;
  FOR I := 1 TO N DO
    WITH STUDENT[I] DO
      BEGIN
        WRITE('ENTER STUDENT #',I,': ');
        READLN(NAME);
        WRITE('      ID NUMBER: ');
        READLN(IDNO);
        WRITE('     (PASS/FAIL): ');
        READLN(STATUS);
        WRITELN
      END; (* WITH STUDENT *)

  (* DETERMINE PASS OR FAIL *)

  P:=1;
  F:=1;
  FOR I := 1 TO N DO
    BEGIN
      IF STUDENT[I].STATUS = 'P' THEN
        BEGIN
          PASS[P]:=STUDENT[I];
          P:=P+1
        END
      ELSE
        BEGIN
          FAIL[F]:=STUDENT[I];
          F:=F+1
        END; (* IF STUDENT *)
    END; (* FOR I *)
```

*(*program continued on next page*)*

*(*program continued from previous page*)*

```
  (* PRINT PASS RECORD *)

  WRITELN('PASS RECORD');
  WRITELN('-----------');
  FOR I := 1 TO P-1 DO
    BEGIN
      WITH PASS[I] DO
          WRITELN(NAME,'      ',IDNO)
    END; (* FOR I *)
END. (* PASSFAIL *)
```

2. Trace the program manually and predict the output.
   a. What happens if you change the value of the constant N?
   b. Why were the variables P and F assigned a value of 1?
   c. Why were the variables P and F incremented by 1 (that is, P:=P+1 and F:=F+1)?

### Analysis of the Program PASSFAIL

1. This program processes ten student records, and prints out the records of the students who passed.

2. A conceptual block diagram of the program structure is shown below:

```
DECLARATION BLOCK  ◄    CONST
                          N=10;
                        TYPE
                          STUDSENTREC=RECORD
                                      .
                                      .
                                      .
                                    END;
                        VAR
```

```
MAIN PROGRAM BLOCK  ◄   BEGIN
                          INPUT
                          (*STUDENT INFO*)

                          PROCESSING
                          (*DETERMINE PASS OR FAIL*)

                          OUTPUT
                          (*PRINT PASS RECORD*)

                        END.
```

## Summary

### COMPARISON OF ARRAY, RECORD, AND SET

| ARRAY | RECORD | SET |
|---|---|---|
| A collection of data items all of the same type that have been grouped together and indexed. | A collection of two or more related data items. | A collection of data items all of the same data type. |

**ARRAY**

A collection of data items all of the same type that have been grouped together and indexed.

– An array provides you with another way of assigning many more values to a single variable name.

– The array allows you to arrange your data items so that they can be stored and retrieved easier.

Each item of an array can be accessed via a single name with a unique subscript or index (for example, A[1]).

**RECORD**

A collection of two or more related data items.

– Unlike an array, individual components of a record can contain data of different types.

– The individual components or fields of a record may be simple data types (that is, INTEGER, REAL, CHAR) and also structured data types (that is, ARRAYS, SETS, or another record).

– You can use records to ·store many kinds of information about a person, place, or thing.

There are three different ways to access values stored in a variable of type RECORD:

1) You can access individual fields using the "field selector" or "record name–period–field name" rotation (for example, ATHLETE.NAME).

2) You can use the **WITH** statement to access fields without having to write the "record name and period" for each field.

3) You can access the complete record using a single statement. (This access method was not covered in this book.)

**SET**

A collection of data items all of the same data type.

– A set is similar to an array, except that there is no indexing (that is, no subscripts).

– The data type of the objects that belong to a set must be a scalar type.

Apple Pascal supports all of the standard constructs for sets, with the following limitations:

– A set may *not* have more than 512 elements assigned to it.

– A set may not have integers less than 0 or greater than 511 assigned to it.

You *cannot* access an element of a set the way you can access elements of an array. You can, however, manipulate sets. You can combine them in various ways, compare them as to their contents, and test them for membership of a set.

– One of the most important uses of sets is to test character input so that you can protect the user of a program from undesired results if the wrong key is pressed when entering data from the keyboard.

## PRACTICE 13–1

### Sets (Digit/Character Check)

a. Write a program to read digits from the keyboard and display the digits as entered. Your program should label the results as shown.

YOUR DIGIT IS (Digit).

b. Write a program to read characters from the keyboard and display the characters as entered. Your program should label your results as shown:

YOUR LETTER IS (Letter).

## PRACTICE 13–2

### PASSFAIL Program

1. Add the necessary program lines to the program in Exercise 13–5 to print out the number of students who failed.

## PRACTICE 13–3

### Programs Using Records to Compute Test Average

1. Write a program to compute student average and class average. The program should do the following:
   a. Read in five student names and ID numbers.
   b. Read in the grades from five tests.
   c. Print out student name, ID number, and test average.
   d. Print out class averages.

Hints:

```
CONST
  N=5;
TYPE
  STUDENTREC=RECORD
                NAME:STRING[20];
                IDNO:INTEGER;
                TEST: ARRAY [1..5] OF REAL;
                TESTAVG:ARRAY [1..N] OF REAL
             END;(*STUDENTREC*)
VAR
  STUDENT:ARRAY[1..N] OF STUDENTREC;
```

*Courtesy of Apple Computer Inc.*

# Chapter 14

# Putting It All Together

## What You Will Learn

Throughout this book, you have learned the basic rules of UCSD Pascal language as used on Apple computers. Most of the examples of programming so far have been short examples; nevertheless, you have acquired enough skills to write simple programs to solve simple problems. But one of the most important things you have learned in this book is how the structure of Pascal will permit you to break large and complex programs into manageable pieces. That is, if you structure your program properly, the main program block of your program will do nothing more than allow the user to select the function he or she wishes to use, and then call a procedure to actually do the work. If you develop your programs this way, you will be taking advantage of the power of Pascal.

In this chapter, we illustrate the technique of using a structured approach to problem solving and programming. More specifically, this chapter covers the following:

- A structured approach to problem solving.

- Starting from the top—step 1.

- Filling in the data boxes—step 2.

- Developing an algorithm—step 3.

- Improving the algorithm—step 4.

- Transforming the algorithm into a program—step 5.

## A Structured Approach to Problem Solving

First, determine what your program is supposed to do. Next, split your problem into the three phases of data processing: input, processing, and output. (See Fig. 14–1.) Then, fill in the information for each of the phases by asking yourself a series of questions: Start with questions about the output, then the input, and finally about processing. For example:

### OUTPUT

1. What are my output requirements?

2. What results are required?

### INPUT

1. What do I know about my input data?

2. What type of input data do I need? Do I have all that I need? If not, can I get it?

### PROCESSING

1. What is the relationship between my input data and output data? Can I express it in words? Can I express it mathematically? How do I use my input data to get the desired output?

2. Is sufficient input data available to compute the required output? If not, how do I get it?

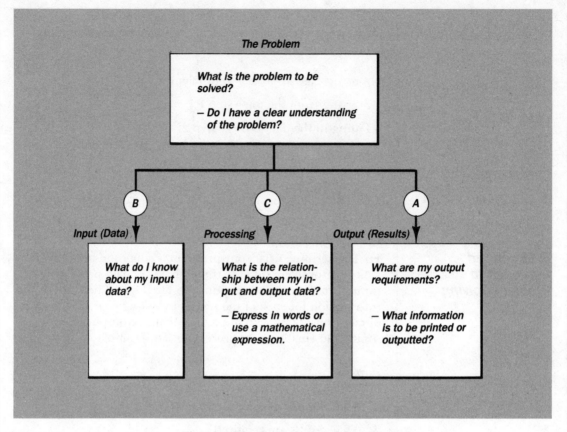

*Fig. 14–1 The three phases of data processing.*

### Starting from the Top—Step 1

*The problem:* Determine the profit/loss for a small business that manufactures widgets.

| INPUT | PROCESSING | OUTPUT |
|---|---|---|
| Here is the input data needed: | What is the relationship between input data and output data? | Here are the results to be printed out: |
| Unit cost ($) | | Total cost ($) |
| Unit price ($) | Compute the total cost. | Total sales ($) |
| Number of units sold | Compute the total sales. | Profit/loss ($) |
| | Compute the profit/loss. | Profit as percentage of sales |
| | Compute percentage of profit. | |

If you understand the problem, then the output or results required should be known. After all, you might not know how to solve the problem initially, but you certainly should have a pretty good idea of what you are looking for. Even if you do not have a computer, you should be able to determine the input data needed in order to process your output.

Think about the relationship between your input and output data. At this point, you should know the input to be processed and the information that will be required for your output. Now all you have to do is develop a strategy for solving your problem. (We will develop the strategy later.)

### Filling in the Data Boxes—Step 2

| *INPUT* | | *PROCESSING* | *OUTPUT* | |
|---|---|---|---|---|
| Variables: | | Other variables: | Variables: | |
| <u>NAME</u> | <u>TYPE</u> | None | <u>NAME</u> | <u>TYPE</u> |
| COST | REAL | | TOTALCOST | REAL |
| PRICE | REAL | | TOTALSALES | REAL |
| UNITS | INTEGER | | PERCENTPROFIT | REAL |
| | | | PROFIT | REAL |

List data whose values are entered via READ statements as input variables, and list variables whose values represent the results required after processing or computation as output variables. For some programs, other variables may be required to store intermediate processing results, but these are not required for this example.

### Developing an Algorithm—Step 3

This section explores the strategy for getting from the input to the output.

**Input**          READ the data items into variables COST, PRICE, and UNITS.

**Processing**     Compute
                   TOTALCOST
                   TOTALSALES
                   PROFIT
                   PERCENTPROFIT

**Output**         Print the values of the variables COST, PRICE, UNITS, TOTALCOST, TOTALSALES, and PERCENTPROFIT.

Most books refer to this step as developing an algorithm. An *algorithm* is a step-by-step procedure or a sequence of instructions that will help you solve problems. In more sophisticated approaches, the algorithm is developed and then refined until it can be easily implemented into Pascal code.

If you are uncomfortable with the term *algorithm,* think of this step as developing your strategy for solving the problem. That is, you will determine how to use your input data to get the desired output. Simply list all the steps in sequence that you need to solve the problem. These steps should be written for you (not for a computer), and they can be somewhat loosely defined initially. A mathematical expression (if you know one) is appropriate here.

## *Improving the Algorithm—Step 4*

**Input**      INPUT(COST)
             INPUT(PRICE)
             INPUT(UNITS)

**Processing**   TOTALCOST = COST*UNITS
             TOTALSALES = PRICE*UNITS
             PROFIT = TOTALSALES–TOTALCOST
             PERCENTPROFIT = PROFIT/TOTALSALES

**Output**     PRINT NO. OF UNITS
             PRINT UNIT COST
             PRINT TOTALCOST
             PRINT UNIT PRICE
             PRINT TOTALSALES
             PRINT PROFIT/LOSS
             PRINT PERCENTPROFIT

To improve the algorithm simply means to refine it until it can be easily transformed to a Pascal program. In this example, we simply added a little more detail about the input and output together with adding the mathematical expressions that use the input data to get the desired output.

Some people find it easy to develop algorithms, while others struggle with the process. It is important to develop your skills in using algorithms. Although most of the problems we have covered thus far could be done without developing a formal algorithm, you will need to understand this process for larger and more complex programs.

It is not the intent here to discuss problem solving in great detail but to merely expose you to some of the techniques.

### Transforming the Algorithm into a Program—Step 5

Now that you have split the problem into more manageable pieces or subtasks, you can use your knowledge of the Pascal programming language to develop a working program. How you attack the program from here depends on your skill as a programmer and the programming tools available to you on your computer. But, for the basic approach, we will take advantage of the features of Pascal to structure our program so that the main program block will simply call procedures to do the work. That is, our structure will look like this:

```
PROGRAM PROFITLOSS;

   (*Global Variables*)


VAR

   (*PROCEDURE BLOCKS*)


PROCEDURE INPUTDATA;


PROCEDURE PROCESSDATA;


PROCEDURE OUTPUTDATA;

   (*MAIN PROGRAM BLOCK*)


BEGIN
   INPUTDATA
   PROCESSDATA;          CALL PROCEDURES
   OUTPUTDATA;
END.(*PROFITLOSS*)
```

We elected to use three procedures for this program: INPUTDATA, PROCESSDATA, and OUTPUTDATA. We then used the main program block to call each procedure as required. The above process is an oversimplification of program development, but it does illustrate how to use the structure of Pascal to break large and complex programs into manageable pieces.

## EXERCISE 14–1

1. Enter the following program.

```
PROGRAM PROFITLOSS;


(* GLOBAL VARIABLE *)

  VAR
    COST,PRICE,TOTALCOST,TOTALSALES,PERCENTPROFIT,PROFIT:REAL;
    UNITS:INTEGER;


(* PROCEDURE BLOCK *)

 PROCEDURE INPUTDATA;

  BEGIN
    WRITE('INPUT UNIT COST($) ');
    READLN(COST);
    WRITE('          PRICE($) ');
    READLN(PRICE);
    WRITE('NO. OF UNITS SOLD: ');
    READLN(UNITS)
  END; (* INPUTDATA *)


 PROCEDURE PROCESSDATA;

  BEGIN
    TOTALCOST:=COST*UNITS;
    TOTALSALES:=PRICE*UNITS;
    PROFIT:=TOTALSALES-TOTALCOST;
    PERCENTPROFIT:=(PROFIT/TOTALSALES)*100
  END; (* PROCESSDATA *)


 PROCEDURE OUTPUTDATA;

  BEGIN
    WRITELN;
    WRITELN;
    WRITELN('NO. OF UNITS    ',UNITS);
    WRITELN('          COST $',COST:2:2);
    WRITELN('   TOTAL COST $',TOTALCOST:8:2);
    WRITELN('         PRICE $',PRICE:2:2);
    WRITELN(' TOTAL SALES $',TOTALSALES:8:2);
    WRITELN('  PROFIT/LOSS $',PROFIT:2:2);
    WRITELN('   % OF SALES %',PERCENTPROFIT:2:2)
  END; (* OUTPUTDATA *)
```

*(*program continued on next page*)*

*(\*program continued from previous page\*)*

```
(* MAIN PROGRAM BLOCK *)

BEGIN

  INPUTDATA;
  PROCESSDATA;
  OUTPUTDATA

END. (* PROFITLOSS *)
```

2. Run it several times with different inputs.

**Summary**

To solve a problem using the Pascal programming language, you start much the same way as you do with many other complex tasks: You must plan your attack. Start from the top and work your way down, step by step, until you solve the problem. After you have a clear idea of what has to be done, attack your problem using the following basic steps:

Step 1: Start from the top (and work your way down).

Step 2: Fill in the data boxes (input, output, and other variables).

Step 3: Develop an algorithm (your strategy for attacking the problem).

Step 4: Improve the algorithm. (This is a refinement process. Several levels of refinement may be required.)

Step 5: Transform the algorithm into a Pascal program. (Use your skills as a programmer and the features of Pascal.)

Pascal is designed to facilitate a structured approach to programming. A structured approach generally results in a clear and well-organized program that is easy to read and to debug. Make certain that your program is clearly documented and well-formatted. Make use of descriptive comments wherever possible, and use indentation of program statements within the program to improve the appearance and readability.

One of the most important things covered in this book is how the structure of Pascal permits you to break large and complex programs into manageable pieces.

If you structure your program properly, the main program block of your program will do nothing more than allow the user to select the function he or she wishes to use, and then call a procedure to actually do the work. If you develop your programs this way, you will be taking advantage of the power of Pascal.

There is much more to learn about structured programming. You have only seen the "tip of the iceberg" in this chapter. For those of you who want to learn more about the Pascal programming language and how to program effectively, you must practice, practice, practice. There is no substitute for it. To quote my eighth-grade math instructor: "There are no short cuts; but to he who has patience, the end is well worth the journey."

Finally, if you feel you have mastered the material in this book, then you should attempt to read some of the manuals available on Apple Pascal. In particular, you should be at a point where you can understand some of the sections of the Apple Pascal operating system reference manual and the Apple Pascal language reference manuals. We have tried to select the right mix of information to get you started. Now that we got you started, there should be no stopping you. You can really say now: "I Speak Pascal."

## PRACTICE 14–1

*Your program should use real variables, and each part (a through d) should be written as a separate procedure that can be called by the main program.*

1. Write a program that uses four procedures to do the following:
   a. Find the area of a circle.
   b. Find the area of a rectangle.
   c. Find the area of a square.
   d. Find the area of a triangle.

# Extra
# Practices

## EXTRA PRACTICE 1

**Making Change from a Dollar (DIV and MOD Functions)**

1. Write a program that outputs the change from a dollar using the least number of coins.
   a. Use pennies, nickels, dimes, quarters, and half-dollars.
   b. Use MOD and DIV operators.
   c. Use headings that are neat for the printout.

## EXTRA PRACTICE 2

**Palindrome (COPY and CONCAT Functions)**

1. A palindrome is a word, line, or verse, that reads the same backward or forward (for example, madam). Write a program that permits you to enter a word from the keyboard, and then determine if it is a palindrome.
   a. The output should print "_____ is a palindrome," or "_____ is not a palindrome." The blank should be filled in with the word you are checking.
   b. Use CONCAT and COPY functions in your program.

## EXTRA PRACTICE 3

**Newsbreak (CONCAT, COPY, Keypress Functions, and the GOTOXY Procedure)**

1. Manually trace the following program.

```
PROGRAM NEWSBREAK;

(*THE OUTPUT OF THIS PROGRAM IS A          *)
(*MESSAGE THAT MOVES ACROSS THE SCREEN*)
(*YOU MAY TYPE UP TO 255 CHARACTERS      *)
(*BEFORE PRESSING RETURN                          *)

USES APPLESTUFF;

VAR
  T1,TEMP,NEWS:STRING[255];
  A:INTEGER;

BEGIN

  WRITELN('YOU WILL BE ASKED TO INPUT A MESSAGE');
  WRITELN;
  WRITELN('PRESS THE SPACEBAR TO STOP THE PRINTING');
  WRITELN;
  WRITELN('WHAT IS THE NEWSBREAK?');
  READLN(NEWS);
  NEWS := CONCAT(NEWS,'***');
  REPEAT
    FOR A := 1 TO 250 DO;(*DELAY LOOP*)
    GOTOXY(0,0);(*LOCATION OF MESSAGE*)
    WRITE(NEWS);
    TEMP := COPY(NEWS,2,LENGTH(NEWS)-1);
    T1 := COPY(NEWS,1,1);
    NEWS := CONCAT(TEMP,T1);(*FILO*)
  UNTIL KEYPRESS;
END.
```

2. Predict the output.

3. Enter and run the program.

*Note:* GOTOXY is a built-in procedure that sends the cursor to a specified position on the screen (for example, top, middle, bottom, and so on). The form of the procedure is:

```
GOTOXY (XCOORD, YCOORD)
```

where XCOORD and YCOORD are integer values interpreted as X (horizontal) and Y (vertical) coordinates. XCOORD must be in the range 0 through 79, and YCOORD must be in the range 0 through 23. The cursor is sent to these coordinates. The upper-left corner of the screen is assumed to be (0,0).

4. Modify the program to make the output read across the middle of the screen.

5. Modify the program to make the output read across the bottom of the screen.

## EXTRA PRACTICE 4

### Exponent: Raising Real Numbers to Real Powers

*(This practice is recommended for students who have had Algebra 2).*

1. Manually trace the program REALTOREAL.
   a. Three procedures are used in this program. What is the purpose of each?
   b. A key program statement in procedure INFO is "ANSWER: = EXP POWER*LN(ABS(BASE))." Why did we take the absolute (ABS) of the base?

2. Enter and run the program several times.

```
PROGRAM REALTOREAL;

USES TRANSCEND;

VAR
  BASE,ANSWER,POWER:REAL;
  NUMPOWER,DENPOWER:INTEGER;

PROCEDURE SIGN;
  BEGIN
      IF (BASE<0) AND (ABS(NUMPOWER) MOD 2 <> 0)
        AND (ABS(DENPOWER) MOD 2 <> 0 )   THEN
          WRITELN(-ANSWER:6:4)
    ELSE
      IF (BASE < 0) AND (ABS(NUMPOWER) MOD 2 <> 0)
        AND (ABS(DENPOWER) MOD 2 = 0) THEN
          WRITELN(ANSWER:6:4,' I, IMAGINARY NUMBER.')
    ELSE
      WRITELN(ANSWER:6:4);
  END;(*SIGN*)


PROCEDURE SIMPLEST;

VAR
  A:INTEGER;
  FOUND:BOOLEAN;

BEGIN
  REPEAT

    IF ABS(NUMPOWER) < ABS(DENPOWER) THEN
        A := ABS(NUMPOWER)
    ELSE
        A := ABS(DENPOWER);
    FOUND := FALSE;


    IF A > 1 THEN
      REPEAT
        IF (ABS(NUMPOWER) MOD A= 0) AND
           (ABS(DENPOWER) MOD A = 0) THEN
          BEGIN
            NUMPOWER := NUMPOWER DIV A;
            DENPOWER := DENPOWER DIV A;
            FOUND := TRUE
          END;
        A := A-1
      UNTIL (FOUND = TRUE) OR (A < 2)
    (*REPEAT UNTIL FRACTION IN LOWEST TERMS*)
  UNTIL A < 2
END;(*SIMPLEST*)
```

*(*program continued on next page*)*

*(\*program continued from previous page\*)*

```
PROCEDURE INFO;

BEGIN

  WRITELN('ENTER BASE');
  READLN(BASE);
  WRITELN('IF EXPONENT < 0 THEN ENTER EITHER ');
  WRITELN('NUMERATOR OR DENOMINATOR AS NEGATIVE.');
  WRITELN;
  WRITELN('ENTER NUMERATOR OF EXPONENT');
  READLN(NUMPOWER);
  WRITELN;
  WRITELN('ENTER DENOMINATOR OF EXPONENT');
  READLN(DENPOWER);
  SIMPLEST;(*CHECK FORM OF EXPONENT*)
  POWER := NUMPOWER/DENPOWER;
  ANSWER := EXP(POWER*LN(ABS(BASE)));
  WRITE(BASE:6:2,' ^(',NUMPOWER,'/',DENPOWER,') = ');
  SIGN
END;(*INFO*)

(*MAIN*)
BEGIN
  WRITELN(' THIS PROGRAM RAISES REALS TO ');
  WRITELN(' REAL POWERS IN THE FORM OF RATIONAL');
  WRITELN(' EXPONENTS (A/B WHERE A AND B ARE');
  WRITELN(' INTEGERS AND B <>0 ) REDUCED TO');
  WRITELN(' SIMPLEST FORM.');
  WRITELN(' FOR EXAMPLE;  -27^-6/9 WOULD');
  WRITELN(' BE REDUCED TO -27^-2/3');
  WRITELN(' YOU WILL BE ASKED TO ENTER THE');
  WRITELN(' BASE (A REAL), AND NUMERATOR');
  WRITELN(' AND DENOMINATOR OF THE EXPONENT ');
  WRITELN(' SEPARATELY.');
  WRITELN;WRITELN;
  INFO
END.(*PROGRAM*)
```

## EXTRA PRACTICE 5

### Factorial (Long Integers)

1. Write a program that will print the factorials for each of the numbers 1 through 20. (Note: The factorial is the product of all integers from 1 to n.) For example:

   1! = 1
   2! = 1X2 = 2
   3! = 1X2X3 = 6

   and so on.

## EXTRA PRACTICE 6

**FIBONACCI Numbers (Long Integers)**

1. A FIBONACCI number is an integer in the infinite sequence 1, 1, 2, 3, 5, 8, 13, and so on, of which the first two numbers of the sequence equal 1, and each succeeding number from there on may be found by taking the sum of the previous two terms in the sequence. Write a program that will output 150 numbers. (Note: The FIBONACCI numbers will exceed the MAXINT (32767); therefore, you must use the long integer, which can have up to 36 digits.

## EXTRA PRACTICE 7

**BUBBLE SORT (Arrays and Procedures)**

1. A BUBBLE SORT is a sort in which succeeding pairs of items in a set are examined. If the items in a pair are out of sequence according to the specified criteria, the positions of the items are exchanged. This process is repeated until all items are sorted.

2. Manually trace the program ALFA.
   a. This program sorts items into ascending order. Do you understand how it does this?
   b. If you wanted to change the program to sort in descending order, what changes would you have to make?
   c. If you want this program to just sort integers, what change(s) would you make?

3. Enter and run this program.

```
PROGRAM ALPHA;

(* THE PURPOSE OF THIS PROGRAM IS TO *)
(* ILLUSTRATE THE BUBBLE SORT METHOD *)
(* OF ORDERING AN ARRAY .            *)
```

*(*program continued on next page*)*

```
CONST
  MAX = 5;

VAR
  I:INTEGER;
  MATA:ARRAY[1..MAX] OF STRING;

PROCEDURE SORT;

VAR
  TEMP:STRING;
  SWAP : BOOLEAN;
  PASS : INTEGER;

PROCEDURE PRINTIT;

BEGIN
  FOR I := 1 TO MAX DO
    WRITELN(MATA[I])
END;(*PRINTIT*)

BEGIN
  PASS := 0;

  REPEAT
    SWAP := FALSE;
    PASS := PASS + 1;

    FOR I := 1 TO MAX-1 DO
      BEGIN
        IF MATA[I] > MATA[I+1] THEN
          BEGIN
            SWAP := TRUE;
            TEMP := MATA[I+1];
            MATA[I+1] := MATA[I];
            MATA[I] := TEMP
          END;(*IF*)
      END(*I LOOP*);


  UNTIL SWAP = FALSE;

  WRITELN('IT TOOK ',PASS,' PASSES TO CHECK AND/OR ');
  WRITELN('PUT THE ARRAY INTO ASCENDING ORDER');


  PRINTIT

END;(*SORT*)
```

```
PROCEDURE INFO;

BEGIN
  FOR I := 1 TO MAX DO
    BEGIN
      WRITE('ENTER ITEM ---> ',I,' ');
      READLN(MATA[I]);
      WRITELN
    END;

  SORT;

END;(*INFO*)



BEGIN
  WRITELN('YOU ARE TO INPUT MAX(5) ITEMS ');
  WRITELN('IN ANY ORDER.  THE OUTPUT WILL ');
  WRITELN('BE THE ITEMS IN ASCENDING ORDER');
  WRITELN('NOTE NUMERIC PRECEDE ALPHA STRINGS');
  INFO
END.(*PROGRAM*)
```

---

## EXTRA PRACTICE 8

**WORDLIST (CONCAT, COPY, DELETE, INSERT)**

1. Manually trace the program WORDLIST and predict the output.
   a. What is the purpose of the procedure CLEAROUTPUNCTUATION?
   b. What is the purpose of the procedure FINDSWORDS?
   c. Can you think of an application for this program?

2. Enter and run this program.

```
PROGRAM WORDLIST;

(* PROGRAM WORDLIST COMBINES TWO PROCEDURES, *)
(* CLEAROUTPUNCTUATION AND FINDSWORDS.        *)
(* ADD MORE CHARACTERS TO THE SET PUNCTUATION*)
(* AS NEEDED.                                 *)

VAR
  S:STRING[255];
```

*(*program continued on next page*)*

*(\*program continued from previous page\*)*

```
PROCEDURE FINDSWORDS;

CONST BLANK = ' ';

VAR
  FIRST:INTEGER;
  WORD:STRING;

  BEGIN
    S := CONCAT(S,BLANK);
    WHILE LENGTH(S) > 1 DO
      BEGIN
        FIRST := POS(BLANK,S);
        IF FIRST > 1 THEN
          BEGIN
            WORD := COPY(S,1,FIRST-1);
            WRITELN(WORD)
          END;(*IF*)
        DELETE(S,1,FIRST)
      END(*WHILE*)

  END;(*FINDSWORDS*)

PROCEDURE CLEAROUTPUNCTUATION;

VAR
  PUNCTUATION : SET OF CHAR;
  I:INTEGER;

  BEGIN
    PUNCTUATION :=[',',';','.','-','?',':','"','!'];
    I :=1;
    WHILE I <= LENGTH(S) DO
      BEGIN
        IF S[I] IN PUNCTUATION THEN
          BEGIN
            DELETE (S,I,1);
            INSERT (' ',S,I)
          END;(*IF*)
        I := I+1
      END;(*WHILE*)
    FINDSWORDS
  END;(*CLEAROUTPUNCTUATION*)

  (*MAIN PROGRAM*)

BEGIN
  WRITELN('ENTER ONE OR MORE  SENTENCES OF TOTAL');
  WRITELN('LENGTH LESS THAN 256 BEFORE YOU');
  WRITELN('PRESS RETURN.');
  WRITELN;
  READLN(S);
  CLEAROUTPUNCTUATION
END.(*PROGRAM*)
```

## EXTRA PRACTICE 9

**Prime Numbers (SQRT FCN, MAXINT, *Loops, and Procedures*)**

1. Manually trace the program PRIMENUMS.
   a. How does the procedure TESTNUM determine if a number is a prime number?
   b. What is the purpose of the MOD function in the procedure LISTPRIMES?
   c. The number 2 is the only even prime. Why?

2. Enter and run the program.

```
PROGRAM PRIMENUMS; (*LESS THAN MAXINT*)

(*THIS PROGRAM OUTPUTS PRIMES LESS THAN   *)
(*MAXINT USING THE MOD OPERATOR WHICH     *)
(*CANNOT BE USED ON LONG INTEGERS.        *)

USES TRANSCEND; (*SQRT FCN*)

VAR
  COUNT,NUM,INDEX:INTEGER;
  PRIME:BOOLEAN;
  ANSWER:CHAR;

PROCEDURE LISTPRIMES;
VAR
  HOWMANY:INTEGER; (* < MAXINT *)

  BEGIN
    WRITELN('HOW MANY PRIMES  DO YOU WISH TO PRINT?');
    READLN(HOWMANY);
    WRITELN('BELOW IS A LIST OF THE FIRST');
    WRITELN(HOWMANY,' PRIMES');
    WRITELN('----------');
    IF HOWMANY = 1 THEN
      WRITELN('2')
    ELSE
      BEGIN
        WRITE('2 ');
        COUNT :=2;NUM :=1;
        REPEAT
          NUM := NUM +2; (*ONLY TESTING ODDS FOR PRIMES*)
          PRIME := TRUE; (*ASSUME PRIME UNLESS PROVEN OTHERWISE*)
          INDEX :=3;
          WHILE (PRIME) AND (INDEX<=ROUND(SQRT(NUM)))  DO
            BEGIN
              IF NUM MOD INDEX = 0 THEN
                PRIME := FALSE
              ELSE
                INDEX := INDEX+2;
          END; (*WHILE*)
```

```
                (*program continued from previous page*)

            IF (PRIME) AND (COUNT MOD 5 <> 0) THEN
              WRITE(NUM,' ')
            ELSE
              IF PRIME THEN
                WRITELN(NUM);(*OUTPUT FIVE ON A LINE*)
              IF PRIME THEN
                COUNT := COUNT +1
          UNTIL COUNT > HOWMANY
      END;(*ELSE*)
  END;(*LISTPRIMES*)

PROCEDURE TESTNUM;

  BEGIN
    WRITELN('ENTER A NUMBER TO BE TESTED AS PRIME.');
    READLN(NUM);
    IF NUM = 2 THEN
      WRITELN(NUM,' IS PRIME.')
    ELSE
      IF NUM MOD 2 = 0 THEN
        WRITELN(NUM,' IS NOT PRIME. IT IS AN EVEN NUMBER.')
      ELSE
        BEGIN
          PRIME := TRUE;
          INDEX := 3;
          WHILE (PRIME) AND (INDEX<=ROUND(SQRT(NUM)))  DO
        (*NO NEED TO TEST FURTHER IF NUM IS NOT PRIME*)
        (*OR BEYOND THE SQRT(NUM) FOR DIVISORS        *)
            BEGIN
              IF NUM MOD INDEX = 0 THEN
                PRIME := FALSE
              ELSE
                INDEX := INDEX+2;
            END;(*WHILE*)
          WRITE(NUM);
          CASE PRIME OF
            TRUE:WRITELN(' IS PRIME.');
            FALSE:WRITELN(' IS NOT PRIME. ',INDEX, ' DIVIDES ',NUM,'.');
          END;(*CASE*)
        END;(*ELSE*)
    END;(*TESTNUM*)
```

```
                         (*MAIN PROGRAM*)

                    BEGIN

                      WRITELN('THIS PROGRAM TESTS INTEGERS AS  PRIMES');
                      WRITELN('CHOOSE T OR L FOR ');
                      WRITELN;
                      WRITELN('T)EST ONE NUMBER AS PRIME');
                      WRITELN;
                      WRITELN('L)IST OF PRIMES');
                      READ(ANSWER);
                      PAGE(OUTPUT);
                      CASE ANSWER OF
                        'T':TESTNUM;
                        'L':LISTPRIMES
                      END;(*CASE*)

                    END.(*PROGRAM*)
```

## EXTRA PRACTICE 10

### Baseball Records (Records and Procedures)

1. Write a program that will allow the user to create and list an array of records. A record should include the following data:

> NAME
> POSITION
> RBIS (RUNS BATTED IN)
> AVERAGE

a. The user should be able to add or change a record.
b. Initially, write your program to handle three records.
c. Modify your program to handle as many records as you desire.

## EXTRA PRACTICE 11

### Character Swap (Sets, Procedures, and Loops)

1. Write a program that reads in a sentence from the keyboard, echo prints the sentence, and then replaces all vowels with V's and all consonants with C's. (Note: *Echo print* simply means to print the information entered from the keyboard.)

## EXTRA PRACTICE 12

### Character Checker
### (Sets, ORD, ASCII)

1. Manually trace the program CHCHECKER.
   a. What is the purpose of "KEYBOARD" in the statement: READ (KEYBOARD, CHOICE) in the main program block?
   b. What are ASCII codes? (hint: see the Glossary.)

2. Enter and run the program.

```
PROGRAM CHCHECKER;

(*PROGRAM CHCHECKER ILLUSTRATES THE USE*)
(*OF KEYBOARD(WITH READ), CHR AND ORD  *)
(*FUNCTIONS ALONG WITH SETS TO  ANALYZE*)
(*AND RETRIEVE THE ASCII CODES OF THE  *)
(*KEYBOARD CHARACTERS.*)

VAR
   LETTER:SET OF CHAR;
   DIGIT:SET OF CHAR;
   CHOICE,CH,SPECIALCHAR,BLANK:CHAR;

PROCEDURE MANUALLY;

 BEGIN
   WRITELN;
   WRITELN('TO END PROGRAM TYPE Q');
   WRITELN('PRESS ANY KEY ON THE KEYBOARD.');
   WRITELN('(EXCEPT RESET!!).');
   WRITELN('THERE ARE THREE KEYS WHEN PRESSED ALONE');
   WRITELN('DO NOT RESPOND TO READ(KEYBOARD,CH).');
   WRITELN('CAN YOU FIND THEM?');
   WRITELN('BEGIN TO PRESS THE KEYBOARD.');
   WRITELN;WRITELN;
   REPEAT
     READ(KEYBOARD,CH);
     IF CH <> 'Q' THEN
       BEGIN
         WRITE('CHR(',ORD(CH),') = ',CH);
         IF CH IN LETTER THEN
           WRITELN(' IS A LETTER')
         ELSE
           IF CH IN DIGIT THEN
             WRITELN(' IS A DIGIT')
           ELSE
             IF CH = BLANK THEN
               WRITELN(' IS A BLANK')
             ELSE
               WRITELN(' IS A SPECIAL CHARACTER')
       END;(*IF*)
     WRITELN;
   UNTIL CH = 'Q'
 END;(*MANNUALLY*)
```

```
PROCEDURE APPLESKEYS;

VAR
  I:INTEGER;

 BEGIN
   WRITELN;
   WRITELN('BELOW IS A LIST OF THE ASCII CHARACTER CODES');
   WRITELN('FROM 33 TO 96 IN DECIMAL. IF YOU HAVE LOWER');
   WRITELN('CASE LETTERS, EXTEND THE LOOP TO 127 ');
   WRITELN('SEE APPLE PASCAL LANGUAGE MANUAL FOR ');
   WRITELN('CODES FROM 0..32.');
   WRITELN;WRITELN;
   FOR I := 33 TO 96 DO
     BEGIN
       CH := (CHR(I));
       WRITE('CHR(',I,') = ',CH);
       IF CH IN LETTER THEN
         WRITELN(' IS A LETTER')
       ELSE
         IF CH IN DIGIT THEN
           WRITELN(' IS A DIGIT')
         ELSE
           IF CH = BLANK THEN
             WRITELN(' IS A BLANK')
           ELSE
             WRITELN(' IS A SPECIAL CHARACTER')
     END;(*FOR*)
 END;(*APPLESKEYS*)


  (*MAIN PROGRAM*)

BEGIN

  LETTER :=['A'..'Z'];
  DIGIT := ['0'..'9'];
  BLANK := ' ';
  WRITELN('TYPE M : TO MANUALLY PRESS THE KEYBOARD');
  WRITELN('TYPE L : TO SEE A LIST OF THE CHARACTER ');
  WRITELN('CODES AND THEIR CATAGORIES');
  READ(KEYBOARD,CHOICE);
  CASE CHOICE OF
    'M':MANUALLY;
    'L':APPLESKEYS
    END(*CASE*)

END.(*PROGRAM*)
```

# Appendixes

## APPENDIX A: Moving Program Files Around

You have learned the basic vocabulary of the Apple Pascal programming language. You have also learned some of the basic techniques for writing programs in Pascal. You will now learn how to store, retrieve, and print the programs you write.

### Transferring, Getting, Saving, and Printing Program Files

As we learned earlier, the Filer handles most of the tasks of transferring information from one place to another. Saving information on disks, moving and deleting files, and sending information to the computer or the printer from a diskette file are some of the functions of the Filer. The general file moving command is T(RANSFER. You can use the T(RANSFER command to:

• Transfer a file from one diskette to another. This is useful for making a back-up copy of a file or relocating a file on another diskette.

• Transfer a file from one place on a diskette to another place on the same diskette. This is useful when you wish to relocate a file on the same diskette.

- Transfer a file to the printer. This is useful for printing a file.

- Transfer a file to the console. This is useful for a quick screen listing of a file.

- Copy an entire disk. This is useful for making extra copies of the whole diskette. (You did this earlier when you made a back-up copy of Apple1:, Apple2:, and Apple3: system diskettes.)

### Specifying a Diskette File

Many Apple Pascal operating system commands require you to specify at least one volume. A complete volume specification consists of the volume name or volume number for the desired device followed by a colon (:). For example,

MYDISK: SHAWN.TEXT

DISK1: GAMES.CODE

DISK2: MAIL.TEXT

The format is as follows:

**VOLUME NAME:**

The diskette name must be seven or fewer characters long.

The diskette name may *not* contain an equal sign ( = ), dollar sign ($), question mark (?), or comma (,).

*The colon (:) tells the system that the name or number preceding the colon is a volume specification and not a diskette file name.*

**FILE NAME**

The file name can have up to fifteen characters (including the suffix),

– In order for the file to be run, the last five characters must be .TEXT or .CODE.

All characters are legal file names. However, you *should not* type file names that include the following characters: dollar sign ($), left square bracket ([), equal sign ( = ), question mark (?), RETURN, and the CTRL characters C, F, M, S, U, and @.

The volume number may be specified instead of name. For example:

#4:FILENAME (for boot drive or Drive #1)

#5:FILENAME (for Drive #2)

## Some Things You Should Know About Diskette Files

A device may be referred to by its volume number or by its volume name. The volume name of a diskette drive is the name of the diskette currently in that disk drive. That is,

| VOLUME NUMBER | VOLUME NAME | WHERE USED |
|---|---|---|
| #4: | <Diskette Name> | Drive #1 (boot drive) |
| #5: | <Diskette Name> | Drive #2 |
| * | <Diskette Name> | Drive #1 (*specifies boot diskette) |

Make sure that the diskettes you use have different volume names. A diskette's volume name must be no more than seven characters long and may not contain an equal sign ( = ), dollar sign ($), question mark (?), or comma (,).

An asterisk (*) can be used as a shorthand notation specifying the volume name of the boot diskette (Vol #4).

If a file name is specified with no preceding volume name or number, or if volume is only specified with a colon (:), the Apple Pascal system supplies the volume name of the "prefix" volume. Booting the system sets the prefix to the name of the boot diskette. To change the name at any time, use the P(REFIX command from the Filer options.

The T(RANSFER command will accept the dollar sign ($) as the second specified file name. This means that the transferred copy of the file is to have the same file name as the original file.

## EXERCISE A–1

### Transferring, Saving, and Getting Program Files

This exercise will permit you to do the following:

- Enter a sample program.

- Print the workfile using the T(RANSFER command.

- Save the workfile on another diskette.

- Get the file you saved on another diskette.

- Run the program stored in the file designated by the GET command.

### A. Entering a Sample Program

*Diskettes needed:* APPLE1: in Drive #1 (Vol #4) and APPLE2: in Drive #2 (Vol #5).

1. Boot up the system.

2. Go to the Editor (that is, press E from the Command level).

3. Type in the sample program shown.

```
PROGRAM SAMPLE;

BEGIN
  WRITELN('I AM A SAMPLE PROGRAM.');
  WRITELN;
  WRITELN('I WILL LET YOU MOVE');
  WRITELN('ME AROUND THE SYSTEM.');
  WRITELN;
  WRITELN('FIRST, ENTER ME AND');
  WRITELN('SEND ME TO THE WORKFILE.');
  WRITELN;
  WRITELN('NEXT, PRINT ME.');
  WRITELN;
  WRITELN('THEN, S(AVE ME IN A FILE');
  WRITELN('ON ANOTHER DISKETTE.');
  WRITELN;
  WRITELN('NEXT, G(ET ME BACK FROM');
  WRITELN('THAT FILE AND DESIGNATE');
  WRITELN('ME AS THE NEXT WORKFILE.');
  WRITELN;
  WRITELN('FINALLY, RUN ME.');
  WRITELN;
  WRITELN('HAVE FUN !!')
END. (* SAMPLE *)
```

4. Exit the Editor and update the workfile (press Q U ).

5. Run the program and read the output.

## B. Printing the Workfile (Using the T(RANSFER Command)

*Diskettes needed:* APPLE1: in Drive #1 (Vol #4).

1. From the Command level, go to the Filer (that is, press F ).

2. Type T For T(RANSFER. You will see the prompt

   TRANSFER?.

3. You want to transfer the workfile. It is stored on the APPLE1: diskette and the file name is SYSTEM.WRK.TEXT, so type in *APPLE1:SYSTEM.WRK.TEXT.* (Don't forget the colon and the periods.)

4. Press RETURN . You will see the prompt

   TO WHERE?

5. Since you want a printout, respond with

   PRINTER:

   *(Don't forget the colon.)*

6. Press RETURN .

   The printer should start printing after you press RETURN . When the printer finishes printing, you should see the message

   APPLE1:SYSTEM.WRK.TEXT ----> PRINTER

This means that the file named SYSTEM.WRK.TEXT on the APPLE1: diskette was transferred to the printer.

## C. Saving the Workfile on Another Diskette

*Diskettes needed:* APPLE1: in Drive #1 (Vol #4) and a Pascal formatted disk in Drive #2 (Vol #5).

**NOTE:** *Do not specify a suffix because it is supplied automatically. If you are S(AVING the workfile under another filename on the boot diskette, the workfile (which is already on the diskette) is simply renamed.*

1. Go to the Filer. (You should still be in the Filer from Part B above.)

2. Type ⬚S⬚ for S(AVE. You will see the message

   ```
   SAVE AS?
   ```

3. Type in a file name of 10 or fewer characters, observing the file name conventions discussed earlier. If your disk in Drive #2 has the name JONES:, you would type in

   ```
   JONES:TESTFILE.
   ```

4. Press ⬚RETURN⬚ .
   a. When your workfile is saved, you will see the message

   ```
   APPLE1:SYSTEM.WRK.TEXT---->JONES:TESTFILE.TEXT
   ```

   The message tells you that the workfile named SYSTEM.WRK.TEXT on the boot diskette named APPLE1: has been successfully transferred to the file named TESTFILE.TEXT on the diskette named JONES:.

   b. If there is no diskette named JONES: in Drive #2 (Vol #5), you will see the message

   ```
   PUT IN JONES: TYPE <SPACE> TO CONTINUE
   ```

   This gives you the chance to insert a diskette named JONES: into the disk drive.

   c. If you specified the diskette JONES: by accident, press the space bar anyway. The system will not find JONES:, and the command will be terminated.

## D. Getting a File from Another Diskette for the Workfile

*Diskettes needed:* APPLE1: in drive #1 (Vol #4) and any Pascal formatted disk in Drive #2 (Vol #5).

1. If you wish to designate a file stored on the boot diskette or another diskette as the next workfile, you would use the G(ET command. Go to the Filer (if you are not still there).

2. The file you wish to G(ET is the one previously saved under the file name TESTFILE.TEXT on the diskette JONES:. To get this file, type ⃞G (Get).
   a. If there is already a workfile SYSTEM.WRK.TEXT present on the boot diskette when you issue the G(ET command, you are asked the question:

      THROW AWAY CURRENT WORKFILE?

   b. Respond by typing ⃞Y . Typing ⃞Y will clear the workfile, removing all files SYSTEM.WRK.TEXT from the boot diskette. If you type ⃞N , you will see the Filer prompt line return.
   c. After you type ⃞Y , you will see

      GET?

      (meaning what file?").

3. Respond by typing *JONES:TESTFILE*

   You do not need to type the text suffix.

4. Press ⃞RETURN . You will then see

   TEXT & CODE FILE LOADED

   Although you are told that the specified file has been "loaded," the GET command does *not* actually transfer the specified file to boot the diskette workfile. But the next time you attempt to EDIT, COMPILE, or RUN, the designated file (TESTFILE) will be used.

### E. Executing the Program Stored on the File Designated by the GET Command

1.  Exit the Filer (type ⎡Q⎤). You will see the Command prompt line.
2.  Run the program (type ⎡R⎤). The program should run, and the message you typed in the sample program should be on the screen.

### Summary

The T(RANSFER command is used to move or save any diskette file (the same or another diskette), copy an entire diskette (back-up), and send files to the printer or other devices. In short, it is the general-purpose file-moving command.

In comparison, the S(AVE command saves all versions of the workfile only. It cannot by itself save or transfer other files. The workfile (SYSTEM.WRK) is usually created by updating the workfile when you Q(UIT the Editor. Any file, however, can be designated as a workfile by use of the G(ET command.

The T(RANSFER command transfers a copy of the file to a specified destination without destroying the original. To delete a file from the source after it is transferred to its destination, you would use the R(EMOVE command. This command is discussed on page 48 in the Filer section of your Apple Pascal Operating System Reference Manual.

The G(ET and S(AVE commands are used together to transfer files from another file to the workfile. Basically, the G(ET command designates the file to be transferred, and the S(AVE command transfers the designated file to the workfile.

## PRACTICE A–1

### Transferring a File from One Diskette to Another

#### A. Transfer File

*Diskettes needed:* Source diskette (with files), destination diskette (formatted), APPLE1:.

1. Boot up the system (if needed).

2. Type [F] to select Filer.

3. Remove APPLE1: from Drive #1 and insert your source diskette in Drive #1 (Vol #4) (that is, the diskette with the file you wish to transfer).

4. Insert your destination diskette in Drive #2 (Vol #5).

5. Note: Make certain that each of the diskettes have different volume names. If they do have the same name, C(HANGE the name of the diskette, at least for the duration of the transfer.

6. Press [T] for Transfer; a prompt will appear:

   ```
   TRANSFER?
   ```

7. Respond by typing in the file you wish to transfer. For example, in order to transfer the file SAMPLE.TEXT from a diskette named DISK1: to a diskette named DISK2:, you would type

   ```
   DISK1:SAMPLE.TEXT
   ```

   (Don't forget the colon (:) and the period (.).)

8. Press RETURN .
   a. If DISK1: is not in any drive, you will see the message

   ```
   DISK1:SAMPLE.TEXT
   NO SUCH VOL ON-LINE <SOURCE>
   ```

   b. If the source diskette is found in a drive, the system checks to be sure the specified file name is on that diskette. If the diskette DISK1: is in the drive but it has no file named SAMPLE.TEXT, you will see the message

   ```
   DISK1:SAMPLE.TEXT
   FILE NOT FOUND <SOURCE>
   ```

   In either case, the Filer prompt will appear on the screen. When it appears, just insert the correct source diskette in any drive and type T again.

   Let's assume the source diskette and file are found. Respond to the system by typing

   ```
   TO WHERE? DISK2:NAME.TEXT
   ```

9. Press RETURN .
   a. When you press RETURN , the system checks to be sure the destination diskette is in the disk drive. If it is not, you will get the prompt

   ```
   PUT IN DISK2:
   TYPE <SPACE> TO CONTINUE
   ```

   b. If the destination diskette is in a disk drive, the transfer begins. When the transfer is complete, the Filer will give the message

   ```
   DISK1:SAMPLE.TEXT---> DISK2:NAME.TEXT
   ```

   which means the Filer has made a copy of the SAMPLE.TEXT as found on the diskette named DISK1:, and has stored that copy on the diskette DISK2: under the file name NAME.TEXT.

### B. Using the R(EMOVE Command to Remove a File from the Source Diskette

The T(RANSFER command transfers only a copy of a file to another location. To delete the file from the source diskette (or any diskette), you must use the R(EMOVE command.

1. Go to the Filer.

2. If you wish to remove the file SAMPLE.TEXT from DISK1: (used in Part A above), you would type R (for REMOVE). Then you should see REMOVE? (meaning remove what file?).

3. Respond by typing

REMOVE? *SAMPLE.TEXT*

Typing this response tells the system to remove the file SAMPLE.TEXT from the directory of DISK1:. The system considers that file erased from the diskette, although *only the directory* has been changed.

To remove SYSTEM.WRK.TEXT and/or SYSTEM.WRK.CODE, the FILER's N(EW command should be used; otherwise, the system might get confused. Then you can use the R(EMOVE command for all files *except* SYSTEM.WRK.TEXT and SYSTEM.WRK.CODE.

**APPENDIX B:**
**Summary of the**
**Program Structure,**
**the Block Format,**
**and Data Types**

## Key Points to Remember about Program Structure

Every Pascal program begins with a program name. Every name must begin with a letter, and the name must consist of only letters (A to Z) and digits (0 to 9). The letters may be upper- or lowercase. Blank spaces must not be included in names; do *not* use any of the Pascal reserved words. Only the first eight characters of a name are "looked at" by the computer. A semicolon must follow the program name. The reserved words **BEGIN** and **END** serve to bracket program statements. Consecutive Pascal statements between **BEGIN** and **END** must be separated by semicolons. The last program statement before **END** does not require a semicolon, but a period is required after the word **END** if it is used as the last Pascal statement.

Use blank spaces and indentation throughout your program to enhance the appearance and readability of your program. Carefully worded comments should be included wherever possible. The operation of each program module should be thoroughly explained by comments: Supply a sufficient number of comments to clarify the intent of each step of your program, but not too many to clutter your program, making it difficult to read.

Use functions and procedures wherever possible in your program to take full advantage of the features of Pascal. Use meaningful names for variables and program names to help improve the clarity of your program.

## The Pascal Program Structure

**PROGRAM HEADING**

```
PROGRAM NAME;
```

**GLOBAL DECLARATIONS**
**DATA DESCRIPTION**

```
  USES
    APPLESTUFF, TRANSCEND, TURTLEGRAPHICS;

  CONST
    <GLOBAL CONSTANT DEFINITIONS>;

  TYPE
    <GLOBAL TYPE DEFINITIONS>;

  VAR
    <GLOBAL VARIABLE DECLARATIONS>;
```

**PROCEDURE DECLARATION**

```
  PROCEDURE <PROCEDURE NAME> (FORMAL PARAMETER LIST)

  CONST
    <LOCAL CONSTANT DEFINITIONS>;
  TYPE
    <LOCAL TYPE DEFINITIONS>;
  VAR
    <LOCAL VARIABLE DECLARATIONS>;

  BEGIN
    <PROCEDURE STATEMENTS OR INSTRUCTIONS>;
  END;
```

**FUNCTION DECLARATION**

```
  FUNCTION <FUNCTION> (FORMAL PARAMETER):<FUNCTION>
            NAME           LIST            NAME

  CONST
    <LOCAL CONSTANT DEFINITIONS>;
  VAR
    <LOCAL VARIABLE DECLARATIONS>;

  BEGIN
    <FUNCTION STATEMENTS TO DO SOMETHING>;
  END;
```

**MAIN PROGRAM BLOCK**

```
BEGIN
  <PROGRAM STATEMENTS>;
  <PROCEDURE CALL>;
  <FUNCTION CALL>;
  <MORE PROGRAM STATEMENTS>;
END.
```

## The Declarations Block Format
## (CONST, TYPE, VAR)

| *FORMAT* | *EXAMPLES* |
|---|---|

CONST

```
NAME = CONSTANT;
```

CONST

```
ROWMAX=6;
COLMAX=3;
PI   =3.14159;
```

TYPE

```
<SCALARTYPE>=(VALUE1,VALUE2,..VALUEN);


<SUBRANGETYPE>=(LOWER VALUE..UPPERVALUE);



(*ONE DIMENSIONAL ARRAY*)
<ARRAY TYPE>=ARRAY [0..N] OF <TYPE>

(*TWO DIMENSIONAL ARRAY*)
<ARRAYTYPE>=ARRAY[0..N,0..N] OF <TYPE>;

<RECORDTYPE>=RECORD

            <FIELD1NAME>:<FIELD1TYPE>;

            <FIELD2NAME>:<FIELD2TYPE>;
                    .
                    .
                    .
                    .
            END;(*RECORD*)
```

TYPE

```
WEEK=(MON,TUE,WED,THU,
        FRI,SAT,SUN);

YEAR=1984..1990;
WEEKDAY=MON..FRI;
LETTER='A'..'Z';



ROW=ARRAY[1..6] OF REAL;


ROWCOL=ARRAY[1..6,1..3]OF REAL;

STUDENT=RECORD

            NAME:STRING[20];
            AGE:INTEGER;
            IDNO:1000..9999;
            GRADEPT:REAL;
            GRADE:'A'..'F'
        END;(*STUDENT*)
```

VAR

```
NAME:TYPE;
    OR
NAME1,NAME2,..NAMEN:TYPE;
```

VAR

```
GRADE:INTEGER;

LENGTH,WIDTH, HEIGHT:REAL;
```

A summary of Apple Pascal data types is shown in Fig. B–1.

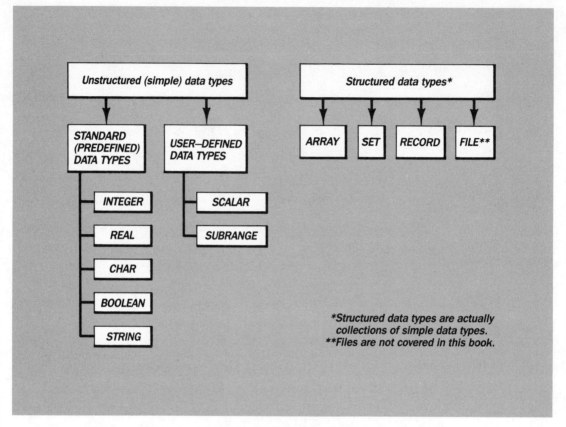

*Fig. B–1 Apple Pascal data types.*

**APPENDIX C:
The One-Drive
System Startup**

This appendix is a tutorial session to get you started using Pascal on an Apple II plus or IIe system with one diskette drive. If you have a dual diskette drive system, refer to Chapters 3 and 4 for instructions.

It is a very awkward and tedious procedure to use Pascal on a one-drive system (especially the Apple IIe). It is much better to use a dual-drive system because you will reduce the number of times you will have to switch the diskette when using the Pascal operating system.

The following is covered in this appendix:

- Equipment required.
- Exercise C–1: Booting up Pascal (a one-drive Apple II Plus system).
- Special instructions for booting up Pascal on one-drive Apple IIe systems.
- Exercise C–2: Formatting a new diskette (one-drive system).
- Exercise C–3: Making back-up copies (one-drive system).

### The One-Drive System Equipment Summary

#### EQUIPMENT REQUIRED

☑ 48K Apple computer with a language card installed.

☑ A TV set or video monitor properly connected to your Apple.

☑ A single disk drive attached to the connector marked "DRIVE 1" on the disk controller card.

☑ APPLE3: and APPLE0: system diskettes (needed to start the system).

☑ Formatted blank diskette (see Exercise C–3).

☑ A clear head.

A diskette marked "APPLE2:" is also included with the system diskette. You will *not* need this diskette since it adds some extra features (assembler and linker) not covered in this book. Also, the APPLE2: diskette contains the compiler and is normally used with the dual-drive system.

## EXERCISE C–1

### Booting Up Pascal (One-Drive System) for the Apple II Plus System

<table>
<tr><th>ACTION</th><th>DISPLAY</th></tr>
<tr><td>

1. Make certain that the system is connected properly.

2. Place the diskette marked APPLE3: in the disk drive. If you are not familiar with handling diskettes, refer to the material that came with your disk drives.

3. Close the door to the disk drive and turn on the Apple. The message shown appears.

(a) The disk drive "IN USE" light comes on. The disk drive makes a whirring, clicking sound that lets you know everything is working.

(b) The screen lights up for an instant with a display as shown.

</td><td>

```
                 APPLE ][
```

```
@@@@@@@@@@@@@@@@@@@@@@@@@@@@@@@@@@@@@@@
@@@@@@@@@@@@@@@@@@@@@@@@@@@@@@@@@@@@@@@
@@@@@@@@@@@@@@@@@@@@@@@@@@@@@@@@@@@@@@@
@@@@@@@@@@@@@@@@@@@@@@@@@@@@@@@@@@@@@@@
@@@@@@@@@@@@@@@@@@@@@@@@@@@@@@@@@@@@@@@
@@@@@@@@@@@@@@@@@@@@@@@@@@@@@@@@@@@@@@@
@@@@@@@@@@@@@@@@@@@@@@@@@@@@@@@@@@@@@@@
@@@@@@@@@@@@@@@@@@@@@@@@@@@@@@@@@@@@@@@
```

</td></tr>
</table>

*(c)* Then this message appears. Remove the diskette marked APPLE3: from the disk drive. Place the diskette marked APPLE0: in the disk drive. Close the door to the disk drive and press the CTRL and RESET keys.

*(d)* Again, the disk drive "IN USE" light comes on. The disk drive makes a whirring, clicking sound that lets you know that everything is working. The @ sign comes back on the screen for an instant.

*(e)* When the disk drive stops, the message (or equivalent) shown appears. The line at the top of the screen, called the Command "prompt line," lets you know that your Apple computer is running the Apple Pascal system. That is, the system is now "booted" and ready for use.

```
INSERT BOOT DISK WITH SYSTEM.PASCAL
ON IT, THEN PRESS RESET█
```

```
@@@@@@@@@@@@@@@@@@@@@@@@@@@@@@@@@@@@@@
@@@@@@@@@@@@@@@@@@@@@@@@@@@@@@@@@@@@@@
@@@@@@@@@@@@@@@@@@@@@@@@@@@@@@@@@@@@@@
@@@@@@@@@@@@@@@@@@@@@@@@@@@@@@@@@@@@@@
@@@@@@@@@@@@@@@@@@@@@@@@@@@@@@@@@@@@@@
@@@@@@@@@@@@@@@@@@@@@@@@@@@@@@@@@@@@@@
@@@@@@@@@@@@@@@@@@@@@@@@@@@@@@@@@@@@@@
@@@@@@@@@@@@@@@@@@@@@@@@@@@@@@@@@@@@@@
```

```
COMMAND: E(DIT, R(UN, F(ILE, C(OMP, L(IN

WELCOME APPLE0, TO APPLE II PASCAL 1.1
BASED ON UCSD PASCAL II.1
CURRENT DATE IS XX-XXX-XX



(c) APPLE COMPUTER INC. 1979, 1980
(c) U.C. REGENTS 1979
```

Your system can now do all the things you will normally want to do in Apple Pascal: filing, editing, running, and compiling. However, diskette Apple0: is missing one file that is needed for the initial start-up when you first turn Apple's power on. That is why you must use diskette APPLE3: to start up the system.

## EXERCISE C–2

### Booting Up Pascal (One-Drive System) for the Apple IIe

It is very "tricky" to boot up Pascal on the Apple IIe system. (Another reason why you should use a dual-drive system.) But it can be done if you have patience and fast hands. Here is how you do it.

1. Insert APPLE3: in the disk drive.

2. Close the disk drive door and turn on the Apple IIe.

3. Have diskette APPLE0: in your hand, and ready to be inserted into the diskette drive *as soon as you see the @ signs appear on the screen.* This is when you must remove APPLE1: and replace it with APPLE0: as fast as you can (make sure the red "in use" light is not on). Sounds crazy? Well, this is one way to get the Apple IIe to boot on a one-drive system. If you try the approach shown in Exercise C–1, you can complete it up to a point. But when you try to insert APPLE0: and press CTRL RESET on Apple IIe, the following message will appear:

    NO FILE SYSTEM.APPLE

    If this happens, reboot the system using APPLE3:, and then try again to replace APPLE3: with APPLE0: when you see the @'s.

4. Once you boot your Apple IIe, everything else should work the same as with the Apple II Plus.

I recommend that you use Pascal with a dual-drive system only. (This is *not* a commercial for Apple but a recommendation based on experience.)

### Dual APPLE0: Method

1. Make an extra copy of the APPLE0: diskette.

2. Delete the file SYSTEM.COMPILER from *one* of your APPLE0: diskettes.

3. Copy the file SYSTEM.APPLE from your APPLE3: diskette onto the APPLE0: (that is, add the file SYSTEM.APPLE to the same APPLE0: diskette in which you deleted the file SYSTEM.COMPILER).

4. You should now have two APPLE0: diskettes:
   a. One APPLE0: as it came with your system (that is, it has a compiler).
   b. Another APPLE0: (the one you changed) without the file SYSTEM.COMPILER but now having the file SYSTEM.APPLE.

5. Label your APPLE0: diskette as follows:
   a. Label one APPLE0: "w/compiler."
   b. Label the other APPLE0: "w/o compiler."

6. Now follow the procedure in Exercise C–1 with the following exceptions:
   a. Use APPLE0: (w/o compiler) just to turn on the system.
   b. Remove APPLE0: (w/o compiler) and replace it with APPLE0: (with compiler) when the boot is complete.
   *Caution:* Do *not* press the [RESET] key because the system acts as if it has the original APPLE0: diskette in it.

Your system can now do all of the things you will normally want it to do in Pascal: filing, editing, running, and compiling. However, the diskette APPLE0: that is currently in the disk drive is missing one file that is needed for the initial start-up when you first turn the Apple's power on. If you have to [RESET] or start up the system again, you must use the APPLE0: diskette without the compiler (but with the SYSTEM.APPLE).

*You may need to get help from your dealer in order to use the dual APPLE0 method.*

## EXERCISE C–3

### Formatting New Diskettes (One-Disk System)

| ACTION | DISPLAY |
|---|---|

**ACTION**

1. Be sure the Apple is turned off.

2. Boot up Pascal (refer to Exercise C–1).

3. When the Command prompt line is showing at the top of the screen, remove system diskette APPLE0: from the disk drive.

4. Place diskette APPLE3: in the disk drive. The APPLE3: diskette is needed because the FORMATTER program is on APPLE3:.

5. If you can't see the other part of the Command prompt line, hold down the CTRL key and then press A.

6. Type X and the message shown should appear. This action selects X(ECUTE. (If the screen is blank, press CTRL A.)

**DISPLAY**

```
COMMAND: E(DIT, R(UN, F(ILE, C(OMP, L(IN
```

```
K, X(ECUTE, A(SSEM, D(EBUG,? [1.1]
```

```
EXECUTE WHAT FILE?
```

7. *Type*
   *APPLE3:FORMATTER*
   *and then press*
   *the* RETURN *key. If*
   *you make a mistake*
   *before pressing*
   RETURN *, use* <---- 
   *to erase.*

8. *Take all of the <u>new,</u>*
   *<u>blank</u> diskettes that*
   *you are going to use*
   *with the Pascal*
   *System and place*
   *them in a pile.*

9. *Remove the diskette*
   *in drive (APPLE3:)*
   *and put one of the*
   *<u>new, blank</u> diskettes*
   *into that drive.*

10. *Type* 4 *and press*
    RETURN *.*

    *If the diskette in*
    *drive #4 has already*
    *been formatted, you*
    *will see:*
    *For example, if you*
    *left APPLE3: in that*
    *drive, you would be*
    *warned with the*
    *message shown.*

    *If you do not want to*
    *destroy the directory,*
    *you would type N (for*
    *"No").*

```
APPLE DISK FORMATTER PROGRAM
FORMAT WHICH DISK (4,5,9..12)?
```

```
DESTROY DIRECTORY OF APPLE3:?
```

11. *Let's assume you have a new unformatted diskette. Then you will not get any warning, but the Apple will place this message on its screen. (Note: The disk drive will make some clickings and buzzings. The process takes about 32 seconds.)*

```
NOW FORMATTING DISKETTE IN DRIVE 4
```

12. *When formatting is complete, the screen again shows the message.*

```
FORMAT WHICH DISK (4,5,9 ..12)?
```

13. *Now you have a formatted disk. Write "Pascal" at the top of the diskette's label using a felt-tip pen.*

14. *Repeat the process at step 9 to format other diskettes or all new diskettes that you want to use with the Apple Pascal system.*

15. *When you have finished formatting all of your new diskettes and have written the word "Pascal" on each of them, press* RETURN. *Note: By SYSTEM DISK, the Apple means APPLE0: (or the disk that completed the boot-up.)*

```
PUT SYSTEM DISK IN #4 AND PRESS RETURN
```

16. *Do as it says: Place the diskette marked APPLE0: in the disk drive and press the* RETURN *key.*

THAT'S ALL FOLKS . . .

17. *You should see the Command prompt line appear.*

COMMAND: E(DIT, R(UN, F(ILE, C(OMP, L(IN

18. *Finally, remove the newly formatted diskettes, and put them away in a safe place until you need them.*

---

## EXERCISE C–4

### Making Back-Up Copies (One-Drive System)

**ACTION**                                    **DISPLAY**

1. *If you just finished formatting new diskettes, the system should be at the Command level. If it is not, make certain that you reboot the system.*

COMMAND: E(DIT, R(UN, F(ILE, C(OMP, L(IN

2. *Now press* F *for Filer.*

FILER: G, S, N, L, R, C, T, D, Q [1.1]

3. *Now Press* T *for T(RANSFER.*

TRANSFER?

4. *Let's say you want to make a backup of APPLE1: (that is, to copy APPLE1: onto your newly formatted diskette). Type "APPLE1:" and then press* RETURN *. Note: When you press* RETURN *, if APPLE1: is not in the drive, you will see the message shown.*

```
TRANSFER? APPLE1:
TO WHERE?
```

```
NO SUCH VOL ON-LINE <SOURCE>
```

5. *Answer the question "TO WHERE?" by typing in the name of the newly formatted diskette, which has been assigned the name BLANK: by the formatter program. Type "BLANK:" and press* RETURN *.*

```
TO WHERE?
```

(a) *The phrase "280 BLOCKS" merely means the "whole diskette."*

(b) *Type "Y" (for "Yes").*

```
TO WHERE? BLANK:
TRANSFER 280 BLOCKS? (Y/N)
```

6. *Put in the newly formatted disk when you see this message; then press the space bar.*

```
PUT IN BLANK:
TYPE <SPACE> TO CONTINUE
```

7. *Since you want to turn "BLANK:" into a perfect copy of APPLE1:, the answer to destroy blank is "Y."*

```
DESTROY BLANK:?
```

(a) When you type "Y," the process begins. The computer will tell you to first put in one diskette, and then the other. Follow the instructions. Your screen should look like this.

(b) You will have to insert two diskettes a total of 20 times, and press the [SPACEBAR] 20 times to copy the entire diskette.

(c) When this process is done, the display message will appear. This means that the contents of APPLE1:, including the diskette name, have been copied onto the diskette that used to be called BLANK:.

8. When you have finished copying APPLE1:, make certain that you remove the new copy immediately.

9. Use a felt-tip pen to write APPLE1: on the new diskette's label. (It is important to label diskettes immediately so you know what information is stored on them.)

```
PUT APPLE1: IN UNIT #4
TYPE <SPACE> TO CONTINUE
PUT BLANK: IN UNIT #4
TYPE <SPACE> TO CONTINUE
PUT APPLE1: IN UNIT #4
TYPE <SPACE> TO CONTINUE
PUT BLANK: IN UNIT #4
TYPE <SPACE> TO CONTINUE
PUT APPLE1: IN UNIT #4
TYPE <SPACE> TO CONTINUE
PUT BLANK: IN UNIT #4
TYPE <SPACE> TO CONTINUE
PUT APPLE 1: IN UNIT #4
TYPE <SPACE> TO CONTINUE
PUT BLANK: IN UNIT #4
TYPE <SPACE> TO CONTINUE
```

```
APPLE1:    ---> BLANK:
```

**APPENDIX D:
Operating System
Summary**

The Apple Pascal Operating System includes a Filer for handling disk files, a text Editor for writing and changing programs, a Pascal Compiler to convert programs into executable P-Code, a 6502 Assembler to convert assembly-language routines into machine-language code, and a Linker to combine other routines into your program. All components of the operating system were covered in this book except the Assembler and Linker.

This appendix includes a summary of the following:

• The Pascal Operating System.

• The Command level.

• The Filer.

• The Editor.

• Some Files used with the Apple Pascal system.

• Command structure tree for the Apple Pascal system.

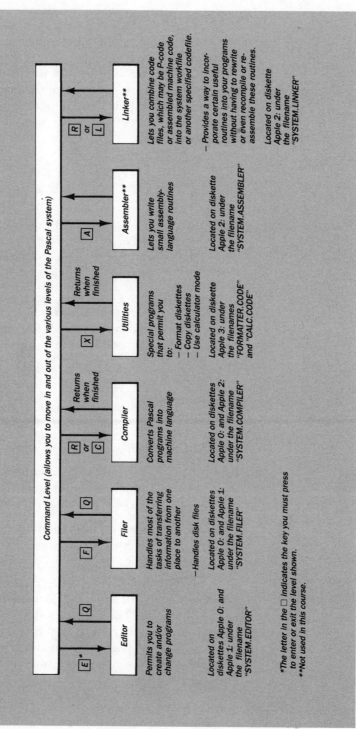

*Fig. D–1 The Pascal operating system.*

## The Command Level

The Command level allows you to move in and out of the
various levels of the Pascal system. It is at the top level of the
Pascal system; therefore, you must use the various options of
the Command level to select any of the main subdivisions or
lower levels of the Apple Pascal Operating System. Some of the
options you can select from the Command level include the
following:

| OPTION | FUNCTION |
|---|---|
| C(OMPILE | Selects the Pascal Compiler, which converts the text of a Pascal program (found in the workfile or other specified textfile) into executable P-Code. |
| E(DIT | Selects the Editor, which is used to create and modify text. Reads the workfile or other specified textfile into the Apple for editing. |
| F(ILE | Selects the Filer, which is used to save, move, and retrieve information stored on diskettes. |
| H(ALT | Does a "cold boot" of the system, like turning the Apple's power off and then on again. |
| I(NITIALIZE | Does a "warm boot" of the system. |
| R(UN | Executes the current workfile, automatically compiling and linking (from SYSTEM.LIBRARY) first, if necessary. |
| X(ECUTE | Loads and runs a utility program or other P-Code files. |

The Command level portion of the operating system is located
on diskettes APPLE0: and APPLE1: under the file name
SYSTEM.PASCAL. The Command level is reached
automatically each time the system is booted, reset, or
initialized. It is also reached when any program, including any
part of the operating system, is terminated.

### The Filer

The Filer handles most of the tasks of transferring information from one place to another. Saving information on diskette, moving and deleting diskette files, and sending information to the computer or to the printer are some of the functions of the Apple Pascal Filer. The Filer also tells you where files have been placed on the diskettes, and what devices and diskettes are available for your system's use.

The following are some of the Filer commands available for your use:

| COMMAND | FUNCTION |
|---------|----------|
| C(HANGE | Renames a file or diskette. |
| D(ATE | Sets the current date. |
| E(XT-DIR | Shows what files are on a diskette, supplying more information than L(IST. |
| G(ET | Designates a file to be used as the next workfile. |
| K(RUNCH | Packs all files together on a diskette. |
| L(IST-DIR | Shows what files are on a diskette. |
| M(AKE | Creates a dummy file on diskette. |
| N(EW | Clears the workfile. |
| Q(UIT | Leaves the Filer and returns to the Command level. (Be sure your boot diskette is in the boot drive.) |
| R(EMOVE | Erases a file from its diskette directory. |
| T(RANSFER | Copies a file or entire diskette to another diskette or device. (The source diskette must be in a drive to begin (for example, send a file to the printer). |
| S(AVE | Saves the workfile on diskette. |
| V(OLUMES | Shows which devices and diskettes are in the system. |
| W(HAT | Tells the original name of the current workfile. |
| Z(ERO | Erases a directory and renames the diskette. |

The Filer is found on the diskettes APPLE0: and APPLE1: under the file name SYSTEM.FILER. Typing [F] while at the Command level selects the Filer mode. (This assumes that your diskette with SYSTEM.FILER is in the disk drive.) When the Filer prompt line appears, the diskette containing SYSTEM.FILER may be removed from the system to make room for other diskettes.

Typing [Q] let's you QUIT (exit) the Filer, but the diskette with the file SYSTEM.PASCAL must be on the boot diskette (that is, APPLE1:) in the boot drive.

### The Editor

The Editor lets you make and change text. To enter text from the keyboard, you must use the Editor. Use the Editor commands to I(nsert, D(elete, X(change, and move text. When you are through, Q(uit and U(pdate the workfile. The following are some of the Editor commands available for your use:

| COMMAND | FUNCTION |
|---|---|
| A(DJUST | Moves line at cursor right and left. The Adjust mode is designed to make it easy to adjust the indentation of a line or a whole group of lines. |
| D(ELETE | Moving the cursor erases text. |
| F(IND /X/ | Moves the cursor to the next "X." |
| I(NSERT | Inserts typed text at the cursor. |
| P(AGE | Moves cursor one page in the set direction. (The set direction is determined by the first character displayed on the Editor prompt line.) |
| Q(UIT | Leaves or exits the Editor. You may U(pdate the workfile, E(xit without updating, or W(rite to any file before returning to the Command level or S(aving your original file. |
| R(EPLACE /X// Y/ | Replaces next "X" by "Y." |

The Editor is found on the diskettes APPLE0: and APPLE1: under the file name SYSTEM.EDITOR.

Typing E while at the Command level selects the Editor. This assumes that your diskette with SYSTEM.EDITOR is in the disk drive. When the Editor prompt line appears, the diskette containing SYSTEM.EDITOR may be removed from the system to make room for other diskettes.

Typing Q lets you Quit the Editor, and will then permit you to select one of the following options:

U(PDATE THE WORKFILE AND LEAVE

E(XIT WITHOUT UPDATING

R(ETURN TO EDITOR WITHOUT UPDATING

W(RITE TO A FILE NAME AND RETURN

S(AVE WITH SAME NAME AND RETURN

The command structure for the Apple Pascal system appears on page 330.

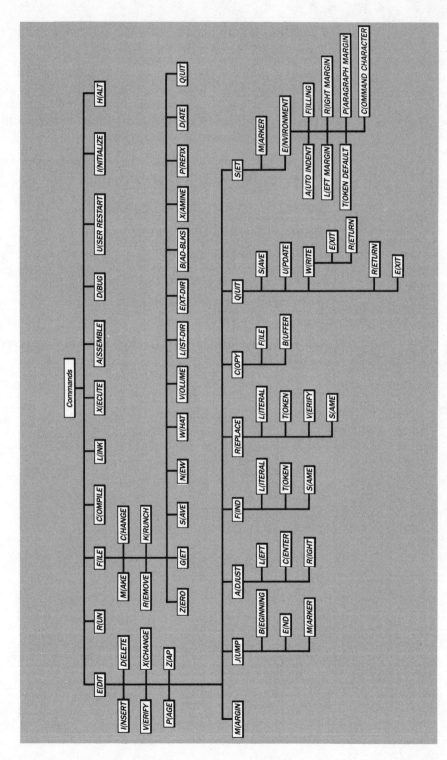

*Fig. D–2 The command structure for the Apple Pascal system.*

The following is a summary of some of the files used with the Apple Pascal System.

| FILE NAME | STORED ON DISKETTE | | | | USE OF FILE |
|---|---|---|---|---|---|
| | APPLE0: | APPLE1: | APPLE2: | APPLE3:* | |
| SYSTEM.APPLE | | X | | X | Executes the P-Code (Interpreter) needed for power-on and halt. |
| SYSTEM.COMPILER | X | | X | | Converts Pascal program text to P-Code. |
| SYSTEM.CHARSET | X | X | | | Lets you put text on the graphics screen. |
| SYSTEM.EDITOR | X | X | | | Lets you create and change text. |
| SYSTEM.FILER | X | X | | | Lets you store, delete, and move disk files. |
| SYSTEM.LIBRARY | X | X | | | Provides standard routines for use by Pascal programs. |
| SYSTEM.PASCAL | X | X | | | Contains the Command level . Needed for power-on, halt, reset, and initialize. |
| SYSTEM.SYNTAX | X | X | | | Contains Compiler error messages. |
| CALC.CODE | | | | X | A utility program that lets you use the computer as a calculator. |
| FORMATTER.CODE | | | | X | A utility program that formats new diskettes. |
| FORMATTER.DATA | | | | X | |

*One-drive system start-up diskette.

# *Glossary*

**Acoustic Coupler**  A device that transmits data over phone lines by converting electrical signals into audio signals, and vice versa.

**Address**  A number used to identify a location in the computer's memory.

**Algorithm**  1) A step-by-step procedure or a sequence of instructions that will help you solve problems. 2) A finite set of well-defined rules for the solution of a problem in a finite number of steps.

**Alphanumeric**  A character set that contains letters, digits, and usually symbols such as punctuation marks.

**Application**  A specific program or task, such as sorting student records, to which a computer solution can be applied.

**Application Program**  A computer program designed to meet specific user needs, such as a program that performs word processing or controls inventory.

**Array** 1) A lineup, an arrangement, or an orderly grouping of things in one or more dimensions. 2) A collection of items, all of the same type, that are grouped together and are indexed so that each item of the array can be accessed through a single label with a unique subscript or index.

**ASCII (American Standard Code for Information Interchange)** An information code that has assigned a binary number to each alphanumeric character and several nonprinting control characters. The ASCII code is used for representing text inside a computer, and for transmitting text between computers or between a computer and a peripheral device.

**Assembler** A language translator that converts a program written in assembly language into an equivalent program in machine language.

**Assembly Language** A low-level programming language in which individual machine-language instructions are written in a symbolic form more easily read by a person than machine language.

**Back-Up** Copying of one or more files onto a storage medium for safekeeping, in case the original becomes damaged or lost.

**BASIC (Beginner's All-Purpose Symbolic Instruction Code)** A high-level programming language designed to be easy to learn and use. BASIC is available on most microcomputers.

**Baud** A unit of data transmitting/receiving speed, roughly equal to a single bit per second. Common baud rates are 110, 300, 1200, 2400, 4800, and 9600.

**Binary** Pertains to a selection, choice, or condition that has two possible different values or states (for example, YES or NO, START or STOP, 1 or 0). The digits 0 and 1 are commonly used in computers, since 0 and 1 can easily represent such states as the presence or absence of electric current, positive or negative voltage, and a white or black dot on the screen.

**Binary Code** A code that makes use of exactly two distinct characters, usually 0 and 1.

**Boolean** Pertaining to the process used in the algebra formulated by George Boole.

**Boolean Operation**   1) Any operation in which each of the operators and the result take one of two values. 2) An operation that follows the rules of Boolean algebra.

**Boot (Boot-Up)**   To start a computer by loading a program into memory from an external storage medium such as a disk. Typically, a small program, whose purpose is to read the larger program into memory, is loaded first. That is, this smaller program is sufficient to bring the rest of "itself" into the computer from an input device. The program is said to "pull itself up by its own bootstraps"; hence the term "booting."

**Branch**   In the execution of a program, to select a set of instructions from a number of alternative sets of instructions.

**Bubble Sort**   A sort in which succeeding pairs of items in a set are examined. If the items in a pair are out of sequence according to the specified criteria, the positions of the items are exchanged. This process is repeated until all items are sorted.

**Buffer**   An area of the computer's memory reserved for a specific purpose, such as to hold graphical information to be displayed on the screen, or text characters being read from the keyboard or some peripheral device. Typically, it is used as an intermediate holding area to compensate for a difference in the rate of flow of data when transferring data between devices operating at different speeds, such as the computer's processor and a printer or disk drive. Information can be stored into a buffer by one device and then read by the other at a different speed.

**Bug**   An error in a program that prevents the program from working as intended.

**Bus**   One or more conductors used for transmitting signals or power.

**Byte**   A unit of information consisting of a fixed number of bits. Typically, one byte consists of eight bits and can hold a value from 0 to 255.

**Call**   To request the execution of a subroutine, function, or procedure.

**Character**   A letter (A to Z), digit (0 to 9), punctuation mark, or other symbol used in printing or displaying information that can be read by people. (This also includes some text symbols that are not visible as characters, such as a space, a tab, or a carriage return.)

**Chip**   The small piece of semiconducting material (usually silicon) on which an integrated circuit is fabricated. The word *chip* refers only to the piece of silicon itself, which is often used for an integrated circuit and its package.

**Cold Boot**   The process of starting up the computer when power is first turned on by loading the operating system into main memory, then loading and running a program.

**Command Level**   The top level of the Pascal Operating System. It is the level where you enter the Pascal system. From this level, you can move in and out of the various levels of the Pascal system.

**Compiler**   A computer program used to translate a programming language (for example, Pascal) into machine language.

**Control Character**   A character that controls or modifies the way information is printed, displayed, or transmitted. A control character is not a graphic character but may have a graphic representation in some circumstances. Control characters have ASCII codes between 0 and 31 and are typed from the keyboard by holding down `CONTROL` while typing some other character; for example, you would type `CONTROL` `A` to see the other half of a 40-column screen.

**CP/M (Control Program for Microprocessors)**   An operating system used by many personal computers.

**CPU (Central Processing Unit)**   The heart of the microcomputer is the microprocessor, often called the CPU. It interprets and controls the execution of instructions in the computer.

**Cursor**   A movable, blinking marker, usually a box or a line, on a video display that defines the next point of character entry or change.

**Daisy Wheel (Printer)**   A print head that forms full characters rather than characters formed by dots (that is, dot matrix). It is shaped like a wheel with many spokes, with a letter, numeral, or symbol at the end of each spoke. The print method used is similar to that of a standard typewriter.

**Debug**   To detect, trace, and correct an error or the cause of the problem or malfunction in a computer system, typically used to refer to software-related problems.

**Diagnostic Program**   A computer program that recognizes, locates, and explains a fault in equipment or a mistake in a computer program.

**Digit**   One of the characters 0 to 9 used to express numbers in decimal form.

**Disk**   An information storage medium consisting of a circular magnetic surface on which information can be recorded in small magnetized spots, similar to the way sounds are stored on magnetic type.

**Diskette (Floppy Disk)**   A term sometimes used for the small (5¼ inch) flexible disk. Because these diskettes are flexible, they are sometimes called "floppy" diskettes, as compared with the more rigid or hard disks used with computer systems.

**Disk/Diskette Drive**   A peripheral device used to read data from or write data onto one or more diskettes.

**Dot Matrix (Printer)**   A printer that forms characters from a two-dimensional array or matrix of dots. Each character is represented by a pattern of dots. More dots in a given space produce characters that are more legible.

**DOS (Disk Operating System)**   DOS is a set of programs that comes with your computer system if your system has a diskette drive. It manages the resource of your microcomputer and provides a wide variety of services to the user. For example, DOS controls all disk operations, tells the computer how to save and retrieve programs, and controls the transferring of information to and from all files.

**Double Density**   A special recording method for disk/diskettes that allows the disk to store twice as much as normal, or single density, recordings.

**Editor**   A program which is part of the Pascal Operating System that lets you create and change text. To enter text from the keyboard, you must use the Editor.

**Element**   A member of a set or collection.

**Empty Set**   A set that has no elements. It is synonymous with the null set.

**EPROM (Erasable Programmable Read Only Memory)**
Much like ROM with one added feature. You can erase the information that you have programmed in it by using ultraviolet light and then reprogram it with different information.

**File**   1) A set of related records treated as a unit. 2) A file is the means by which data are stored on a disk or diskette so it can be used at a later date.

**Filename**   The sequence of alphanumeric characters assigned by a user to identify a file that can be read by both the computer and the user.

**Filer**   A program that is part of the Pascal Operating System. It permits you to store, delete, and move diskette files. It handles most of the tasks of transferring information from one place to another.

**Function**   A preprogrammed calculation that can be carried out on a request from any point in the program. You may use the standard Pascal functions such as the mathematical function (for example, SIN(X), COS(X), and so on), or you may define your own.

**Global**   Pertains to that which is defined in one subdivision of a computer program and is used in at least one other subdivision of the program; for example, a global variable that can be used in procedures, functions, and the main program block of a Pascal program.

**Graphics**   The use of lines and figures to display data, as opposed to the use of printed characters.

**Hardcopy**   Output in a permanent form (usually on paper) rather than in temporary form, such as a visual display.

**Hard Disk**   A disk that is rigid. It is more expensive than a flexible disk (floppy diskette) but is capable of storing much more data.

**Hardware**   The physical components of a computer system (electronic or mechanical devices).

**High-Level Data**   A programming language that does not reflect the structure of any one given computer or that of any given class of computers. A high-level language is usually close to the English language, as compared to the much lower-level machine language (0's and 1's). Examples of high-level language are BASIC, Fortran, and Pascal.

**IC (Integrated Circuit)**   An electric component consisting of many elements fabricated on a single piece of semiconductor material, such as silicon. (Same as Chip.)

**Initialize (Format)**   1) To set to an initial state or value in preparation for some calculation; that is, to set counters, switches, addresses, or contents of storage to zero or other starting values. 2) To preface a blank disk to receive information by dividing its surface into tracks and sectors.

**I/O (Input/Output)**   Pertains to a device that may be involved in an input process, and, at a different time, in an output process. For example, a disk drive can read (Input) or write (Output) data.

**Interactive**   A system that is capable of carrying on a dialogue through a keyboard with the user, rather than simply responding to commands.

**Interpreter**   A program that translates and executes each source language statement of a computer program before translating and executing the next statement. In contrast, a compiler translates the entire source program into machine language before it is executed. As a result, a compiled program will usually run faster than an interpreted program.

**K (Kilo)**   From the Greek root kilo meaning one thousand. For example, 64K memory means 64,000 bytes. (To be more exact, since a Kbyte = $2^{10}$ = 1024, then 64 × 1024 = 65,536. But most people refer to it as 64K.)

**Kilobyte**   A unit of information consisting of 1K (1024) bytes or one thousand bytes. *See* K.

**Long Integer**   In Apple Pascal, a predefined integer type that can have a maximum of 36 digits. The long integer is suitable for business, scientific, or other applications which need extended number lengths with complete accuracy.

**Machine Language**   A language that is used directly by a machine. It is the form (consisting of 0's and 1's) in which instructions to a computer are stored in memory for direct execution by the computer's processor. Each model of computer processors has its own form of machine language.

**Main Memory**   The memory component of a computer system that is built into the computer itself and whose contents are directly accessible to the processsor.

**Matrix**   A rectangular array of elements arranged in rows and columns that may be manipulated according to the rules of matrix algebra.

**Memory**   A hardware component of a computer system that can store information for later retrieval.

**Memory Location**   A unit of main memory that is identified by an address and can hold a single item of information of a fixed size. In the Apple II, a memory location holds one byte of information.

**Microprocessor**   A very small computer processor usually contained on a single integrated circuit.

**Modem (Modulator–Demodulator)**   A device that connects your computer and extends its capabilities by permitting your computer to transmit over data communications facilities.

**Monitor**   A TV-like computer display with better resolution than a TV set.

**Nonvolatile Memory**   Memory that does not lose its contents when a computer's power supply is shut off or disrupted.

**Object Code**   Output from a compiler or assembler which is itself executable machine code or is suitable for processing to produce executable machine code.

**Operating System**   Software that oversees the operation of a computer system. All programs must be written for a specific operating system.

**Output**   1) Information transferred from a computer to an external destination such as a display screen, disk drive, printer, or modem. 2) The process of transferring such information.

**Parameter**   A variable that is a constant value for a specified application, and that may denote the application.

**Pascal**   A high-level programming language.

**P-Code**   The output of the Apple Pascal Compiler. The P-Code is the "machine language" of the Pascal pseudo-machine, or P-Machine. The P-Code version of your program can then be run on virtually any computer for which the P-Machine interpreter has been implemented.

**Peripheral Equipment**   1) Any equipment distinct from the central processing unit that may provide the system with outside communication or additional facilities. 2) A piece of equipment that is external (peripheral) to the computer itself (for example, disk drives, printers, and so on).

**Pixel**   1) The smallest picture element (dot) on a computer screen. 2) A measure of resolution.

**P-Machine or Pseudo-Machine**   A software-generated device which executes P-Code as its machine language. Every computer operating under a form of UCSD Pascal has been programmed to "look like" this common P-Machine, from the viewpoint of a program being executed.

**Port**   A computer connector (to plug in printers, game controllers, and so on).

**Program**   A set of instructions that tells the computer what to do.

**Programmer**   A person who writes (creates) programs.

**Prompt**   To remind or signal the user that some action is expected, typically by displaying a reminder message, or a menu of choices, on the display screen.

**RAM (Random Access Memory)**   Memory in which the contents of individual locations can be referenced in an arbitrary or random order. It is used to temporarily store programs and data in a computer.

**Read**   To transfer information into the computer's memory from a source external to the computer (such as a disk drive or a modem), or into the computer's processor from a source external to the processor (such as the keyboard or main memory).

**Record**   A collection of related data items.

**Resolution**   The amount of detail in an image that is displayed.

**RF Modulator (Radio Frequency Modulator)**   A device that connects a computer to a television set.

**ROM (Read Only Memory)**   Memory whose contents can only be read; used for storing programs permanently. Information in the ROM remains intact even when the power to the computer is turned off.

**Save**   To store a program on a magnetic disk or cassette.

**Scalar**   A quantity characterized by a single number.

**Sector**   A portion of the recording surface of a disk consisting of a fixed fraction of a track.

**Set**   A finite or infinite number of objects of any kind, of entities, or of concepts, that have a given property or properties in common.

**Single Density**   Describes the normal recording density for diskettes.

**Software (Programs)**   Instructions that tell the computer what to do.

**Source Code**   A program before it has been translated into machine language.

**Subroutine**   A part of a program that can be executed on request from any point in the program, and which retains control to the point of the request on completion.

**Subscript**  An index number used to identify a particular element of an array.

**Syntax**  The rules governing the structure of statements or instructions in a programming language.

**Text**  Information presented in the form of characters readable by humans.

**Track**  A portion of the recording surface of a disk consisting of a single circular band at a fixed distance from the center of the disk.

**Truth Table**  A table that describes a logic function by listing all possible combinations of input values and indicating for each combination the true output value.

**Utility Program**  A computer program in general support of the processor of a computer; for instance, a diagnostic program, a sort program, or a copy program.

**Variable**  1) A quantity that can assume any of a given set of values. 2) A location in the computer's memory where a value can be stored.

**Volatile Storage**  A storage whose contents are lost when the power to the computer is turned off.

**Warm Boot**  The process of restarting the computer after the power is already on, without reloading the operating system into the main memory and often without losing the program or information already in the main memory.

**Write**  To transfer information from the computer to a destination external to the computer, such as a disk drive, printer, or modem; or from the computer's processor to a destination external to the processor, such as main memory.

**Write-Enable Notch**  A square cutout in one edge of a disk's jacket that permits information to be written on the disk. If there is no write-enable notch, or if it is covered, information can be read from the disk but not written onto it.

**Write-Protect**   To protect the information on a disk by covering the write-enable notch with a write-protect tab, preventing any new information from being written onto the disk.

**Write-Protect Tab**   A small adhesive sticker used to write-protect a disk by covering the write-enable notch.

# INDEX